Finance
for the
Nonfinancial
Manager

HERBERT T. SPIRO

A WILEY-INTERSCIENCE PUBLICATION

JOHN WILEY & SONS, New York · London · Sydney · Toronto

Copyright © 1977 by John Wiley & Sons, Inc.

All rights reserved. Published simultaneously in Canada.

Reproduction or translation of any part of this work beyond that
permitted by Sections 107 or 108 of the 1976 United States Copyright Act without the permission of the copyright owner is unlaw-
ful. Requests for permission or further information should be
addressed to the Permissions Department, John Wiley & Sons, Inc.

This publication is designed to provide accurate and
authoritative information in regard to the subject
matter covered. It is sold with the understanding that
the publisher is not engaged in rendering legal, accounting, or other professional service. If legal advice or
other expert assistance is required, the services of a
competent professional person should be sought.

From a Declaration of Principles jointly adopted by a
Committee of the American Bar Association and a
Committee of Publishers.

Library of Congress Cataloging in Publication Data:

Spiro, Herbert T
    Finance for the nonfinancial manager.

    "A Wiley-Interscience publication."
    Includes index.
    1. Finance. I. Title.

HG173.S67   332   76-56371
ISBN 0-471-01788-4

Printed in the United States of America

10 9 8 7 6 5 4

To midcareer students
— Inspiring teachers all!

Preface

This book originated in a series of seminars and short courses conducted for managers who sought to increase their understanding of financial management. Three issues surfaced repeatedly during these courses:

1. Individuals in their midcareers who seek to broaden their knowledge have unusually high motivation and great untapped capacity for learning new concepts. Old dogs can indeed be taught new tricks!

2. The need for increased understanding of financial management is not limited to managers of profit oriented organizations. A large percentage of managers seeking this information serve in hospitals, libraries, school districts, and governmental organizations.

3. Textbooks in use for introductory finance courses are not suitable for meeting the needs of these individuals. These books either presume a considerable body of knowledge in economics, accounting, and statistics as prerequisites or are geared to very young, inexperienced, and unsophisticated students.

This book attempts to address the needs of mature and motivated readers. It is not a how-to book but rather an exposition of relevant financial concepts coupled with selected demonstrations of their application to solve the problems of financial management. The book is geared to meet the needs of managers who wish to broaden their understanding of decision making processes within their organizations.

Three individuals were instrumental in the execution of this venture. Ronald E. Brennan helped to crystallize the need for this project. Barbara E. Amantea had the patience to read, correct, and assess the draft manuscript. Most important were the contributions of Oliver P. Steele IV as all-around project assistant. My continuing indebtedness is to my students who have stimulated my interest in midcareer education and who keep prompting me to rethink many of the issues that I have taken for granted.

HERBERT T. SPIRO

Northridge, California
November 1976

Contents

Tables

Figures

1 The Functions of Finance

From obscure notices on the back pages, financial information has gained headline prominence in daily newspapers and on network broadcasts. The reasons for this heightened interest lie in the impact that financial matters have on all segments of society. Employee, administrator, or self-employed, no one is immune to the effects of financial decisions. Furthermore, the consequences of governmental financing are of continuing concern to most citizens, certainly to all taxpayers.

An understanding of the activities encompassing the finance function has become necessary for the successful discharge of managerial responsibilities in most organizational settings. While specific procedures and applications may vary according to customs, personalities, and needs, certain general principles are adhered to and practiced by financial management in almost all types of organizations. It is the intent of this book to describe and explain these practices and to identify the contributions that finance can make to good management.

Finance engages in two primary types of functions for top management: recording, monitoring, and controlling of financial consequences of past and current operations, and acquiring funds to meet current and future needs. The first set of functions is predominately internal to the organization and is customarily handled by the controller. The second set, which interfaces the organization with outside institutions, is usually the treasurer's sphere of activities.

In performing these functions financial executives employ the theoretical constructs of economics and utilize the data systems organized by accountants. While their orientation is toward the future — how to allocate today's resources to reap benefits tomorrow — they also have a managerial responsibility to assure that agreed upon plans are followed and that organizational objectives are pursued. Through these efforts finance touches on the activities of most functional areas of the organization.

A general description of their respective functions is to view the controller's responsibilities as encompasing those financial management issues that are summarized and reported in the Income Statement and reflected on the left hand side of the Balance Sheet, while the treasurer's functions are oriented to issues of financial structure reflected on the right hand side of the Balance Sheet. The development and interpretation of these statements is presented in Chapter 4.

The controller's responsibilities are best described in terms of the financial management accounting functions he performs. The orientation of financial accounting is historical: a portrayal, consonant with a series of conventions (generally accepted accounting principles, or GAAP), of financial events that have occurred. It provides an answer to the question "what happened," rather than concerning itself with what should happen. The emphasis in this process is on accuracy, consistency and reasonableness. It also serves as the basis for providing information on the financial posture of the organization to interested outsiders such as creditors, lenders, and investors. Furthermore, it serves to meet the legal requirements imposed by taxing authorities and regulatory bodies.

Managerial accounting is the term used to describe the control aspects of the finance function. It deals with the preparation of financial forecasts, the development and monitoring of performance budgets and product costing. These endeavors require considerable reliance on the historical data and expenditure patterns developed by financial accounting. Yet, since they are oriented primarily towards the future, they differ in perspective and orientation. In discharging these responsibilities financial management forecasts utilize the framework and tools of economics and financial analysis.

Almost all of the activities of concern to managerial accounting are relevant to other functions of the organization. For example, the determination of profit and cash break even points (or regions) for selected products and services are of great significance to the production and marketing functions. Similarly, flexible budgets are an accepted tool for measuring performance of organizational components. These measurements can serve as a basis for initiating remedial action, if required, and for structuring managerial reward systems. The budgeting process also serves an important ancillary purpose. The very act of developing budgets and monitoring performance opens valuable communication channels between different functions and echelons of the organization. Consequently management's objectives are properly disseminated throughout the organization, and problems that could impair the attainment of these objectives are brought to the attention of management.

An emerging view of the controller's function is that he develops and maintains a management information system, capturing in almost real time the past, present, and emerging developments within the organization and presenting to the organizational components involved and to top management the financial implications of these behavior patterns. An unresolved problem with respect to these systems is the determination of the proper detail and mix of performance data that will enable financial managers to utilize such information and to initiate timely intervention in current operations.

In contrast to the controller's function, the treasurer's responsibilities are oriented primarily outside the organization: relationships with lenders, stockholders, security markets, and regulatory agencies. He is the management member most likely to negotiate with banks regarding the organization's short term debt, with underwriters regarding long term obligations and stock issues, and with the Securities and Exchange Commission (SEC) in meeting regulatory requirements. Often, relations with stockholders will also be handled by the treasurer's office, frequently in conjunction with the corporate secretary and corporate public relations.

As in all similar divisions of labor, the dividing line between the functions of the controller and the treasurer is not absolute; it is heavily dependent on the personalities of the incumbents and the interests of top management. For example, in some organizations the chief executive officer may prefer to handle all external negotiations himself. By serving as the primary contact with banks, underwriters, and regulatory agencies he necessarily preempts many customary activities of the treasurer. In other organizations the controller may adopt a restrictive view of his mission, limiting himself to financial accounting, and thereby allotting greater scope to other members of the management team. Another variant on the division of labor in the exercise of financial management functions is that of an aggressive controller who extends his responsibilities to bank loan negotiations and SEC relationships.

While the specific organizational arrangements are of no particular significance, it is essential that the functions identified above be discharged successfully. All of the activities enumerated, be they part of the controller's sphere of interest or designed as treasurer's functions, are within the scope of finance. The important issue for the success of an organization is not to whom specific responsibilities have been assigned, but rather that these functions are addressed in a timely fashion and are handled effectively.

The functions of finance should be handled in accordance with the basic goal of the organization. In a profit oriented enterprise this goal should be maximization of the wealth of the organization's shareholders. In a not-for-profit organization it should be the delivery of the maximum attainable level of benefits to designated clients that is feasible with the resources entrusted to the organization. The attainment of these goals requires the active involvement of finance.

THE RELEVANCE OF FINANCE

Finance impacts on all segments of organizational activity. It acquires funds, allocates resources, and tracks performance. In a profit oriented enterprise, its statements form the basis for the stockholders' assessment of management's record; in a not-for-profit organization its analyses may constrain management from meeting all the desires of its constituents. In either case it becomes the focal point for managerial attention, decision making, and accountability. Methods utilized by finance in performing these functions are important and relevant to managers in all types of organizations.

A traditional role for finance is that of scorekeeping. In this function finance reports historical events to management and outsiders such as the SEC, stockholders, and creditors, and pinpoints responsibility for deviating from previously approved plans for specific components of the organization. The extent to which these deviations may be attributed to organizational components depends on the degree of sophistication built into the budgeting and control system. Chapter 9 deals with the specifics of this issue. In some organizations profit center accountability is established, in which deviations from plans are tracked and the ability of specific organizational components to manage the resources allocated to them is judged. Attempts are made in these instances to develop an almost full set of financial statements for organizational components reflecting each component's performance over specified time periods.

A sophisticated scorekeeping system not only identifies deviations from previously formulated plans but also pinpoints proper responsibility for these deviations. Thus the system should prevent penalizing an organizational component for nonattainment of stipulated targets if such nonattainment was caused by the lack of performance of another organizational element. For example, a final assembly line cannot perform in accordance with previously established targets if required parts are not delivered on time.

Although scorekeeping is an important function for all types of organizations, to remain effective it must always be viewed as a tool and not an end in itself. If the system becomes overly rigid and loses sight of its objectives, it will invite countermeasures and subterfuges that will destroy its effectiveness. The ability of entrenched bureaucracies to subvert threatening directives is boundless, not only in a governmental setting but also in profit oriented organizations. Effective scorekeeping functions will therefore solicit organizational compliance by demonstrating the utility of this approach to all levels of management.

The allocation of existing resources to derive future benefits is one of the key responsibilities of top management. Determining the financial feasibility and desirability of such commitments is an important task for finance. Since analyses for these objectives require the determination of future costs and benefits rather than the reconciliation of past expenditures, the framework of financial accounting is unsuitable for this task. Financial management relies instead on the framework of microeconomic theory, discussed in Chapter 2. Basic to this approach is the analysis of future costs and future benefits for a particular project as incremental to the costs and the benefits that would otherwise be expected to be realized by the organization.

The repeated assessment that finance must make for allocation decision is an answer to the following question: Are the long run benefits (adjusted for risk) anticipated from the proposed project commensurate with the long run costs it is expected to incur? In the broadest sense all expenditures can be handled by this framework, including those undertaken for reasons other than financial gain (e.g., improved waste management). Most projects, however, will be undertaken with the expectation of financial gain. In these particular areas finance will contribute to top management decision making. Details of the tools of analysis employed are presented in Chapter 8.

Closely related to decisions regarding capital expenditures are those that concern the magnitude and characteristics of financing that must be obtained from external sources. Here, financial management is instrumental in identifying the need, determining the timing, and negotiating with potential sources of outside capital. Decisions of whether to engage in short term bank borrowing or long term bonds or stock issues are dependent on cash flow expectations, capital structure determination, and the cost of capital considerations. To discharge this function effectively, finance must maintain close contact with financial markets and be sensitive to macroeconomic development that may influence the availability and cost of the capital to be acquired. (Appropriate considerations are presented in Chapters 10, 11, 16, 17, 18, 19, and 20.)

Finally, Finance is the focal point for information requested by creditors, contributors, and stockholders regarding the financial posture of the organization. The preparation of legally and contractually required information and the maintenance of proper relationships with past and potential sources of capital has become a significant and time consuming activity in recent years. This function also provides one of the key continuing interfaces between suppliers and users of capital. Accuracy, timeliness, and tactfulness are the primary characteristics required for these activities. Close working relationships with the public relations and legal departments are frequently maintained in this area.

Historically, finance functions have been viewed solely in the context of a for-profit enterprise. This restrictive view of finance is neither necessary nor appropriate. With very few exceptions, all the functions discussed above apply equally to the management of hospitals, universities, libraries, museums, and governmental agencies. The fact that benefits cannot always be expressed in quantitative, monetary form does not detract from the need to marshal the best tools of analysis available for determining the desirability of the contemplated allocation of resources. In a similar vein, the absence of stockholders does not diminish the need for the presentation of information to potential suppliers of capital, be they taxpayers, contributors, suppliers, or lenders.

Given the increasing role that government and other not-for-profit organizations play in the economy, the stake that the public has in good financial management of these organizations and institutions is mounting. Good scorekeeping systems, rational procedures for the allocation of capital, and proper dissemination of relevant financial information are essential tools for avoiding the undue waste of resources that might otherwise plague this sector of our economy. Thus finance's role clearly includes not-for-profit organizations. Actually, in the absence of the verdict of the marketplace, its responsibilities in this arena are even greater than those in profit oriented organizations.

FINANCE AND THE NONFINANCIAL MANAGER

The previous discussion highlighted the many areas of involvement between finance and other organizational components. The role of finance, particularly in the areas of scorekeeping and capital allocation, is all pervasive and impacts on the managerial discretion of nonfinance activities. All managers must develop an understanding of the objectives, tools, and functions of finance. Lacking such an understanding, they will not be in a position to contribute effectively to and utilize the results of financial analyses undertaken on behalf of their activities.

In a profit oriented enterprise finance also presents the result of management's effort to the public. It is the language of business. Nonfinancial managers have a direct stake in understanding this language and using it to set forth their departmental requirements and contributions. Thus finance facilitates the communication process, not only between the organization and the public, but also between different departments within the organization.

A matter of immediate concern for all managers is an appreciation of the purpose, underlying assumptions, and interpretation of the budgeting process. In the absence of firsthand familiarity with these aspects, the manager is at a disadvantage within the organization he serves. The ability to present a case for a budget and to discuss it with financial management on its own grounds is almost a prerequisite for organizational survival.

A related skill is the ability to develop and provide the data required for top management's project approval. Any major allocation request evaluated by finance will require forecasts of benefits over the life of the project. Good management practice dictates that nonfinancial managers analyze their appropriation request prior to submission in the same framework in which it will be evaluated by approving authorities. Familiarity with the theory and practices of capital budgeting will accomplish this.

Finally, the language of finance imposes a desirable discipline on all organizational components. It forces the expression of organizational plans in quantifiable terms, even if the assumptions underlying these plans are sometimes tenuous. The specificity of these expressions contributes to a more fruitful dialogue between managers and thereby improves overall management.

PERSPECTIVE FOR OUTSIDERS

Effective financial management must take into account the needs and concerns of those who supply capital to the organization: lenders and stockholders. The obverse is also true: effective lending and investment requires a thorough understanding of the tools and practices of financial management.

In assessing the desirability of a loan to a potential borrower, the lender wishes to assure himself of the viability and financial potential of the enterprise. Analysis of past financial statements, prevailing financial plans, and control procedures in effect provide much relevant information. Similarly, a supplier may wish to assure himself of the strength and credit worthiness of a customer, or a purchaser who depends on a particular source of supply on the financial strength of his supplier. All of these outsiders have a vested interest in understanding and interpreting the financial systems in effect.

Contributors to charitable institutions have a similar interest. Knowledge of financial control procedures permit them to judge the worthwhileness of their contribution in accordance with their objectives. Legislators and trustees of public agencies have a responsibility to their constituents in interpreting and assessing the relationships between operating costs and expected benefits. A generalized knowledge of finance is a necessary step in discharging these responsibilities.

Finally, investors in private enterprises wish to ascertain the potential for their investments. By understanding the language, tools, and procedures of financial management, investors can place themselves in the decision and information framework of corporate management, thereby gaining a better appreciation of the risks their capital is exposed to and the returns they may realize. The deliberate entertaining of risk/return trade-off considerations actually becomes the meeting ground between investors and corporate management. Both must base their decisions on their perception of the facts provided primarily by finance.

ROAD MAP AND TERMINOLOGY

Any applied discipline, be it engineering, law, or medicine, is built on a basic body of knowledge, employs certain common tools of analysis, and

is practiced within an accepted institutional framework. Finance follows
this pattern. It is based on economic theory, employs specialized tools,
and operates within well-defined institutional channels. The vocabulary of
finance has evolved from this setting. To properly understand and utilize
the concepts, tools, and vocabulary of finance a certain investment (beyond the cost of this book) is required by the reader.

Learning requires the exercise of effort by the student; to date no effective shortcuts have been found. Gaining sufficient familiarity with the
field of finance is no exception. A number of basic concepts must be understood, tools must be mastered, and a vocabulary acquired. Chapters 2
to 6 are devoted to this objective. Although only those issues that are ger-
mane to the understanding required by nonfinancial managers were included, the study of some economics, some accounting, some mathematics, and an appreciation of tax laws is also required.

Readers who have previously been exposed to this material may find it
a highly condensed review, worth scanning for refresher purposes prior to
reading the remainder of this book; those who have never been exposed
are encouraged to proceed slowly and make the investment required to
master these chapters. They will find, as hoped for in all good investments, that the required effort will yield appropriate returns. The concepts and tools developed are for the most part equally applicable to problems of profit oriented and not-for-profit organizations. Managers in both
types of organizations are therefore encouraged to take the time required
to absorb this material. The remainder of the book will be easier to understand, more meaningful in its presentation and, once mastered, much
easier to apply.

Chapters 7 to 15 analyze the problems of the controller in managing
the assets of the organization, utilizing the framework developed in Chapters 2 to 6. These chapters discuss issues associated with the management
of working capital as well as the management of long term investments.
Again, this segment is almost equally applicable to profit oriented as well
as not-for-profit organizations.

Chapters 16 to 20 are concerned with the establishment of proper relationships with lenders and investors. About one half of the material presented applies to both profit oriented and not-for-profit organizations.
The other half, dealing with security markets and investor relationships, is
primarily applicable to profit oriented organizations.

It is the objective of this book to familiarize managers with the financial
functions which they are likely to encounter in their daily activities. These
functions are presented in the context of their theoretical and institutional
rationale.

Financial functions are performed by many members of the management team. The controller and treasurer have already been mentioned.
Long range planners, marketing managers, production managers, and often

the chief executive officer also contribute extensively to the analysis of asset management and product pricing problems. The aim of this book is to clarify the functions of finance, rather than to define the job responsibilities of any particular manager, which vary from one organization to another. Since it would be futile to attempt an all-encompassing definition, the term "financial management" is used throughout this book. The implication is that the considerations enumerated are applicable to any manager, regardless of his primary responsibilities, who has to deal with the issues identified. Thus, for example, in some organizations problems of financial management pertaining to the acquisition of long term assets might actually be handled by the production manager. Only in some instances, primarily those where the issues are highly specialized, such as cash management, is the financial manager (whatever his title may be) always identifiable as the responsible specialist.

Finally, an additional comment on the distinction between profit and not-for-profit organizations is in order. Neither the literature of finance nor that of economics or management has yet arrived at a theoretically tight and unambiguous definition of those organizations in our society who deliver desired services but are not operated for the long run benefit of shareholders. Our interest in not-for-profit organizations is not dogmatic. This book is not intended to debate their role and place in an economic system whose basic commitment is to profit oriented enterprise. Thus, whether they provide a better or poorer level of service for the total costs to society associated with their existence is a moot issue in this context. What is important is that the number and scope of involvement of these organizations has increased dramatically and is still rising.

Among not-for-profit organizations one must enumerate governmental agencies at all levels: federal, state, local, school districts, and so on; all are included here. In addition, governmental operations that compete with the private sector, such as waterworks and electric utilities, postal operations, irrigation districts, and passenger railroad operations qualify for this definition. Furthermore, libraries, museums, and universities belong to this category, whether they are publicly funded or privately endowed. Finally, many delivery services of the health industries are not-for-profit organizations, from insurance companies such as Blue Cross and Blue Shield to hospitals and health maintenance organizations (HMO).

All of these organizations are referred to as not-for-profit, although their methods of financing and operation may differ widely. Essentially their common attribute is the absence of marketable equity participation by outsiders. Otherwise their financial management problems are very similar to profit oriented firms delivering the identical product or service.

A final word to the reader before he or she tackles the task of mastering the tools. It is very unlikely that a manager will find the material presented here totally new. Having worked in either profit or not-for-profit organizations, a manager will doubtless have encountered many of the terms and methods presented here. Experience has revealed, however, that many, even those who successfully meet the demand imposed on them by financial management, are not quite sure why they are doing, what ever they are doing in this area. The success of this book, then, will be the spontaneous voicing of "aha" by the reader — so this is *why* we have been doing what might have appeared to be a silly and useless exercise. The more such exclamations, the greater the learning experience!

SUMMARY

An understanding of the activities encompasing the finance function has become necessary for all managers. This function can be divided into two categories: recording the financial consequences of past activities and acquiring funds to meet current and future needs. Responsibilities of the Controller usually include internally directed activities, while the duties of the Treasurer require his interfacing with the financial community.

Most of the functions of finance are applicable to profit as well as not-for-profit organizations. All managers should master the objectives and structure of performance budgets and capital budgeting to discharge their job responsibilities more effectively. An understanding of basic economic and accounting concepts will prove of value. The objective of this book is to explain and clarify practices to which nonfinancial managers are continually exposed.

2 Economic Concepts

This book deals with the field of finance — its tools, its institutional setting, and its application. To develop the relevant concepts appropriately, it is important to acknowledge its continuing debt to its parent discipline — economics. The concepts applied in finance are those of economic theory; the tools used are those of economic analysis; the institutions described are those established for facilitating economic activity.

A very brief exposure to the field of economics is therefore appropriate. The scope is limited to broad delineation of areas of investigation presently pursued by economists, description of concepts and tools most useful in financial analysis, and discussion of several topical issues of particular concern to financial managers.

Economics deals with the allocation of resources to meet mankind's wants. It is one of the social sciences, entailing explicit or implicit behavioral assumptions about mankind. Although great strides have been made in recent years to quantify many of the observed or deduced relationships, it is important to remember that these abstractions are predicated on behavioral preferences of individuals acting on their own or within institutional settings. Economic behavior is analyzed in terms of transactions between economic agents. An economic agent can be an individual, a household, a not-for-profit organization, a business organization, or a governmental unit.

Contemporary economic thought distinguishes between microeconomics, and macroeconomics. Microeconomics deals with the decisions of individual economic agents — households, firms, or institutions. Macroeconomics is concerned with the aggregate interaction of these agents, their impact on society at large, and the role that governmental action can assume in attaining specified objectives. As in all such distinctions the dividing line is somewhat arbitrary. Furthermore, evidence appears to be ac-

11

cumulating that macroeconomic phenomena are best understood in the context of the microeconomic foundations underlying them.

Financial managers require familiarity with selected concepts and terms developed in economics. Some of the terminology that is used is self-explanatory, while other terms have specialized meaning deserving particular attention. In this book only the most widely used concepts and terms will be identified. To facilitate presentation, the customary distinction between micro and macro is observed.

MICROECONOMICS

Supply and Demand

Supply and demand are terms that are used indiscriminately in casual discussions of economic events. A comment such as "there is an ample supply of gasoline" may appropriately reflect the stock of gasoline on hand but does not convey information regarding the conditions under which sellers are willing to part with their stock of gasoline. Economists, therefore, define supply in terms of the quantity of a specific commodity offered at a given price. Thus the available physical supply of gold may indeed be 1,000,000 ounces, but it is unlikely that this supply will be offered to prospective buyers at the depression price of $35 per ounce.

As the price that can be attained for a commodity increases, more owners of that commodity are willing to part with it, and thus the quantity offered increases. In addition, producers who were not interested in producing the commodity at lower prices will be encouraged by the higher prices to acquire the necessary equipment and manpower required to supply the commodity. Suitable examples are oil wells and gold mines. As the price of crude oil and gold increases, the exploitation of wells and mines that was uneconomical at the old prices now becomes financially attractive. Consequently, new suppliers enter the market as the price increases.

Figure 1 illustrates these relationships. P denotes the price obtainable for a given commodity. Q denotes the quantity offered at that price. For example, at a price of $2, two units are offered, while at a price of $3, four units are offered. The line SS, depicting quantities offered at increasing prices, is called the supply curve of the commodity under consideration.

Similar considerations apply to the demand for a commodity. At high prices consumers tend to acquire only small quantities of the commodity. As prices demanded by the suppliers decrease, consumers are willing to absorb increasing quantities of the commodity. A prominent example of this is the reduction in the prices of automobiles in the 1920s. From a high-priced luxury item with limited unit sales, automobile sales soared to

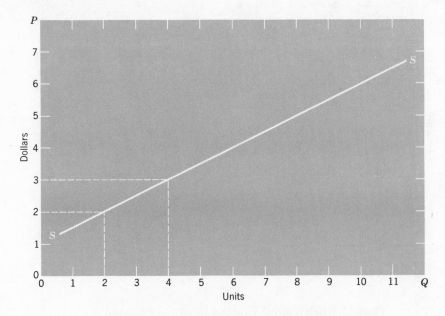

Figure 1. Supply curve for a commodity.

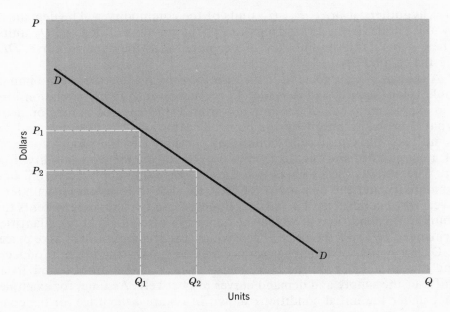

Figure 2. Demand curve for a commodity.

million of units per year as the economies of mass production encouraged competitive reductions in unit price.

Figure 2 depicts the relationship between the price charged for a commodity and the demand for a commodity at that price. Thus for example,

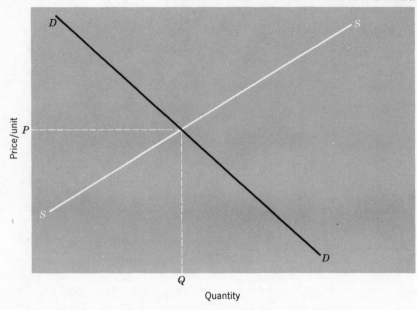

Figure 3. Relationship between supply and demand curve.

at a hypothetical price, P_1, Q_1 units of the commodity will be demanded by the public. If the price drops to P_2, the public will demand Q_2 units. These general relationships are incorporated into the demand curve, DD, for the commodity.

Although it may come as a surprise to some readers there is no immutable law of supply and demand! In economics one observes relationships and equilibrium conditions but not irrevocable laws of nature or men. What is probably meant by the popular notion of "law of supply and demand" are the equilibrium conditions pertaining to the supply curve SS of a commodity and the demand curve DD for the same commodity. Figure 3 represents the basic relationships between the supply curve, SS, of a commodity and the demand curve, DD, for that same commodity under a given set of conditions. The intersection of these two curves represents the equilibrium conditions at which the quantities offered equal the quantities demanded (Q) and the price (P) at which the transaction will take place.

Over a period of time changes occur in the cost structure of producers and the preference of the consumers. These changes are referred to as shifts in the supply and demand curves respectively. Assume, for example, that under the initial conditions shown in Figure 4 the price for the commodity was P_0 and the quantity supplied and demanded at that price was Q_0. Now assume that a uniform cost increase affects the supply curve, SS, in Figure 4. For example, all suppliers of the commodity experience an increase in the price of fertilizers needed in the production of the given commodity. This increase in cost is expected to shift the supply curve to $S'S'$ with a new equilibrium price of P_1 for the equilibrium quantity, Q_1.

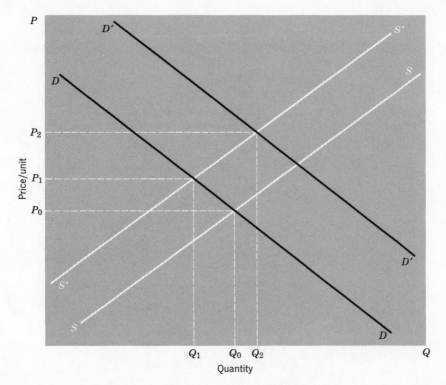

Figure 4. Shifts in the supply and demand curves.

Assume also that consumers generally exhibit an increasing preference for this particular commodity. An example would be the Food and Drug Administration (FDA) ban on cyclamate diet drinks resulting in increased consumption of sugar-based soft drinks. If such a change in preference occurs, the demand curve, DD, can be expected to shift to $D'D'$, with a new equilibrium price of P_2 for the commodity for quantity, Q_2.

Average Costs

In most production processes — agricultural, manufacturing, or service — certain fixed costs are incurred regardless of the volume of output. The greater the volume of production the smaller the fixed charges that each unit must absorb. At the same time, as output increases and productive capacity is reached, inefficiencies are incurred in the process. These may be overtime payments, lack of close supervision, and repeated breakdowns due to excess utilization of equipment. As a result of the first phenomenon (absorption of fixed costs), the average cost per unit decreases as the volume of production increases. The second phenomenon, the inefficiencies resulting from higher than planned output levels, increases the average

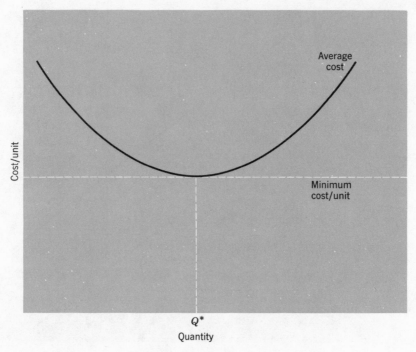

Figure 5. Average cost curve.

unit cost of production. For each production facility, such as a farm, a manufacturing plant, or a hospital, a certain level of output exists at which unit costs are at a minimum. This is shown in Figure 5, where Q^* signifies the quantity of output at which average costs per unit are at a minimum.

Average costs can be computed by dividing total costs incurred by the quantity produced. They provided a historical perspective for management and answer the question: "How much did it cost per unit to produce the quantity we sold?". Most managerial problems, however, are oriented towards the future. Management interests lie in determining the additional costs that will be incurred if production is increased.

Marginal Costs

This leads to the concept of marginal costs. Marginal costs are defined as the addition to total costs required to produce one additional unit at a given level of output. As output increases, marginal costs increase due to the inefficiencies incurred at higher levels of output. A plot of marginal costs is presented in Figure 6. It can be shown that when average costs are at a minimum they are intersected by the marginal cost curve. The interpretation of this is that from that level of output on additional units will

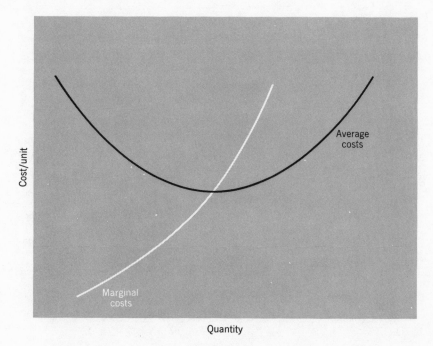

Figure 6.   Intersection of marginal and average cost curves.

cost more to produce than the average cost per unit up to that point. This should be a signal for management's attention. If the selling price per unit remains above the marginal costs, it is still worthwhile to expand production. If, however, marginal costs exceed the selling price that can be realized per unit, production should be curtailed. As a general rule production should be supported up to the point where the price obtained per unit equals marginal costs.

Assume the market price for a product is P' dollars per unit. Management should increase output up to the point where the marginal cost equals this price. In Figure 7 the appropriate level of output is designated Q'. Should the price fall to P'', the organization would be well advised to curtail production to Q''.

In summary, as long as average costs decrease, marginal costs are less than average costs, a signal that an additional unit will cost less to produce than the average of the units up to that volume of output. As soon as average costs rise above their minimum value, however, marginal costs are higher than average costs, a warning that the cost of an additional unit of output exceeds the average cost per unit experienced up to that point. Output decisions should be based on market prices and marginal costs.

An additional concept should be mentioned in passing. Each product requires a certain level of output in order to achieve its minimum average cost point. Take automobiles, for example: An assembly plant producing 100 automobiles per year will incur higher average costs per car than a plant producing the same car at a rate of 100 per day. On the other hand, a dentist who insists on treating all his patients personally may actually

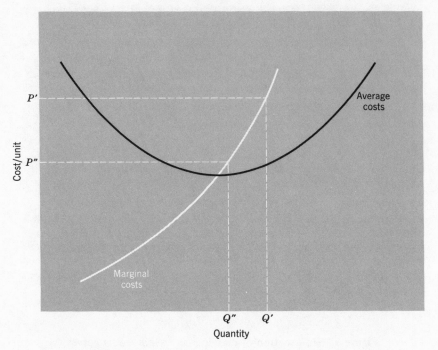

Figure 7.   Increased production to where marginal costs equal price.

increase his average costs by expanding his facilities. Leasing additional space, buying additional equipment, and hiring additional clerical help will not greatly expand his capability to treat patients. In fact, the additional space and equipment may result in excess capacity and substantially increase his costs for only small increases in output.

Thus average costs for some products decrease with increasing outputs while they increase for others. When average costs are expected to decrease with increasing output the, concept of *economies of scale* prevails. The implication of this statement is that if sales are sufficiently increased to justify the planning of production facilities for higher levels of output, then average costs for the product will fall. If such is the case, an organization must be ready to marshal the financial resources required to achieve these economies of scale; otherwise it will probably not be in a position to compete.

The concepts of average costs, marginal costs, and economies of scale apply to public agencies and not-for-profit organizations as directly as they pertain to profit oriented firms. Although the pressure exerted by competitive market prices may not prevail, good management practice dictates that when the cost of providing additional services rises above the average cost of services previously provided, administrative changes are in order. These may consist of the expansion of facilities, the acquisition of computing equipment, and the hiring of more skilled personnel.

A final point: The determination of marginal costs in any given organization, public or private, are simple in concept but extremely complex in actual practice. Although prevailing accounting systems are not geared in many instances to provide the necessary detailed data, this should not discourage a manager from adopting these concepts and analyzing his order output decisions with estimated data. Marginal analysis is one of the cornerstones of good management.

Cost Benefit Analysis

In recent years the concept of cost benefit analysis had gained much currency. Although the label is new, the approach is not. Any time a manager examines alternate courses of action he engages in cost benefit analysis, whether or not he labels it as such. It is and has always been the very essence of economic analysis to examine the trade-offs that must be made in exchanging one commodity or policy for another. What is new is the deliberate effort to apply analytical tools to areas that were previously the private domain of policymakers and to increasingly supplant judgment based on experience with rigor based on analysis.

The tools of cost benefit analysis are those of microeconomics fortified with the capital budgeting concepts presented in this book. The recurring problem in cost benefit analysis is the danger of ignoring secondary costs or benefits in formulating a solution. For example, in computing the costs of cleaning a stream, does one include unemployment compensation for paper mill workers who might lose their jobs as a result of tighter pollution standards? Should a decrease in ear and eye infections among swimmers be included as benefits? Often the economic agents paying the costs are not the same as those who reap the benefits.

An additional problem is the data issue. Even if costs and benefits have been conceptually delineated to the analyst's satisfaction, representative estimates are difficult to develop. Furthermore, the validity of the assumptions underlying the data diminishes rapidly the further out the proposed action takes place. Yet this is a universal problem as any manager knows, and decisions must be made in the face of uncertainty!

MACROECONOMICS

When managers express concern about the economic environment they are referring to macroeconomic events. Gross national product (GNP), employment levels, budget deficits, tax policy and government regulation are all relevant. Although they are beyond the control of managers, these factors directly influence their ability to perform in both profit oriented and not-for-profit organizations.

Macroeconomics is an area where politics and economics intermingle.

After decades of professional debates, some macroeconomic phenomena are still assessed according to the gospel of the particular school of thought to which its proponents adhere. This in turn makes it a fertile and welcome arena for political intervention in the economic process. Economists who emphasize the role of monetary policy for economic stability are customarily classified as conservatives, while those stressing fiscal initiatives are categorized as liberals. Unfortunately neither group can claim startling success for its approach. Since the evidence is inconclusive, the field is rife for grandstand political actions that are often counterproductive insofar as the economy is concerned.

These complications are due to the magnitude of the problem and the lack of opportunity to establish scientifically sound experiments to test economic hypotheses. A chemist has a laboratory for experimentation; a nuclear physicist may require a $1 billion facility to validate his hypotheses, yet he can probably obtain access to such an installation. However, the laboratory of the macroeconomist is the United States economy. No economist has yet established such unanimity of credibility that the elected representatives of the people are willing to subordinate their judgment to his hypotheses!

These complications do not relieve managers from their responsibility to forecast the economic environment as it is likely to impact on their organizations. Financial managers should be particularly sensitive to these issues since they influence the availability and cost of funds. The brief discussion below, which summarizes contemporary thinking on these issues, should not be interpreted as dogmatic statements of revealed truisms.

Concepts of GNP

The gross national product (GNP) is a measure of total spending of all economic units on final products during a stated period. Conventionally the appropriate period is a calendar year. "All economic units" is a term encompassing households, business and not-for-profit organizations as well as local, state, and federal government. The concept of GNP excludes products passing through intermediate manufacturing phases. It also excludes services that are provided but not sold on the market, such as housewifely chores or the value of labor provided by an owner in repairing his own car. GNP reflects the total gross value, at market prices, of goods and services produced in the economy during the period delineated.

The concept of GNP has received wide acceptance and is often used as a proxy for the overall health of the economy. Thus economic growth, recessions, and so on are frequently defined in relation to previously experienced levels of GNP. In view of the highly aggregate nature of this measure, care must be exercised that unusual swings are fully understood before long run implications are attributed to these changes.

Inflation

A major distortion in the reported value of GNP is due to the effect of price inflation. Recall that GNP is computed on the basis of market prices: as prices rise so does GNP. Clearly, this does not represent increased vigor and health in the economy since, if all other factors (number of employees, output per employee, kilowatt-hours of electricity consumed, etc.) remain at their previous levels of activity, real output remains unaffected. To compensate for this, GNP is often expressed in "real terms" in addition to current prices. This is accomplished by means of a GNP deflator, an index number by which current, or money GNP is divided each year to determine what GNP would have been in comparison to a stated base year if prices had not changed. Any increase in constant prices must be attributed to increased economic activity.

For example: The reported GNP for the first quarter of 1975 happened to be identical to that reported for the third quarter of 1974 — $1416 billion. However, when stated in terms of constant 1958 prices, the picture presented changes dramatically. In the third quarter of 1974 the GNP amounted to $823 billion in 1958 prices, while the first quarter 1975 GNP deflated to 1958 prices amounted to only $780 billion, a drop of 5% in real terms. This is the same percentage by which the GNP deflator rose between these two periods.

The effects of inflation are obviously not limited to the difficulties of keeping proper score of the GNP. As prices rise, lenders and investors wish to protect themselves against the expected erosion in purchasing power and demand higher returns. In view of the uncertainty of economic prospects, businessmen may hesitate to borrow at these high rates and may prefer instead to curtail their purchases of new equipment. This in turn may lead to lessened output, requiring fewer employees, and so on. Inflation can thus induce reduction in real GNP despite increases in monetary GNP.

Another effect of inflation is on the market value of securities held by investors and on the purchasing power of pensioners. As the real value of fixed money assets and of guaranteed payments declines, the economic position of their owners deteriorates. A third impact is caused by the progressive nature of income taxes. In an effort to maintain real purchasing power, money wages increase by approximately the amount of price inflation experienced. However, the higher income results in an even higher percentage increase in tax liability, thus reducing real disposable income from that obtained in previous periods.

The pernicious effect of inflation is not limited to individuals but influences the economy as a whole via distortion of economic activity from the equilibrium it had attained at stable prices. In a world of constant prices economic agents base their investment decisions on long run expectation of return. Thus the acquisition of capital assets, pricing decisions, and capital structure delineations are all based on anticipation of profit levels commensurate with the risk exposure of the economic agent. These long term decisions lead to economies of scale in output and the employment of land, labor, and facilities in their most productive mode. Changing price levels due to inflationary pressures change the output equilibrium previously attained and channel economic resources into activities promising high short run returns. Economic activity is thus distorted and productivity and output can decrease.

Employment

Of continuing interest to policymakers is the level of employment in the economy. It is clearly an area where economics and politics share mutual concern. A difference exists, however, in the time perspective that is brought to bear on the problem by these respective groups. Economists are likely to take an unemotional, detached view of this issue and propose actions that assure the long run health of the economy, encompassing high levels of employment. Policymakers, on the other hand, are concerned with the short run, since high levels of unemployment entail human hardships and create politically explosive situations.

During the 1960s the Phillips Curve presented in Figure 8, was accepted by many economists as a proper observation of the relationship between wages and unemployment. According to this concept, decreases in unemployment are likely to result in inflation. Thus, for example, as unemployment dropped from %A to %D, wages were predicted to increase from %E per annum to %F.

On theoretical as well as empirical grounds the Phillips Curve is no longer uniformly accepted by economists as a proper long term observation of the relationship between changes in wage rates and unemployment. Current controversies pertaining to the attainment of higher levels of employment involve the function of the federal government in creating employment opportunities. Economists usually identified as sympathetic to conservatively inclined policymakers argue that long-term economic health is best assured by a prosperous and expanding private sector. The role of government should therefore be the encouragement of this sector through the removal of excess restrictions and taxes. Such actions are expected to stimulate economic activity and thereby increase employment.

Other economists, often sympathetic to liberal policymakers, argue that the private sector solution takes too long to benefit the unemployed and, furthermore, that most of these benefits are likely to accrue to the owners of capital rather than potential employees. Their recommended solutions to the unemployment problem range from federal financing of public projects such as dams, highways, reclamation, to the generation of direct employment opportunities by the government as the employer of last resort. Defense and space spending has also been tacitly accepted as benefit-

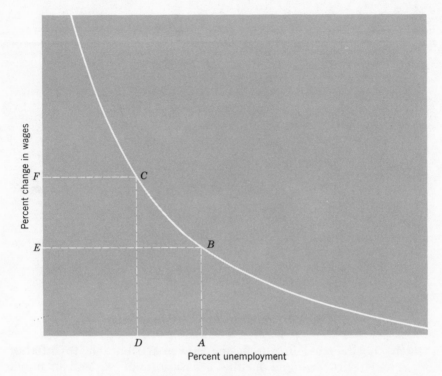

Figure 8. Phillips Curve.

ing employment. For political reasons, however, the constellation of supporters for this approach usually differs from that customarily associated with other public projects.

Interest Rates

As was indicated earlier, interest rates play a most significant role in investment decisions. The mathematical treatment of interest is discussed in Chapter 6, the institutional setting in Chapter 16, and the implications of financial management in Chapter 8. The treatment at this point is limited to sharpening the terminology frequently associated with a discussion of interest rates.

Interest is viewed as the price of money; it arises from the ever present choice between spending (consuming) today or postponing such consumption until a later date (investing). By lending to a venture or partaking directly in it as a stockholder, possible immediate consumption is postponed. The incentive for this postponement is interest. An economy will have a fundamental interest rate based on its stage of development reflecting its productivity, investment needs, and so on. In times of inflation, lenders expect to receive the basic interest rate plus a premium that will neutralize

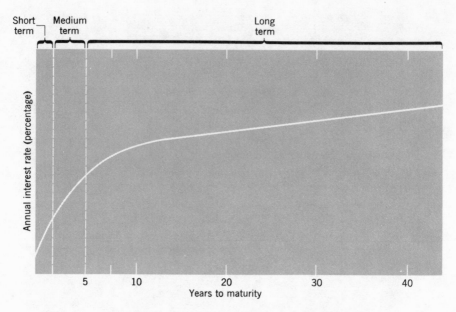

Figure 9. Term structure of interest rates.

for them the decrease in purchasing power attributable to inflation of their principal. For example, assume a basic rate of 3%, and an annual inflation rate of 6%. Lenders would not be willing to lend funds at less than 9%.

Similar considerations apply to risk. Since a lender can realize a certain return on a risk-free investment (interest on a government bond), he expects a premium over that interest rate in order to lend his funds to a hazardous venture. The greater the risk, the higher the premium required.

Capital markets make a distinction between funds borrowed for relatively short periods of time (months) and those for long periods (decades). A customary way of displaying this phenomenon is by plotting the interest that must be paid on an equivalent risk loan as the period of borrowing increases. Customarily, interest rates for short term loans (short rates) are lower than interest rates charged for long periods (long rates), resulting in a curve shaped as shown in Figure 9. There have been periods, however, when these relationships did not hold and short rates were higher than long rates.

Fluctuation in interest rates causes movement of capital between financial institutions. For example, as long as savings institutions are regulated in terms of the maximum rate they can pay savers, heavy withdrawals are likely to occur whenever market rates exceed the limit. This in turn restricts the ability of those institutions to lend funds to potential investors for the acquisition of capital assets. Another effect of rapid fluctuation is on international capital movement. In times of high domestic rates compared to prevailing foreign rates, capital is attracted to domestic institutions. In times of low domestic rates, capital is likely to seek foreign opportunities.

Monetary Policy

A prominent school of economic thought holds that the supply of money in the economy determines economic activity and the prevailing price level. Attention is therefore focused on the Federal Reserve System (FRS) and its attempt to regulate the money supply (discussed in greater detail in Chapter 16). The money supply is defined as currency held by the public and their deposits held by banks. The latter is by far the larger percentage of the money supply and is deemed to be under the regulation of the FRS.

Currently, these economists believe that if the money supply increases beyond the normal increase in economic activity (about 4 to 5% per annum) inflationary spending ensues. Similarly, if the growth in the money supply is throttled below this range recessionary tendencies increase. Adherents of the monetary school argue, therefore, for automatic increases in the money supply, removing it from discretionary action by the policymakers.

Another group of economists argues that monetary expansion induces economic activity, causing increased employment. It looks to the FRS to increase the money supply with the hope that as a result the cost of money (interest rates) will drop, thereby stimulating investment in the private sector. At times both the executive and legislative branches of the federal government try to stimulate action along these lines by the independent FRS.

Fiscal Policy

An alternative approach to governmental initiative in regulating economic behavior is that of fiscal policy. Measures that are normally characterized as belonging in this category are tax policy, federal budgets, and deficit financing. It is generally agreed that these measures generate a more rapid impact on economic activity, for better or for worse, than monetary policy.

Tax policy addresses the issue of stimulating activity in a specific segment of the economy by providing tax benefits to this segment. Chapter 5 details some of the approaches that have been developed. The investment tax credit, for example, is geared to stimulate investment in capital goods, with the intention that this will facilitate increased private employment.

The federal budget, by its very magnitude, exerts considerable influence on overall economic activity. Federal expenditures translate into purchasing power and through it into economic activity and employment. Opponents to this point of view would argue that unless revenues are increased simultaneously, increased expenditures can only be realized through deficit spending. Increasing revenues requires the imposition of additional taxes. Such action, by reducing the returns that investors are likely to realize, may have the effect of slowing economic activity contrary to the result desired.

Federal budget deficits generate demand in the short run. Some economists would argue that the implication of such action is increased inflationary pressures on the economy which, in the long run, might stifle economic activity. Also, if federal deficits are financed through the sale of debt obligations to the public, they may compete for capital with private investments and thus defeat the desire to expand economic activity. Finally, a word about the economic burden of existing debt on the public. In addition to the issues enumerated above, annual service payments redistribute income from taxpayers to the holders of federal debt instruments.

Government Regulation

A policy issue that straddles conventional definitions of macro- and microeconomics is government regulation of business. Through regulatory agencies such as the Interstate Commerce Commission (ICC) and the Civil Aeronautics Board (CAB), and the legal authority vested in other commissions and bureaus, the federal government narrows the decision making capability of affected business regarding product characteristics, employment conditions, frequency of service, and quantity of output.

The initial intent of the legislation in each case was to safeguard the public interest, yet it is argued that the aggregate effect is the diminution of economic activity and the encouragement of wasteful practices. Microeconomic analysis supports the contention that output decisions are distorted from what they would be under fully competitive conditions and, as a consequence, that prevailing prices are higher than required.

A special type of government regulation is applied to activities that affect public goods — those assets that belong to the community at large rather than to any individual or organization. Prominent examples include the environment and the airwaves. Various members of the community seek to derive different benefits from these assets. The role of regulation in this case is to assure that any one use of a given public good does not detract from its value to the rest of the community.

A manufacturer who pollutes a stream in the process of production prevents other members of the community from swimming, fishing, or otherwise enjoying this asset. Regulation, in this example, strives to force the manufacturer to pay all the costs associated with restoring the stream to its previous condition. Costs incurred in this restoration are incorporated into overall production costs. If this were not done, the public goods used in production would be free of cost to the manufacturer and all members of the community would in effect subsidize his profit oriented use of public resources.

SUMMARY

Since financial concepts are rooted in economic theory, a brief exposure to economics is appropriate. Economics deals with the allocation of resources to meet mankind's wants. Economic behavior is analyzed in terms of transactions between economic agents. Microeconomics deals with decisions of individual economic agents while macroeconomics deals with aggregate economic activities.

Important microeconomic concepts for financial managers are supply and demand, average and marginal costs, and cost benefit analysis. Macroeconomic terms with which managers should be familiar are GNP, inflation, employment, interest rates, fiscal and monetary policy, and government regulation. Economists are in general agreement on microeconomic behavior but not on policy recommendations for influencing aggregate economic activity.

3 Future Orientation

One of the key functions of financial management is the allocation of existing resources with the expectation of reaping benefits in the future. The relationships between investment (allocation of resources) and returns (future benefits) is asymmetrical. While existing resources are expended with certainty, the benefit stream anticipated to result from the investment is not guaranteed — it is uncertain. This stream may fall considerably short of the expected returns or may exceed the initial estimate. Thus at the time the investment is made, returns may deviate from those expected in either direction. In finance, this deviation from expected returns serves as the definition of uncertainty or risk.

UNCERTAINTY

A numerical example will help to illustrate this concept. Assume that a governmental unit has decided to build a toll bridge. The investment of $15 million is financed through the issuance of bonds. Expected returns for this project are based on a forecast of expected traffic of 7000 cars per day (on average) in each direction. Preliminary analysis also indicates that the public appears willing to pay up to $1 per car each way and that the annual cash flow required for operation and maintenance of the bridge as well as retirement of the debt is $3.5 million. Based on these estimates, the bridge authority establishes a toll of $0.75, expected to generate $0.75 × 2 × 7000 × 365 = $3.83 million in revenue. This revenue is based on the expectation that 7000 motorists per day will be willing to pay $0.75 each way. If fewer motorists use the toll bridge, returns will be less than expected. If more motorists elect to use the bridge, returns will be greater than anticipated.

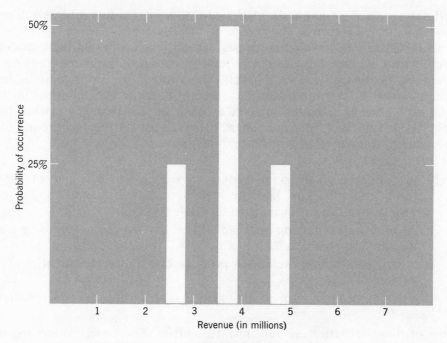

Figure 10. Probability distribution of revenues.

The key to the revenue forecast is predicting traffic volume — an extremely uncertain prospect. Even if the bridge has a monopoly of access to an important destination in terms of employment, shopping, and governmental services, motorists may elect to change their shopping habits or places of employment, or to join a car pool or switch to public transportation to avoid part or all of the toll charge. If only 5000 motorists use the bridge each way per day, annual revenues fall to $2.74 million. On the other hand, using the bridge may result in substantial savings in driving time and motorists who previously carpooled or used public transportation may decide to drive separately and thereby increase the traffic from that originally anticipated. Thus, if 9000 motorists pay the bridge toll, revenues will be $4.93 million. Further, assume that the probability of 7000 motorists actually using the bridge daily is estimated at 50%, and that of 5000 and 9000 motorists using it is estimated at 25% each, Figure 10 portrays the revenue that may be realized under each of these possible utilizations.

The actual outcome may be either one of the three defined conditions. Since deviations from the estimate of 7000 cars a day are likely to occur, the outcome is uncertain. Anticipated returns are at best averages of all possible returns that can be expected from very low to very high estimates. In the language of statistics they are expected values. The greater the uncertainty associated with the expected value, the greater the probability that actual returns will differ from the expected returns. If the uncertainty is small, it implies a high probability that actual returns will approach expected returns.

Uncertainty can have many causes, to that even a partial list becomes lengthy and overlapping. Therefore possible causes of uncertainty are best described in the context of a specific investment decision. Assume, for example, that a food manufacturer observes that the decline in the birthrate may have been halted and, as a consequence, that the market for baby food is likely to expand. These observations are the background for subsequent investment of corporate funds in the following:

1. A development program leading to a complete new line of baby food, encompassing latest evidence of nutritional requirements, taste appeal, and packaging to facilitate serving.
2. A pilot market-testing program to identify suitable advertising and distribution channels.
3. A new production facility to produce efficiently the quantities expected.
4. Training programs for producing and distributing the new product.

Any of these activities can run into difficulties. The observed leveling of the birthrate may only be a temporary phenomenon, preceding a continuing decline. The development program may not produce a product sufficiently different from those currently on the market; the pilot market test may identify low consumer acceptance; the production facility may require investment in excess of the amount originally visualized; the personnel department may find it difficult to recruit the necessary labor force. Thus, even the most carefully planned programs face great uncertainties as to the potential outcome of the course of events envisioned during the investment phase. Each of the events described will have implications on the cash flow and accounting profit emanating from the contemplated investment. Thus planned benefits are not assured: They may deviate in either direction from those assumed initially. They are uncertain.

The specific uncertainties identified above may occur in addition to political and economic events impinging on all business activities at that time. War or peace, recession or prosperity, inflation and unemployment are all events that are likely to influence the degree of success associated with a particular investment. These are issues over which the investing firm has no control. Nevertheless, these events can have great impact on the actual returns realized from the investment. The greater the dependency of expected returns on a particular state of nature, the greater the uncertainty associated with the investment. Similarly, the smaller the likelihood that a given state of nature on which expected returns depend is going to prevail, the greater the uncertainty facing the investment.

For example: At the time of the 6-day Arab-Israeli war in 1967, very little excess capacity existed in the world's oil tanker fleet. The closing of the Suez Canal lengthened tanker routes, and a shortage of vessels developed immediately. This in turn prompted a supertanker construction boom. Those who invested in oil tankers stood to reap respectable profits if the international situation remained as it was in 1967. The oil boycott in 1973 and the subsequent reopening of the Suez Canal changed this situation dramatically. Returns were for the most part substantially less than expected. The deviation in outcome experienced by investors was not caused by faulty products or insufficient advertising, nor could it be remedied by altering management practices. It was due solely to changes in the state of nature.

Since uncertainty cannot be avoided, it must be treated explicitly in the financial planning process. This can be accomplished by stipulating a range of likely outcomes, varying these stipulations, and observing the changes that occur in expected benefits as the assumptions are altered. Thus, in addition to examining only a probable sales forecast, management may wish to inspect both a forecast at the high end of the range of possible outcomes and one at the low end. For each of these forecasts probable returns can be developed.

This approach will provide a clue to management as to whether a proposed investment should be undertaken, even if the probability is considerable that returns will be less than expected. In the previous example, an analysis of world tanker needs in case of stabilized oil consumption and the reopening of the Suez Canal could be conducted. A subjective probability assessment of such development might also be made. Assume that if the demand persists an annual return of $30 million will be realized. On the other hand, if the demand for tankers slackens, a $10 million annual loss will be experienced. An assessment of the political outlook leads to a probability assessment of 60% that the Canal will remain closed and 40% that it will reopen. The expected return is therefore 40% × (−10,000,000) + 60% × 30,000,000 or $14 million. The range of outcome, from a loss of $10 million to a gain of $30 million, is an indication of the riskiness of this investment. The decision will depend on the willingness of management to accept risk and an assessment of whether the expected return of $14 million is commensurate with this risk. More on that later.

THE FUTURE ENVIRONMENT

The study of domestic politics, international relations, and macroeconomics is clearly beyond the scope of this volume. Nevertheless, as demonstrated earlier, all these factors influence the returns an organization may realize from its investments. Emerging developments in the future environment that may influence the nature and direction of the financial decisions of the organization must be tracked and evaluated. This requires a rudimentary understanding of these disciplines. Management must be sensitive to developments in these areas since they often influence sales revenue and profits. It must also be prepared to adopt appropriate financial strategies to capitalize on opportunities and hedge against adverse developments that result from economic and political factors beyond its control.

Larger organizations handle this problem by means of staff specialists and the use of consultants. Smaller organizations, with limited resources, must of necessity compromise in this area and utilize the judgment of the management team. Either approach, however — whether full staff capabilities are available to the financial manager or whether the individual must rely on his or her own resources — requires that the manager keep attuned to the external environment by reading, listening, and investigating. Uncertainties facing the financial manager cannot be controlled, yet the manager must be explicitly aware of this uncertainty and include appropriate considerations in the financial planning process.

Financial forecasting and planning are discussed in Chapter 7, and recommended approaches based on the considerations enumerated here are indicated. At this point it suffices to restate that the orientation of financial management is towards the future. While past events are tracked for the purpose of understanding trends and rewarding performance, for reporting to stockholders, tax collectors, and regulatory agencies, the basic function of financial management remains the direction of corporate assets to realize returns in the future. Therefore the uncertain external environment must be considered part of the framework within which financial management operates.

The significance of the external environment to financial management is not limited to business firms. Management of not-for-profit institutions requires a high degree of sensitivity to emerging political and economic trends. Charitable institutions, for example, must keep abreast of economic trends and changes in the tax laws as these may significantly influence charitable contributions. Governmental agencies are particularly sensitive to changing attitudes regarding the political priorities of funding proposed programs. Here, as in profit oriented organizations, good management dictates that contingency planning be undertaken in a timely fashion.

SUMMARY

Financial management allocates existing resources with the expectation of reaping benefits in the future. Returns may not materialize as expected. This deviation from anticipated results is termed uncertainty or risk. Some of these deviations, such as advertising budgets and quality assurance, are under the control of the organization while others, such as the weather and the economy, are beyond its control.

It is the responsibility of financial management to keep abreast of external developments that might influence the financial health of the organization. Contingencies should be assessed with respect to their probable impact on financial returns and needs. Sensitivity to the significance of emerging trends is a necessary trait for successful management.

4 Accounting Conventions

Financial decisions are usually formulated on the basis of information generated by the accounting system. Proper interpretation of the data requires an understanding of the assumptions underlying such systems, the convention adopted in recording information, and the limitations inherent in the information presented. To facilitate this understanding, basic accounting concepts are presented and discussed in this chapter. Although the issue of data interpretation is conceptual in nature, the problems encountered in this process are best understood in the context of concrete numerical examples.

Fundamental to an understanding of the accounting system is the differentiation between stock and flow concepts. A *stock* in this context refers to wealth in monetary (dollars, pesos, liras) or other forms (buildings, land, bonds, accounts receivable) available to the owners at a given point in time. Similarly, it refers to obligations due the owners at that point in time. A *flow* refers to the receipt or disbursement of wealth occurring between any two points in time. Thus wealth received during a stated period, in the form of salary, sales revenue, or interest payment, reflects a flow of wealth identified by a beginning and an ending date.

An analogy may prove helpful. The gasoline present in the underground reservoir of a service station is a stock of gasoline; similarly, the gasoline remaining in an automobile tank is a stock of gasoline. Activation of a pump may result in a transfer of gasoline from the reservoir to the tank; this process is a flow of gasoline. The stock of gasoline in the reservoir or tank is measured in gallons; the flow from one to the other is measured in gallons per minute. After the transfer has been in effect for a certain amount of time, the stock in the reservoir is diminished and the stock in the automobile tank is increased.

A numerical example further illustrates this point. Let us assume stocks of 5000 gallons in the reservoir and 2 gallons in the automobile. If the pump generates a flow of 5 gallons per minute, then after 2 minutes a total flow of 10 gallons will have taken place. The stock in the reservoir will be reduced to 4990 gallons and the stock in the tank of the automobile increased to 12 gallons.

Accounting systems recognize the difference between stock and flow. The basic statement of the stock of wealth is termed the Balance Sheet; the flow of wealth is presented in the Income Statement. The Balance Sheet reflects the wealth position at a point in time; the Income Statement presents the flow of wealth between two stated points in time.

Graphically the linkage is as follows:

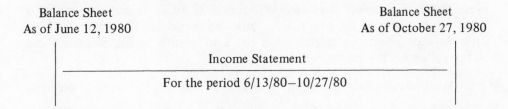

Balance Sheet
As of June 12, 1980

Balance Sheet
As of October 27, 1980

Income Statement

For the period 6/13/80–10/27/80

In the absence of the infusion of new capital from the outside, the change in the net stock of wealth from 6/13/80 to 10/27/80 is due to activities reflected in the Income Statement spanning these dates.

The Balance Sheet and the Income Statement are key documents of financial accounting, the activity concerned with the recording and portrayal of historical financial events.

Accounting, as most disciplines, has evolved a terminology with specialized meanings which appear formidable to outsiders. Often the terms used by accountants have a substantially different meaning in general usage, and a high degree of confusion arises from attempts to understand these terms and the concepts they represent on the basis of conventional usage.

A typical example of this issue is the nomenclature use by accountants to designate transactions. Conventions have evolved that require differentiation between entries made on the left hand side of a column and those made on the right hand side of the same column. Accountants refer to entries on the left as debits and to entries on the right as credits. Regardless of the conventional use of these terms, no value judgment about the nature of the entries made should be based on these designations. Debit simply refers to the left side of the column and credit to right side.

The Balance Sheet serves to illustrate this point. Customarily, the format of presentation consists of a "−T−", with the assets of the organization presented on the left hand side (the debit side) and the liabilities and

	Liabilities
Assets	
	Ownership

ownership on the right hand side (the credit side). Adding to an asset is referred to by accountants as "debiting" that asset, while adding to liabilities or ownership would be termed "crediting" the account involved.

Before proceeding with a more detailed examination of the Balance Sheet, an additional issue deserves clarification. As discussed previously, the Balance Sheet portrays the stock of wealth at any point in time. The question of whose stock of wealth has been skirted until now. In some instances the answer is obvious. The Balance Sheet of a corporation deals with the stock of wealth of a legal entity and describes the net wealth position of its owners. Similarly, if a Balance Sheet is developed for a household, it will detail all assets and liabilities of that entity. Often, however, the entity is not that clearly defined. Consider a college professor who also happens to have an active consulting practice. If he were to draw up a Balance Sheet representing the stock of wealth of his business some of the following problems could arise:

- Are the cash balances in his checking acount for personal or business use?
- Is his car, which is used primarily for contacting clients, a personal or a business asset?
- Are the outstanding bank loans attributable to the business or to the household?

These questions are often difficult to resolve in the abstract and answers must be sought on a case-by-case basis. The essential point to keep in mind is that prior to the development of financial statements the *entity* whose stock and flow of wealth is to be displayed must be delineated and defined.

THE BALANCE SHEET

The Balance Sheet is frequently presented in the format discussed above:

on the left hand side (the debit side) are listed those assets to which the entity has primary claim. Examples of these assets are

- Cash on hand or in bank
- Accounts receivable

- Inventories
- Investments
- Land
- Buildings
- Equipment

All these examples are tangible assets, which can be identified as physical entities or clearly documentable financial claims. The Balance Sheet also lists intangible assets, such as goodwill, patents, and some defered charges. Often these assets arise from prior transactions or accounting treatments.

The right hand side (the credit side of the Balance Sheet) contains outsiders' claims on the assets of the entity. Outsiders fall into two categories: lenders and owners. The accounting term for claims of lenders is liabilities, for the claims of owners it is equity or net worth.

Examples of liabilities are

- Accounts payable
- Mortages
- Bonds outstanding

Examples of equity accounts are

- Preferred stock
- Common stock
- Retained income
- Paid in Surplus

The Balance Sheet can be presented schematically as follows:

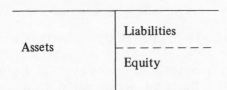

This presentation gives rise to the basic Balance Sheet equation:

assets = liabilities + equity

It has significant implications for financial management and will be discussed repeatedly in Chapters 9 to 17.

Assets are generally grouped into two categories: current assets and fixed assets. Current assets consist of cash or claims on outsiders that are expected to be converted into cash in less than a year. For example, customers are expected to pay their bills within 90 days. Fixed assets, on the other hand, have longer life expectancies. Examples of fixed assets are land and manufacturing equipment. Some asset accounts cannot be differentiated so readily and appropriate judgment must be exercised in categorizing them.

Liabilities are also grouped into two main categories. Current liabilities are expected to be discharged in less than 1 year. Long term liabilities are not due within the next fiscal year. An example of current liabilities is accounts payable. These are payments due to the suppliers of goods and services to the entity. Examples of long term liabilities are mortgages and bonds outstanding.

Components of equity accounts are treated in greater detail throughout this book. For the purpose of understanding the Balance Sheet mechanism, only three accounts are discussed in detail: common stock, paid in surplus, and retained income. Preferred stock is not introduced at this point.

Common stock describes the ownership of the corporation in terms of the number of shares outstanding. Each share is assigned an arbitrary, usually very low, par value for legal reasons. The common stock entry on the Balance Sheet is obtained by multiplying the par value adopted per share times the number of shares issued by the corporation. The resulting total should be viewed for what it is — an arbitrarily adopted number not bearing any particular relationship to the market value of the common stock.

To illustrate, assume for example that 20,000 shares of common stock are issued and that a par value of $2 per share is adopted. The equity account entry on the Balance Sheet would therefore read: 20,000 $2PV shares = $40,000. If, when the corporation was organized, each share was actually sold at $13, the difference between funds received and the common stock account is recorded in the paid in surplus (PIS) account.

In this example,

$$PIS = \$220,000 = (\$13 \times 20,000 - \$40,000)$$

The third equity account that merits explicit treatment at this time is retained income. It reflects the accumulated income after taxes retained in the entity since its inception. This accumulation is the net of any dividend payments that may have been made to stockholders. Recall the earlier discussion about stock and flow of wealth. Retained income represents the summing of past flows of wealth into a stock of wealth.

At this point it is important to clarify an issue that is often misunderstood. The equity accounts represent claims on assets but are not assets in their own right. They reflect past transactions and accounting entries but do not contain funds for future disbursement. Retained income, for example, is to be viewed as a historical record of past transactions and not as a source of future financing. There is absolutely no cash in the retained income account, as there is none in the common stock and paid in surplus accounts. The retained income account cannot provide funds for future acquisitions, regardless of the magnitude of the numbers recorded.

Having clarified the underlying concepts and assumptions, it is now appropriate to introduce a sample Balance Sheet. Assume that a group of investors are encouraged by increased federal spending for health care. To partake in the emerging need for service, they organize a corporation with the objective of providing hospital services to the public: 500,000 shares, with a par value of $1 per share are issued at a price of $10 per share. The proceeds of this public offering are deposited in a corporate checking account. To simplify the illustration all transaction costs and administrative expenses associated with the offering are ignored.

The opening Balance Sheet is as follows:

Hospital Services Corporation
Balance Sheet
As of January 1, 1980

Cash	$5,000,000		
		Common stock $1 PV;	$500,000
		Paid in surplus	$4,500,000
Total assets	$5,000,000	Total equities	$5,000,000

Further assume that during the month of January the following purchases are made:

1. An existing building is acquired for $7 million. The transaction is financed with $2 million in cash and a $5 million mortgage.
2. Equipment worth $300,000 is acquired for cash.
3. Inventories of supplies and pharmaceuticals costing $200,000 are acquired on credit.

These transactions are reflected in the following Balance Sheet for January 31, displayed on page 40.

Several points merit comment. First, total assets more than double without the issuance of additional common stock. This was accomplished by incurring current liabilities (accounts payable) and long term liabilities (mortgages). Second, in spite of the substantial increase in total assets, stockholders' equity remains unchanged. Third, in addition to stockholders, others (suppliers and lenders) now have a claim on the assets of the corporation.

Hospital Service Corporation
Balance Sheet
As of January 31, 1980

Cash	$2,700,000	Accounts payable	$200,000
Inventories	200,000		
Current assets	$2,900,000	Mortgage	5,000,000
		liabilities	$5,200,000
Equipment	300,000		
Building	7,000,000	Common stock $1 PV	$500,000
Fixed assets	$7,300,000	Paid in surplus	4,500,000
		equities	$5,000,000
		Total liabilities	
Total assets	$10,200,000	and equities	$10,200,000

T-ACCOUNTS

A digression is proper at this point to explain the actual mechanics of accounting transactions. Each account on the Balance Sheet or the Income Statement is a summary of numerous transactions previously recorded in subsidiary accounts. For example, accounts receivable is a summary of payment due from all customers as a stated date, January 31, 1980 in this example. The information for each customer, however, is collected separately. The mechanism for collecting the data is the T-Account, listing debits on the left hand side and credits on the right hand side. Data for each customer are collected in a separate T-Account with entries paralleling those of the corresponding affected T-Account on the Balance Sheet.

An illustration clarifies this process. Accounts receivable appear on the debit (left) side of the Balance Sheet. Each customer has a subsidiary T-Account, with the amounts outstanding recorded as debits. Thus, for example:

Customer A	Customer B	Customer C	Accounts receivable
$100	$200	$300	$600

If customers A, B, and C owe $100, $200, and $300 respectively, total accounts receivable are $600. The T-Account, accounts receivable serves as a summary, reflecting the outstanding balances in subsidiary accounts.

Assume now that accounts receivable are $600 and that current cash balances are $1 million.

Accounts receivable		Cash	
$600		$1,000,000	

Now assume that customer B pays his outstanding obligation by sending a check for $200. The effect on our Balance Sheet is to increase cash balances and decrease accounts receivable. In accounting terminology, we debit cash and credit accounts receivable. By dealing in T-Accounts the logic of this becomes apparent. As customer B pays off his debts, our cash balances increase. To record an increase in a Balance Sheet T-Account, we make an entry on the same side on which the T-Account is displayed on the Balance Sheet. Since cash is on the debit side, an increase to cash is a debit entry. Accounts receivable, however, have experienced a decrease in this transaction. To record a decrease, our entry is made in the opposite side of its Balance Sheet position, the credit (right hand) side. The transaction appears as follows:

Accounts receivable		Cash	
$600	$200	$1,000,000	
		200	

and is read by accountants as follows: debit cash $200, credit accounts receivable $200. Note that the one transaction decrease of accounts receivable involves two entries, hence double entry bookkeeping! Eventually our accounts are summarized and appear as follows:

Accounts receivable		Cash	
$400		$1,000,200	

One further example. If customer A pays $50 on his account, the transaction reads: debit cash $50, credit accounts receivable $50.

The opening transactions of the Hospital Service Corporation can now be designated appropriately.

1. The issuance of capital stock
    Debit cash $5,000,000
        Credit common stock $500,000
        Credit paid in surplus $4,500,000

2. Acquisition of building
    Debit building $7,000,000
        Credit cash $2,000,000
        Credit mortgage $5,000,000

3. Purchase of equipment
    Debit equipment $300,000
        Credit cash $300,000

4. Acquisition of inventories
    Debit inventories $200,000
        Credit accounts payable $200,000

Note that a debit represents either an increase in an asset account or a de-crease in a liability account. Thus the acquisition of equipment and the payment of debts outstanding are both debit entries. Similarly, a credit reflects either a decrease in an asset account or an increase in a liability or equity account. Reduction of cash balances and increased debts are both credit entries.

THE INCOME STATEMENT

So far only transactions dealing with the stock of wealth have been dis-cussed. In activities such as sales and payments for services rendered the flow of wealth is involved. Examples are cash receipts and payments for rent, labor, and interest on indebtedness. These transactions are summar-ized in the second basic financial document, the Income Statement.

Referring back to the Hospital Service Corporation, let us assume that normal business activities commenced on February 1, 1980. The following transactions are noted for the month of February. To simplify the presen-tation, assume that no other expenses were incurred in addition to those stated. For example, the absence of expenses for food indicates that pa-tients fasted during the month of February!

1. Receipts from patients for services and pharmaceuticals: $380,000

2. Cost of pharmaceuticals: $114,000

3. Salaries paid to hospital staff and management: $208,000

4. Interest on mortgage: $40,000

Based on these transactions, the Income Statement for the month of February is prepared.

Hospital Service Corporation
Income Statement
February 1 — February 29, 1980

Revenue:

   Sales $380,000

Expenses:

   Cost of goods sold $114,000
   Salaries......................... 208,000
   Interest......................... 40,000   362,000

Net income $18,000

The relevant T-Account entries are as follows:

1. Debit cash $380,000
    Credit sales revenue $380,000

2. Debit cost of goods sold $114,000
    Credit inventories $114,000

3. Debit salary expense $208,000
    Credit cash $208,000

4. Debit interest expense $40,000
    Credit cash $40,000

These activities are reflected in the appropriate T-Accounts below. The numbers in parentheses in these accounts identify the above listed transaction number.

Cash		Sales revenue	
$2,700,000	$208,000 (3)		$380,000 (1)
(1) 380,000	40,000 (4)		

Cost of goods sold		Interest expense	
(2) $114,000		(4) $40,000	

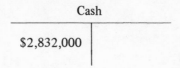

Two types of summarizing entries are now appropriate. The first of these is the netting of debits and credits within each account. For cash, the summary result is

Cash

$2,832,000

For inventories, it is

Inventories

$86,000

The second type of summary involves the revenue and expense accounts that were summarized individually and presented on the Income Statement. These accounts are closed out into the Retained Income account. As they are closed out, their residual value equals the net income previously computed.

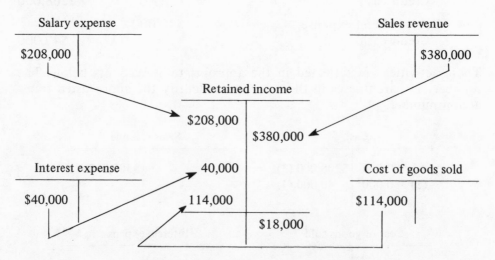

The Retained Income account appears in the equity portion of the Balance Sheet. The residual of the revenue and expense accounts for the current period, $18,000, is added to the balance recorded in the Retained Income account as of January 31, 1980. In this instance, since the corporation is newly established, that balance is zero. Usually, however, positive or negative balances already exist and the profit or loss recorded for a particular period is added to the sum total of all previously recorded profits or losses. In this case the balance becomes $18,000.

If dividends are distributed to stockholders, the retained income account is reduced by the amount of dividends actually paid out. Assume that $.02 a share are distributed on February 28, 1980. The total amount distributed is 500,000 X $0.02 = $10,000. The accounting entries are as follows:

Debit retained income $10,000
Credit cash $10,000

After the distribution, the balances in these accounts are as follows:

Cash	Retained income
$2,822,000	$8,000

To prepare the February 29, 1980 Balance Sheet, we list the accounts presented on the February 1, 1980 Balance Sheet, reflect the changes that resulted from the transactions identified above, and add the new accounts introduced during the month. If our record keeping was correct, the double entry bookkeeping system should again provide us with a conformation to the basic Balance Sheet equation:

Assets = liabilities + equity

Hospital Service Corporation
Balance Sheet
As of February 29, 1980

Cash	$2,822,000	Accounts payable	$200,000
Inventories	86,000	Mortgage	5,000,000
Current assets	$2,908,000	Total liabilities	5,200,000
Equipment	300,000	Common stock $1 PV	$500,000
Building	7,000,000	Paid in surplus	4,500,000
Fixed assets	$7,300,000	Retained income	8,000
		Total equities	$5,008,000
		Total liabilities	
Total assets	$10,208,000	and equities	$10,208,000

Checking according to the equation:

Total assets = total liabilities + total equities

$10,208,000 = $5,200,000 + $5,008,000

The Balance Sheet balances!

GENERALLY ACCEPTED ACCOUNTING PRINCIPLES

A customary phrase in the opinion letters from auditors accompanying corporate financial statements is that these documents "fairly represent the corporate financial position in conformity with generally accepted accounting principles consistently applied." *Generally accepted accounting principles* is an important term and merits some discussion.

While accounting draws on economic theory as an overall framework, specific decisions must be made by practitioners based on their interpretation of the situation at hand. To aid in providing consistency to these judgments, the Accounting Practices Board (APB) and the Financial Accounting Standards Board (FASB) publish guidelines for the resolution of troublesome, frequently encountered issues. Where these guidelines do not exist, or in cases where additional interpretations are feasible, accountants rely on the professional body of knowledge and the practices prevalent at the time the judgment is rendered. All these interpretations, guidelines, and judgments are customarily termed Generally Accepted Accounting Principles (GAAP). It it important to note, however, that unlike principles encountered in some other disciplines, GAAP are not verifiable experimentally nor can they be deduced unequivocally from theoretical premises. Instead they represent the prevalent professional judgment at the time they are applied. Different interpretations of GAAP by professionals are possible, and are indeed made.

DEPRECIATION

Depreciation is an important issue in financial management that deserves explicit discussion. Its treatment influences the availability of cash, the reported income, and the tax liabilities incurred. Thus it concerns not only management and its accountants but also the Internal Revenue Service (IRS). The involvement of the IRS stems from the effect that depreciation practices have on tax liabilities. To present its point of view in a consistent fashion the IRS has published guidelines for practitioners. Since depreciation policies have considerable implications insofar as stockholders' relations and corporate cash positions are concerned, they are also of interest to nonfinancial managers.

Depreciation arises from the recognition that with the exception of land all capital assets have a finite life span. The cause of this may be technological and economic obsolescence or simply wear and tear from ordinary use. In addition to labor and material costs, which are readily observable and are recorded as expenses, production costs must include an allowance for this phenomenon. The accounting mechanism for accomplishing this is the establishment of two accounts: depreciation expense — an Income Statement account, and reserve for depreciation — a Balance Sheet account.

An example illustrates this mechanism. Assume that the equipment acquired by the Hospital Service Corporation is expected to provide the desired services for 8 years. Further, assume that it is estimated it may be sold after 8 years for $60,000. Straight line depreciation computations would then be as follows:

$300,000 − $60,000 = $240,000 (total value to be depreciated)

$240,000 ÷ 8 = $30,000 (annual depreciation charges)

The T-Account entries for 1980 are

Depreciation expense		Reserve for depreciation	
$30,000			$30,000

Reserve for depreciation appears on the Balance Sheet as a counter account against equipment, reducing the purchase price preciously entered.

Equipment	$300,000
Less reserve for depreciation	30,000
Net equipment	$270,000

Depreciation expense is entered on the Income Statement, reducing the reported profit from what it would have been otherwise. However, in contrast to other expenses, depreciation expense does not entail an outflow of cash from the organization. This highly significant point will be amplified later. Since reported profits are now lower than what they would have been without depreciation expense, income taxes, if payable, will also be lower. Depreciation thus serves as a tax shelter.

In addition to straight line depreciation, several other systems are in use. Sum-of-the-years-digits and double-declining-balance are the best known. These systems are based on the observation that the reduction in market value of equipment is greatest in the early years of acquisition and

less in later years. Rather than list as an expense an identical portion of
the cost of the asset each year over the life span of the asset, the largest
depreciation expenses are reported in early years, with continually decreasing entries after that. In addition to the tax shield effect already discussed, these practices directly influence the net profit reported by the
organization. Compared to straight line depreciation methods, profit is
understated in early years and overstated in later years.

Sum-of-the-years-digits depreciation methods are best explained by
means of a numerical example. Assume a capital asset is to be depreciated
over 5 years. To compute each year's depreciation charges, the book value
of the asset is multiplied by a fraction that differs from year to year. The
denominator of the fraction remains the same; it is developed by adding
the digits of the total number of years that the asset is to be depreciated.
In the given example the denominator is: $5 + 4 + 3 + 2 + 1 = 15$. The nu-
merator of this fraction differs from year to year. In the first year it is the
number of years the asset is to be depreciated, in the second year that
number less one, and so forth. Thus, for the given example, depreciation
charges are 5/15, 4/15, 3/15, 2/15 and 1/15. Note that by this method depreciation charges are large in the early years and smaller in the subsequent years.

Consider again the example of the Hospital Service Corporation. The
denominator of the fraction of sum-of-the-years-digits (SYD) depreciation
is $8 + 7 + 6 + 5 + 4 + 3 + 2 + 1 = 36$. The depreciation schedule for the investment of $240,000 is presented in Table 1.

Double-declining-balance (DDB) depreciation is computed by doubling
the straight line depreciation charges computed for the remaining book
value of the capital asset. Assume a life of 3 years for a $10,000 asset
with zero salvage value. Depreciation charges in the first year are: 2 ×
($10,000/3) = $6667. In the second year, the book value is $10,000 −
$6667 = $3333. Depreciation charges according to DDB computations are

Table 1   Sum-of-the-years-digits depreciation for an 8-year $240,000 investment

Year	SYD Fraction	Depreciation
1	8/36	$53,333
2	7/36	46,667
3	6/36	40,000
4	5/36	33,333
5	4/36	26,667
6	3/36	20,000
7	2/36	13,333
8	1/36	6,667
Total	36/36	$240,000

Table 2   Double-declining-balance for an 8-year $240,000 investment

| Year | DDB | |
	Depreciation	Remaining book value
1	$60,000	$180,000
2	45,000	135,000
3	33,750	101,250
4	25,312	75,938
5	18,985	56,953
6	14,238	42,715
7	10,679	32,036
8	8,009	24,027

2($3333/3) = 2222. Remaining book value for the third year computation is $3333 − $2222 = $1111. Third year depreciation charges are therefore 2 × ($1111/3) = $741. Note that a small book value $1111 − 741 = $340 remains at that point.

Depreciating the $240,000 capital asset of the Hospital Services Corporation over 8 years results in the DDB decprciation schedule presented in Table 2.

Table 3 compares the straight line, sum-of-years-digits and double-declining-balance methods for a $240,000, zero salvage value investment to be depreciated over 8 years.

Note the increased deductions that SYD and DDB provide in the early years over straight line depreciation. To determine the crossover point from higher to lower charges, the graphic presentation in Figure 11 is helpful.

Table 3   Comparative depreciation charges for an 8-year $240,000 investment under Straight line, SYD, and DDB depreciation methods

| Year | Depreciation charges | | |
	Straight line	SYD	DDB
1	$30,000	$53,333	$60,000
2	30,000	46,667	45,000
3	30,000	40,000	33,750
4	30,000	33,333	25,312
5	30,000	26,667	18,985
6	30,000	20,000	14,238
7	30,000	13,333	10,679
8	30,000	6,667	8,009
Total	$240,000	$240,000	$215,973
Remaining book value	-0-	-0-	$24,027

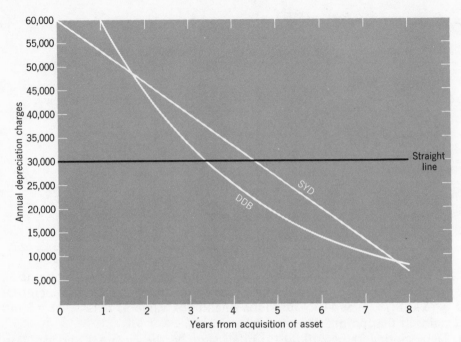

Figure 11. Comparison of changing depreciation write-offs under Straight Line, Sum-of-Year-Digits (SYD), and Double-Declining-Balance (DDB) methods.

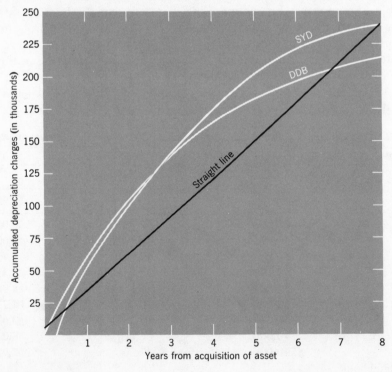

Figure 12. Comparison of accumulating depreciation under Straight Line, SYD, and DDB methods.

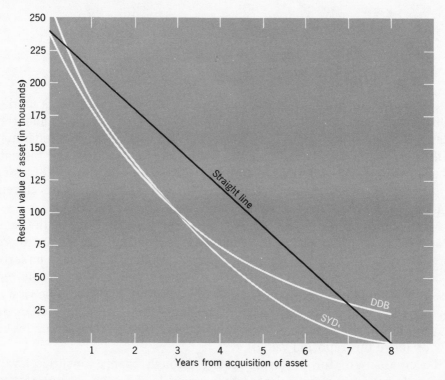

Figure 13. Comparison of residual value Straight Line, SYD, and DDB depreciation methods.

Figures 12 and 13 display the respective balances in the Reserve for Depreciation and Asset accounts for each of these depreciation methods over time. Notes that under DDB the asset is depreciated more rapidly in early years but is never totally written off the balance sheet since some residual net value always remains.

PRICE LEVEL ACCOUNTING

An important issue requiring discussion is the impact of price inflation in the economy on accounting practices. The topic is complex and the proposed solutions to this dilemma are beyond the scope of this book. Nevertheless, it is important to discuss the implications of current practices.

Balance Sheet assets, although acquired in different time periods, are simply added to arrive at the value of total assets. In general these assets are listed at cost less GAAP-sanctioned adjustments. This implies that if the original purchaser of Manhatten Island had incorporated, and the corporation was still intact and had retained title to the purchase, its Balance Sheet would identify the property under land as $24! Let us further assume that this corporation's only other assets today are cash balances of $100,000. Total assets would therefore be reported as follows:

Cash	$100,000
Land	24
Total assets	$100,024

The widely held assumption that reported asset value represents market value is therefore clearly misleading. The understated value of Manhattan Island is obvious and would not cause difficulties if identified separately with a proper explanation about the nature of the property and the date of acquisition (1626). The distortion arises from the addition of this asset, acquired with twenty-four 1626 dollars, to cash which represents current dollars.

Most corporations acquire their assets over time and not in the same year. The value of total assets appearing on the Balance Sheet must therefore be viewed as not necessarily representing current value. Similarly, owner's equity, as reported on the Balance Sheet, does not necessarily represent the liquidation of market value of ownership but should be viewed solely as the residual of past accounting transactions. Actual value of the corporation in liquidation or as a going concern may be considerably below or above this reported value.

To compensate for problems arising through changes in price levels, proposals have been promulgated that would lead to the adoption of inflation-adjusted Balance Sheets. If these are adopted, reported equity will more closely represent the liquidation value of assets, although not necessarily the market value of the corporation.

The Income Statement is not immune to the problem of inflation. The most serious effect is in the cost of goods sold (COGS). Assume, for example, that the Fort Knox Corporation is in the gold selling business. Much of its inventory was acquired during the 1930s at a price of $35 per ounce. As the corporation sells its gold it must replenish its inventory at current wholesale prices, say $180 per ounce. Further assume that the retail sales price is currently $200 per ounce. We learn that 1000 ounces are sold during 1980 and that selling and administrative expenses total $50,000.

To develop an Income Statement, the COGS policy must be stated. Two options are available: first-in-first-out (FIFO) and last-in-first-out (LIFO). Under FIFO, COGS are reported at the earliest price paid (in this example, $35 per ounce). Under LIFO, COGS are reported at the most recent prices paid ($180 per ounce in this case). The alternate Income Statements acceptable under GAAP are as follows:

1. *FIFO*

Fort Knox Corporation
Income Statement
1/1/1980 – 12/31/1980

Sales revenue	$200,000
COGS	35,000
Gross profit	$165,000
Selling and administrative expense	50,000
Net profit	$115,000

2. *LIFO*

Fort Knox Corporation
Income Statement
1/1/1980 – 12/31/1980

Sales revenue	$200,000
COGS	180,000
Gross profit	$20,000
Selling and administrative expense	50,000
Net profit	($30,000)

Under FIFO, the corporation reports a profit, while under LIFO a loss is presented. Furthermore, under FIFO an income tax liability may be incurred; this is not the case under LIFO. In times of stable prices the differences are probably slight; in inflationary periods, however, the impact can be pronounced. Good financial management requires careful consideration of the implications of alternative reporting methods. Furthermore, this example demonstrated that to use reported profit does not suffice as an indicator of the success of the endeavor; an understanding of the accounting practices yielding these profits is required before proper judgments can be formed.

FINANCIAL RATIOS

The Balance Sheet and the Income Statement of any entity can be developed in relative rather than absolute terms. For example, assets can be stated on a percentage basis so that total assets equal 100%. This in turn will result in total liabilities and equities expressed as a percentage of total assets.

As an example, the January 31, 1980 Balance Sheet of the Hospital Service Corporation would appear as follows:

Hospital Service Corporation
Balance Sheet
As of January 31, 1980

Cash	26%	Accounts payable	2%
Inventories	2%	Mortgage	49%
Current assets	28%	Total liabilities	51%
Equipment	3%	Common stock $1 PV	5%
Building	69%	Paid in surplus	44%
Fixed assets	72%	Total equities	49%
		Total liabilities	
Total assets	100%	and equities	100%

Similarly, the Income Statement can be expressed in terms of the percentage of sales revenue.

Hospital Service Corporation
Income Statement
February 1 — February 29, 1980

Revenue:

Sales 100%

Expenses:

Cost of goods sold 30%

Salaries 55%

Interest 10%   95%

Net Income   5%

These presentations are most useful in that they permit the comparison of information related to the composition of assets and liabilities of any given organization to that of other entities engaged in the same type of activity. For example we may wish to compare the percentage held in cash to determine whether, in relation to our total assets, we make adequate use of our cash balances or whether excess amounts are carried. Similarly, we may wish to compare the percentage COGS of our product with that of a similar product to determine whether our purchasing and pricing policies are in line.

In making these comparisons care must be exercised that the basis for comparison is valid. The entities compared must serve similar clientele with similar products, must be reasonably equal in size, and must have reached some maturity in their respective activities. Otherwise misguided conclusions leading to inappropriate management actions may easily be reached.

Over time some of these relationships were judged by financial management and outsiders (investors and lenders) to have particular significance as indicators of financial health and good management. Many of these relationships may be computed directly, without requiring the expression of all entries on the financial statements in percentage form. These relationships are known as financial ratios.

Four main types of financial ratios are commonly used:

- Liquidity ratios
- Profitability ratios
- Activity ratios
- Leverage ratios

Examples of each type of ratio are presented below. The emphasis in the examples presented is on understanding the underlying concepts and on the ability to acquire facility with the nomenclature in use. The numbers presented should not be viewed as typical or representative unless it is specifically stated that they are.

Liquidity Ratios

Liquidity ratios are used as indicators of an entity's ability to discharge its current obligations in times of stress. The best known of these is the current ratio. It is defined as

$$\text{current ratio} = \frac{\text{current assets}}{\text{current liabilities}}$$

and is usually expressed in terms of a ratio, such as $2:1$; $0.8:1$; $2.7:1$.

Another well-known liquidity ratio is the quick ratio, also called the acid test. It is defined as

$$\text{quick ratio} = \frac{\text{current assets} - \text{inventories}}{\text{current liabilities}}$$

This ratio is usually applied when current assets have a high component of inventories that are not readily marketable, such as work-in-process. In such instances the current ratio does not adequately represent the entity's ability to meet its current obligations since inventories may not be subject to rapid liquidation at the recorded value on the Balance Sheet. The quick ratio is stated in the same terms as the current ratio: 0.7:1; 1.3:1; 2:1.

For the Hospital Service Corporation the liquidity ratios as of February 29, 1980 are as follows:

current ratio = 2908/200 = 14.5 : 1

quick ratio   = 2822/200 = 14.1 : 1

These numbers are *not* representative of a going concern. As time passes it may be anticipated that the cash raised through the stock offering will be used for corporate purposes, that inventories will increase and that accounts payable and other current liabilities will also increase. Assume the following partial Balance Sheet for the end of the year.

Hospital Service Corporation
Balance Sheet
December 31, 1980

Cash	$58,932	Accounts payable	$68,351
Accounts receivable	134,000	Accrued expenses	91,725
Inventories	87,435	Income tax payable	9,872
Total current assets	$280,367	Total current liabilities	$169,948

In this example, the current ratio is

$280,367/$169,948 = 1.6 : 1

The quick ratio is

($280,367−$87,435)/$169,948 = 1.1 : 1

Profitability Ratios

The second set of ratios commonly used are the profitability ratios. Here the focus is on the profit realized and its relationship to the revenue generated or its relationship to the resources employed, for example, total assets or equity. As long as one deals with relationships within either stock or flow statements, no particular complications arise. When both statements are involved, however, care must be exercised that the resulting percentage is expressed in terms of the time period covered by the Income Statement. The following example will clarify this point.

For the Hospital Service Corporation, income for the month of February 1, the Balance Sheet reflected total assets of $10.2 million and equities of $5 million. Based on this information, we can compute the following:

$$\text{profit margin on sales} = \frac{\text{net profit}}{\text{sales}} = \frac{\$18,000}{\$380,000} = 4.7\%$$

$$\text{return on total assets} = \frac{\text{net profit}}{\text{total assets}}$$

$$= \frac{\$18,000}{\$10,200,000} = 0.2\% \text{ per month}$$

Note that these returns are computed on the basis of the flow period spanning the Income Statement, in this case 1 month. If one assumes that net income remains identical for each of 12 months, total net income for the year amounts to 12 $\times$ $18,000 = $216,000. Return on total assets for the year then becomes

$$\frac{\$216,000}{\$10,200,000} = \underline{2.1\%}$$

This is the more common form of profitability ratio.

One additional adjustment requires comment. The implication of taxes on financial management is explored in detail in Chapter 5 and need not be developed here. In most cases profitability is reported on an after-tax basis. If the Hospital Service Corporation is a nonprofit organization, and therefore exempt from payment of corporate income taxes, this discussion is not relevant. Assume, however, that the annual tax liability of this corporation is 40% of reported income. Then net earnings after taxes (EAT) are

$$\$216,000 \times (1 - .4) = \$129,600$$

$$\text{return on total assets} = \frac{\text{earnings after taxes}}{\text{total assets}}$$

$$= \frac{\$129,600}{\$10,200,000} = \underline{1.3\%} \text{ per year}$$

Return on equity is computed as

$$\text{return on equity} = \frac{\text{EAT}}{\text{equity}} = \frac{\$129,600}{\$5,000,000} = \underline{2.5\%}$$

Activity Ratios

A third set of financial ratios deals primarily with the utilization of assets entrusted to corporate management. They are particularly useful in tracking the performance of operating managers in charge of specific functions such as inventory management, cash management, and credit policy. The four commonly used ratios of this kind, usually referred to as activity ratios, are

$$\text{fixed asset turnover} = \frac{\text{sales}}{\text{fixed assets}}$$

$$\text{total asset turnover} = \frac{\text{sales}}{\text{total assets}}$$

$$\text{inventory turnover} = \frac{\text{sales}}{\text{inventory}}$$

$$\text{average collection period} = \frac{\text{accounts receivable}}{\text{sales per day}}$$

Using annualized data for the Hospital Service Corporation:

$$\text{fixed assets turnover} = \frac{\$380,000 \times 12}{\$7,300,000} \simeq \underline{\underline{0.6 \text{ times}}}$$

$$\text{total asset turnover} = \frac{\$380,000 \times 12}{\$10,200,000} \simeq \underline{\underline{0.4 \text{ times}}}$$

$$\text{inventory turnover} = \frac{\$380,000 \times 12}{\$200,000} \simeq \underline{\underline{23 \text{ times}}}$$

The Balance Sheet of the Hospital Service Corporation does not include accounts receivable. To demonstrate the use of the ratio, suppose that a total of $450,000 in bills from patients and insurance companies have not yet been collected. They, with sales per day of $13,000 ($380,000/30 = $13,000),

$$\text{average collection period} = \frac{\$450,000}{\$13,000} \simeq \underline{\underline{35 \text{ days}}}$$

Each of these ratios provides feedback for operating managers on the nature of their operations and on the adequacy of the controls instituted.

Leverage Ratios

The final set of ratios in wide usage are termed leverage ratios. These aim at displaying the nature of the methods and sources of financing utilized in acquiring the corporate assets and their impact on the earnings available to common stockholders. The debt to total assets ratio is computed as

$$\text{debt to total assets} = \frac{\text{total debt}}{\text{total assets}}$$

For the Hospital Service Corporation, as of February 29, 1980:

$$\text{debt to total assets} = \frac{\$5,200,000}{\$10,208,000} = 51\%$$

The two other commonly used ratios are defined as follows:

$$\text{fixed charge coverage} = \frac{\text{income available for fixed charges}}{\text{fixed charges}}$$

expenses

and,

$$\text{times interest earned} = \frac{\text{earnings before taxes plus interest charges}}{\text{interest charges}}$$

Assume that salaries reported on the February 1 – February 29 Income Statement for the Hospital Service Corporation are fixed (for example 10-year employment contracts). Then:

$$\text{fixed charge coverage} = \frac{\text{net income} + \text{fixed charges}}{\text{fixed charges}}$$

In this case fixed charges consist of salaries and interest, $208,000 + $40,000 = $248,000.

$$\text{fixed charge coverage} = \frac{\$18,000 + \$248,000}{\$248,000} = \underline{1.07 \text{ times}}$$

Usually, however, fixed charges consist of payments such as lease obligations, property taxes, and interest.

Times interest earned is computed for the Income Statement as defined.

$$\text{times interest earned} = \frac{\$18,000 + \$40,000}{\$40,000} = \underline{1.5 \text{ times}}$$

Table 4 summarizes the ratios described in this section. See page 60.

Several points must be stressed at this time. First, the ratios discussed above have gained acceptance through common usage. Advocates feel that they can gain insight into corporate activities through these analyses. Whether this is indeed true has not been proven conclusively. The fact remains, however, that outsiders are apt to analyze corporate financial statements to determine the correlation between specific corporate ratios and those experienced by a sample of organizations engaged in similar activities. Astute financial management will therefore conduct similar analyses as a defensive measure in order to be prepared to explain any divergences that may exist. An example of available ratios is given in Table 5. See page 61.

The second point worth stressing in this context is that these ratios are not sacrosanct. If a manager discovers that certain other relationships derived from financial statements provide him with useful information for planning or control purposes, he or she should certainly be encouraged to

Table 4 Commonly used ratios

1. Liquidity ratios
   a. Current ratio $= \dfrac{\text{current assets}}{\text{current liabilities}}$

   b. Quick or acid test $= \dfrac{\text{current assets} - \text{inventories}}{\text{current liabilities}}$

2. Profitability ratios

   a. Profit margin on sales $= \dfrac{\text{net profit}}{\text{sales}}$

   b. Return on total assets $= \dfrac{\text{net profit}}{\text{total assets}}$

   c. Return on equity $= \dfrac{\text{earnings after taxes}}{\text{equity}}$

3. Activity ratios

   a. Fixed asset turnover $= \dfrac{\text{sales}}{\text{fixed assets}}$

   b. Total asset turnover $= \dfrac{\text{sales}}{\text{total assets}}$

   c. Inventory turnover $= \dfrac{\text{sales}}{\text{inventory}}$

   d. Average collection period $= \dfrac{\text{accounts receivable}}{\text{sales per day}}$

4. Leverage ratios

   a. Debt to total assets $= \dfrac{\text{total debt}}{\text{total assets}}$

   b. Fixed charge coverage $= \dfrac{\text{income available for fixed charges}}{\text{fixed charges}}$

   c. Times interest earned $= \dfrac{\text{earnings before taxes} + \text{interest charges}}{\text{interest charges}}$

Table 5 Dun & Bradstreet key business ratios

Line of Business (and number of concerns reporting)	Current assets to current debt	Net profits on net sales	Net profits on tangible net worth	Net profits on net working capital	Net sales to tangible net worth	Net sales to net working capital	Collection period	Net sales to inventory	Fixed assets to tangible net worth	Current debt to tangible net worth	Total debt to tangible net worth	Inventory to net working capital	Current debt to inventory	Funded debts to net working capital
	Times	Per cent	Per cent	Per cent	Times	Times	Days	Times	Per cent	Per cent	Per cent	Per cent	Per cent	Per cent
2873-74-75-79 Agricultural Chemicals	3.14	8.25	28.44	52.27	5.56	8.65	23	15.3	18.9	37.8	48.9	38.9	86.1	5.8
	2.26	5.20	18.53	33.73	3.57	5.27	36	8.6	32.4	51.2	117.3	72.1	137.9	35.9
(46)	1.66	2.08	11.68	18.44	2.85	4.08	61	5.6	52.2	103.2	172.0	143.1	211.2	122.9
3724-28 Airplane Parts & Accessories	3.09	6.39	17.92	25.88	4.27	5.72	41	7.3	25.2	32.6	60.8	51.0	65.8	26.4
	2.23	4.50	11.75	16.49	2.90	3.94	52	4.6	46.9	59.5	116.8	95.2	92.8	54.5
(68)	1.77	1.43	5.43	6.20	1.79	2.67	65	3.2	71.4	102.2	202.2	126.2	121.7	74.0
2051-52 Bakery Products	2.92	2.63	12.35	38.31	8.04	27.30	19	33.8	55.5	22.0	46.5	35.9	116.5	18.0
	1.72	1.47	5.77	16.51	4.73	14.88	24	24.5	72.0	45.5	76.4	77.1	181.9	52.5
(54)	1.34	0.51	3.04	7.01	3.66	7.88	35	15.2	98.7	71.3	159.1	138.0	249.5	172.8
3312-13-15-16-17 Blast Furnaces, Steel Wks. & Rolling Mills	2.53	7.20	21.42	52.20	3.83	7.58	31	9.5	52.8	33.6	59.0	72.8	75.0	37.1
	2.03	6.13	16.81	35.38	2.80	5.95	39	7.1	78.6	47.4	75.3	85.0	99.6	62.3
(61)	1.74	4.27	13.93	22.93	2.30	4.42	48	4.9	94.5	70.2	104.5	114.8	159.5	87.3
2331 Blouses & Waists, Women's & Misses'	2.44	2.58	19.65	27.10	12.01	14.29	30	19.8	4.0	64.3	79.1	51.8	114.2	3.2
	1.74	1.52	12.49	14.89	7.82	10.37	38	10.9	9.8	85.5	153.6	96.2	154.5	34.0
(54)	1.32	0.54	4.09	6.76	5.14	5.87	60	6.2	24.8	185.4	250.9	139.6	272.1	66.2
2731-32 Books; Publishing & Printing	3.99	7.39	16.84	22.53	3.32	4.52	46	6.2	11.3	26.5	46.7	57.6	47.4	7.4
	2.38	4.02	10.18	15.48	2.08	2.89	62	3.6	33.2	46.0	86.0	73.4	85.7	24.9
(55)	2.06	2.91	6.11	9.09	1.70	2.03	77	2.9	54.3	79.5	135.5	100.5	146.9	62.7
2211 Broad Woven Fabrics, Cotton	4.54	5.35	13.30	20.54	3.29	5.08	36	8.4	36.9	16.9	54.3	53.5	48.2	21.4
	3.32	3.42	8.40	10.60	2.81	3.98	53	6.0	50.3	33.7	83.6	74.6	64.3	45.7
(56)	2.25	1.34	3.17	4.29	2.00	3.04	65	3.8	64.9	56.0	134.7	98.1	96.4	67.9
2032-33-34-35-37-38 Canned & Preserved Fruits & Vegbls.	2.83	5.34	22.63	36.61	6.09	12.07	15	7.7	41.4	43.0	84.3	78.5	65.3	22.6
	1.79	3.16	14.05	21.11	4.43	6.53	24	5.0	58.7	77.3	117.5	129.3	87.9	44.4
(78)	1.36	1.68	7.72	11.15	3.32	4.92	36	3.7	89.4	165.8	249.4	225.7	122.3	90.7
2751 Commercial Printing except Lithographic	3.40	4.59	14.69	27.93	5.08	9.40	36	**	41.6	21.0	57.9	**	**	15.3
	2.23	2.79	9.65	16.78	3.32	5.40	44	**	60.8	47.1	86.9	**	**	53.3
(74)	1.68	1.32	4.14	9.62	2.04	4.03	60	**	90.6	86.5	136.3	**	**	119.4
3661-62 Communication Equipment	3.89	7.72	19.57	28.88	4.35	4.87	49	6.0	22.2	33.1	54.1	61.9	57.3	23.4
	2.46	4.13	12.06	14.71	3.05	3.55	64	4.5	44.3	60.8	111.3	79.7	85.7	50.2
(78)	1.80	1.79	4.79	5.83	2.18	2.77	86	3.5	64.1	105.2	183.1	99.0	152.2	73.2
3271-72-73-74-75 Concrete, Gypsum & Plaster Products	3.04	5.71	14.71	36.73	3.89	10.73	34	15.9	43.1	19.2	46.1	39.0	79.5	32.9
	2.22	3.56	7.91	18.83	2.46	5.76	46	9.5	64.3	40.9	81.5	61.0	132.6	68.5
(85)	1.45	1.58	3.61	10.81	1.93	4.08	63	6.0	90.2	81.0	130.3	99.2	255.5	150.4
2065-66-67 Confectionery & Related Products	3.91	4.07	11.30	23.13	5.42	11.46	17	9.9	35.6	24.4	35.8	65.6	52.5	13.6
	2.35	2.33	8.00	13.83	3.95	6.40	26	7.5	52.9	38.6	68.8	100.4	75.3	28.9
(40)	1.89	0.38	1.23	2.16	2.73	4.99	42	5.1	67.5	67.2	131.4	146.8	124.8	54.8
3531-32-33-34-35-36-37 Const., Min. & Handling Machy. & Equipt.	3.06	6.04	16.71	23.58	4.88	5.83	43	6.5	24.1	40.5	87.4	75.8	54.0	33.2
	2.18	3.73	12.56	15.42	3.45	4.14	61	3.8	45.9	63.6	114.2	95.0	80.2	49.0
(89)	1.84	1.96	8.29	8.67	2.28	2.71	79	2.8	65.3	103.8	186.9	123.0	117.6	74.0
2641-42-43-45-46-47-48-49 Convtd. Paper & Paperboard Prods.	3.67	5.51	17.80	30.32	4.49	7.85	33	8.5	30.8	25.7	53.1	60.3	61.5	15.9
	2.85	3.77	13.63	18.44	3.34	4.66	43	6.0	51.6	40.7	73.3	91.1	77.1	35.8
(73)	1.78	2.33	9.12	12.67	2.47	3.65	58	4.6	73.7	73.9	119.6	111.0	124.2	66.7
3421-23-25-29 Cutlery, Hand Tools & General Hardware	3.67	5.55	17.08	21.76	3.93	5.39	37	5.9	27.5	25.3	48.9	74.0	47.5	14.3
	2.50	3.79	11.84	15.68	2.76	4.09	45	4.3	39.8	45.8	73.6	94.2	70.7	38.7
(80)	1.90	2.37	7.10	9.95	2.08	3.15	56	3.2	61.6	73.4	134.9	120.6	89.0	59.7
2021-22-23-24-26 Dairy Products	2.04	2.30	14.99	51.25	10.56	32.91	18	32.7	48.2	39.3	73.5	62.6	126.1	29.1
	1.49	1.23	9.24	24.08	7.28	20.79	25	22.0	67.8	69.3	105.8	95.3	207.2	65.6
(103)	1.26	0.42	3.84	10.09	4.97	12.23	31	11.0	94.1	114.1	164.7	157.3	300.9	130.6
2335 Dresses: Women's, Misses' & Junior's	3.09	2.10	14.66	16.52	11.68	13.78	33	16.5	2.6	37.6	67.2	55.8	83.5	4.9
	1.86	0.85	5.91	7.21	7.42	8.30	48	10.0	9.0	95.1	149.9	78.1	138.7	19.4
(98)	1.42	0.16	1.70	2.15	3.86	4.48	58	6.0	23.3	199.6	245.0	121.9	223.1	66.3

** Not computed. Printers carry only current supplies such as paper, ink, and binding materials rather than merchandise inventories for re-sale.

Source. Key Business Ratios, © 1975 by the Business Economics Division of Dun & Bradstreet, Inc. Used by permission.

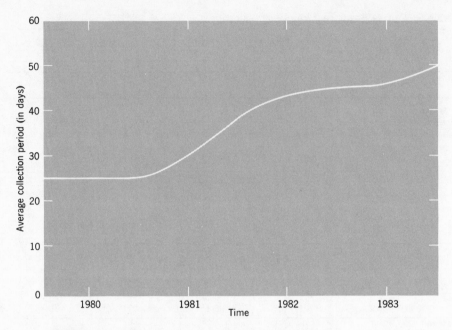

Figure 14. Average collection period – possible shape of curve.

develop and use such ratios. The fact that these relationships are not among the commonly listed ratios should not act as a deterrent.

Finally, ratios may serve as a useful control for managers in plotting selected performance. For example, the credit manager may wish to plot the average collection period over time (Figure 14). This will spotlight changes in customer payment schedules and permit the institution of remedial actions to accelerate payments or secure additional funds. Without such early warning signals, an unanticipated shortage of funds may develop in the organization.

FUND ACCOUNTING

Governmental units, charitable and educational institutions, and other not-for-profit organizations adopt slightly different financial statements. In lieu of equity, the Balance Sheet contains fund balances and retained earnings. Fund balances are the excess of budgeted amounts over expenditures incurred or committed. Retained earnings may arise from those activities for which services are provided at a fee to the public. Each fund is administered as an entity; expenditures may only be committed for amounts budgeted in that particular fund.

This has important implications for financial management in the not-for-profit sector. Allocations in profit oriented organizations reflect management perceptions and interests; as these change, budgets can be revised and reallocation between projects may be made. This method retains considerable flexibility for management in adapting to changing conditions. In the public sector and frequently in other not-for-profit organizations funded allocations are embedded in law, and expenditures may only be incurred if authorized for the designated purpose of the fund.

These legal limitations may introduce severe constraints on management's freedom of action. Suppose that a technological innovation enables an organization to effect worthwhile savings by replacing labor with newly available equipment. An organization subject to fund accounting might not be in a position to transfer funds readily from its operations fund to its capital fund and might therefore have to sacrifice these possible savings.

The accounting principles on which fund accounting is based are generally similar to those discussed above. The peculiarities of governmental and charitable funding give rise, however, to procedures that are unique to this sector of the economy. One example is the absence of capital assets and depreciation charges from the statements. An asset once acquired is no longer listed and is therefore not depreciated. The attitude of management toward excess fund balances may also differ from the attitude of profit oriented management toward retained income.

SUMMARY

The accounting system is best understood in the context of the stock and flow of wealth. The Balance Sheet is the basic document reflecting the stock of wealth of an entity at a given point in time. The Income Statement portrays the flow of wealth between two points in time. T-Accounts are the mechanism for recording accounting transactions. Generally accepted accounting principles (GAAP) reflect currently accepted conventions of recording accounting information.

The depreciation policies adopted by an entity have considerable implications for reported profit, tax liabilities, and cash positions. Double-declining-balance and sum-of-the-years-digits generate earlier write-offs than straight line depreciation. These and other accounting practices must be known before reported profit can be properly interpreted.

Financial ratios are widely used as indicators of financial health of organizations. The four commonly used ratios are liquidity, profitability, activity, and leverage. Managers find it useful to plot selected ratios over time for control purposes. Governmental and many other not-for-profit organizations adopt fund accounting. Statements based on fund accounting pose specialized problems of interpretation and control.

5 Tax Environment

The days when taxes were levied solely for the purpose of raising revenue for the sovereign have long since passed. Indeed it is questionable whether the issue of taxation was ever that simple. For example, the interrelationship of a poll tax and a census of the population some twenty centuries ago, comes to mind. Generally, tax policy encompasses considerations of revenue, redistribution of wealth, and macroeconomic consequences.

The tax structure in effect at any point in time reflects compromises in economic orientation achieved through the political process. Legislators probably consider the position of economists, political scientists, and other spokesmen for particular schools of thought and specific interest groups on issues they deem important during the formative stages of the legislation. These may include considerations of equity, income distribution, incidence and shifting of taxes, ability to pay, work incentives, and morality, to name a few. The final tax legislation is developed, however, by compromising divergent points of view according to dominant voter preferences. This point is emphasized to demonstrate the futility of searching for a consistent economic rationale within prevailing tax codes. Thus, to operate effectively, managers must acquaint themselves with the diverse basic concepts underlying the tax structure and formulate their financial decisions with an awareness of what is and what is likely to be rather than what they believe should be. A financial manager must consider taxes in the decision process since ignoring them results in overstating anticipated income. Consequently investment alternatives may be pursued that do not actually provide adequate return for the risk exposure they entail.

In the United States we are blessed with more than a few taxing authorities. To name only the better known of these authorities, taxes may be levied by local, state, and federal governments, by school districts, water districts, and mosquito abatement districts. Taxes may be levied on property, income, and sales; it is difficult to avoid them. Since they cannot be avoided, financial management often strives to postpone taxes as we all attempt to postpone that other inevitability of life.

Taxing authorities are most ingenious in developing devices that fit the attributes and requirements of a given locale. Since the number of permutations and combinations of authorities and tax schemes is very large, a detailed exposition is beyond the scope of this book. The issue of taxation is, however, too significant to be ignored since it must be included in the basic decision process of managers in profit oriented organizations. Checking into tax implications must become second nature to these managers. Although not-for-profit organizations are not subject to most of the taxes levied, managers in the government sector may find it useful to learn how their actions are likely to affect profit oriented decisions.

To provide the necessary exposure, one particular tax, the federal corporate income tax, is explored here. Since this tax is generally the most pervasive and the largest in magnitude, it has the greatest potential for swaying an investment decision from acceptance to rejection.

A basic concept underlying the federal income tax laws is that as additional income is earned, the percentage tax liability on the incremental income increases. In 1977, for example, the tax liability for the first $25,000 of corporate income was 20%; for the next $25,000 it was 22%; and for all income over $50,000 a tax liability of 48% was incurred.

Thus for example, corporate income of $80,000 was taxed as follows:

```
20% of $25,000 =  $5,000
22% of $25,000 =  $5,500
48% of $30,000 = $14,400
Total  $80,000  $24,900
```

Similarly, the tax liability on income of $180,000 was

```
20% of  $25,000 =  $5,000
22% of  $25,000 =  $5,500
48% of $130,000 = $62,400
Total  $180,000 = $72,900
```

Two terms capture the concept underlying this tax structure: the marginal tax rate and the average tax rate. The marginal tax rate is defined as the percentage liability imposed on the next dollar of earned income. The average tax rate is defined as that rate which, if applied to all taxable income, would result in the reported tax liability.

In the first example, the marginal tax rate at $80,000 and applicable to additional income above that is 48%. The average tax rate experienced at the taxable income of $80,000 is $24,900/$80,000 = 31%. In the second example, the marginal tax rate applicable to income above $180,000 is again 48%, while the average tax rate has increased to 41% ($72,900/$180,000). Note that although the average rate approaches the marginal rate as taxable income increases, it will never actually equal it.

Two additional examples will clarify the relationship between average and marginal tax rates. At an income of $10,000 the marginal rate is 20% which, in this case, is also the average tax rate. At an income level of $40,000 the marginal rate is 22%, while the average rate is ($5000 + $3300)/$40,000 or about 21%.

Since the financial decision maker is concerned with the liability that will be incurred if additional income is earned, the relevant decision input is therefore the marginal rate. The average rate presents obligations incurred to date and may be of general historical interest. For decision purposes, however, the significant information is conveyed by the marginal tax rate. In most corporate settings the applicable marginal tax rate prevailing in 1977 was 48%.

Several additional features of the federal corporate income tax are worth mentioning. They are not introduced to serve as definitive guidelines for applications, but rather as a means of understanding the nomenclature, creating familiarity with the underlying concepts, and stimulating the utilization of expert advice if appropriate. The features discussed below are capital gains, carry-back-carry-forward, certain tax exemptions, and the investment tax credit. Since tax rates are continually subject to change, few specific numbers are introduced.

The tax laws differentiate between income earned in the ordinary conduct of business and that earned from the appreciation in value of capital assets owned by the corporation prior to sale. While the definition of what constitutes a capital asset for the purpose of claiming such a tax treatment is complex, as a general rule it is worthwhile to explore the applicability of this feature since the capital gains tax rate is below the highest marginal rate.

A calendar year is a rather arbitrary time span in the life cycle of a business. It bears no particular resemblance to the time required for conceiving, developing, producing, and marketing a concept or a product. Business activities with highly cyclical markets for their products are liable to alternate between profitable years rather than show constant profits. The loss incurred should be viewed as a cost required to retain organizational capabilities in order to meet the demands of the market in subsequent periods. If the tax laws recognize only one-way relationships — tax liability on earned income but not partial government reimbursement for losses incurred — the business activity described above suffers an inherent disadvantage versus enterprises with more stable customer demand. In profitable years its tax bill is substantial, while in loss years it receives no relief. Its total tax payments as a percentage of revenue received is likely to be higher than those of a less cyclical endeavor.

A simple example will illustrate the dilemma. Suppose that a flat 50% tax rate on all earned income is in effect. Assume further that two corporations, A and B, report the taxable incomes shown in Table 6.

The tax liabilities that would be incurred at a 50% tax rate, in the ab-

Table 6 Taxable incomes for corporations A and B

Year	Taxable income (in millions)	
	Corporation A	Corporation B
1980	$5	$2
1981	($2)	$2
1982	$8	$2
1983	($5)	$2
1984	$4	$2
Total	$10	$10

Table 7 Tax liabilities for corporations A and B

Year	Tax liability (in millions)	
	Corporation A	Corporation B
1980	$2.5	$1
1981	—	$1
1982	$4	$1
1983	—	$1
1984	$2	$1
Total	$8.5	$5

sence of special provisions, are shown in Table 7. Thus with the same aggregate income, corporation A's tax payment would constitute an effective tax rate of 85% versus the 50% rate intended.

The carry-back-carry-forward provision recognizes these complications by permitting corporations to recompute their tax annually by taking into account the totality of profit and losses realized over a longer period of time.

Certain types of corporate income escape partial or total taxation. Prominent examples are as follows: 85% of dividends received by one corporation from another are exempt from taxation. Interest received from municipal bonds — the debt obligations issued by state or local taxing authorities — are totally exempt. Depletion allowances reduce income subject to taxation.

The final feature deserving special attention is the investment tax credit. It provides that up to 10% (in 1977) of the cost of a newly acquired capital asset may be claimed as a credit against the tax liability incurred. Assume for example, that a corporation has a taxable income of $400,000 in the year in which it acquired a capital asset for $900,000. Its tax liability is computed as follows:

$$
\begin{array}{lll}
20\% \text{ of } & \$25,000 = & \$5,000 \\
22\% \text{ of } & \$25,000 = & \$5,500 \\
48\% \text{ of } & \underline{\$350,000} = & \underline{\$168,000} \\
\text{Total} & \$400,000 = & \$178,500 \\
\text{Less:} \quad 10\% \text{ of } \$900,000 = & & \underline{-90,000} \\
\text{Tax liability} & = & \underline{\underline{\$88,500}}
\end{array}
$$

For profitable corporations, the effect of the investment tax credit is to reduce the true cost of the purchase to 90% of the actual purchase price.

Recall that depreciation expense decreases the income subject to taxation. Thus it acts as an effective tax shield. By reducing taxable income, the tax liabilities of the year in which the operating income is realized are reduced. As discussed in Chapter 4, several approved methods exist for shifting the bulk of depreciation charges incurred over the lifetime of a fixed asset to the early years of ownership. The effect of these accelerated depreciation methods is to postpone tax payment and thereby provide the corporation with interest-free working capital.

Assume, for example, Income Statement data consisting of sales revenue of $200,000, cost of goods sold of $70,000, and all other expenses exclusive of depreciation of $60,000. Further assume that at the beginning of the year a capital asset was acquired for $240,000 and that the corporation is subject to a flat 40% income tax rate. Financial management is considering the tax implications of adopting straight line, sum-of-the-years-digits on double-declining-balance depreciation methods. From Chapter 4 we know that first-year depreciation expense for these three methods are $30,000, $53,333, and $60,000 respectively.

Table 8 develops three Income Statements equally valid for tax purposes. Note that with accelerated depreciation accounting the tax liability in the early years is substantially reduced from that computed on the basis of straight line depreciation. In future years the reverse will be true (the

Table 8 Alternative income statements

	Depreciation method				
	Straight line		S-Y-D		DDB
Sales revenue		$200,000		$200,000		$200,000
Less: COGS		70,000		70,000		70,000
Gross profit		$130,000		$130,000		$130,000
Depreciation expense	$30,000		$53,333		$60,000	
Other expenses	60,000		60,000		60,000	
Total expenses		90,000		113,333		120,000
Earnings before taxes		40,000		16,667		10,000
Tax at 40%		16,000		6,667		4,000
Earnings after taxes		$24,000		$10,000		$6,000

reader may wish to verify this as an exercise). It is also important to note that regardless of the indicated accounting profit, financial management has more cash at its disposal if accelerated depreciation is adopted than it has with straight line depreciation.

The effect of depreciation is to shield operating income with expenses that do not entail the outflow of cash. Since expenses increase, taxable income decreases and tax liability is reduced commensurably. This is a particularly significant benefit if depreciation expense keeps the taxpayer in a lower tax bracket than he would otherwise be exposed to.

SUMMARY

The tax policy in effect at any point in time reflects compromises in economic orientation achieved through the political process. It is futile, therefore, to seek a consistent economic rationale within prevailing tax codes. Of particular concern to managers of profit oriented organizations are federal corporate income taxes. Managers of not-for-profit organizations are for the most part exempt from these taxes.

In assessing probable returns, managers should apply the appropriate marginal tax rate. Average rates are computed primarily for historical perspective and not for decision purposes. Depreciation expense serves as a tax shield and should be explicitly considered. Other significant tax features are the carry-back-carry-forward provisions, capital gains treatment, and the investment tax credit.

6 Mathematics of Interest

Interest, the time value of money, is the price paid to potential lenders and investors to induce them to postpone consumption. Even if funds are internally available within the organization, interest must be considered in financial decisions. The use of these funds entails an opportunity cost, that is, they could be invested elsewhere and earn a return. These possible returns will be sacrificed if available funds are earmarked for specific purposes.

Financial decisions encompassing interest considerations include those internal to the organization as well as those that entail interaction with capital markets. An example of the former is an evaluation assessing the desirability of replacing an existing computer with a newer, technologically more advanced model. Analysis of the merits of retiring an outstanding bond issue with a new issue is an example of the latter.

Interest is customarily stated as a percentage of the original sum involved, on a per annum basis. For example, 8% interest on a $500 loan would entail an obligation to pay $40 to the lender at the end of 1 year in addition to repaying the $500 loan. If the loan is renewed for a second year, and no interest payment is made by the borrower to the lender at the end of the first year, then the total payment due the lender at the end of the second year is $540 + $540 × 8% = $583.20. This total is composed of the repayment of the principal, the $500 originally borrowed, and $83.20 in compound interest charges.

PRESENT AND FUTURE VALUES

Algebraic notations are helpful in arriving at generalized solutions and should be viewed as efficient aids to communication rather than as formidable barriers. The development of general relationships helps to simplify calculations and to facilitate transactions. Readers lacking prior exposure to algebra may wish to skim the exposition of the formulas and use the interest tables.

For the purpose of this discussion let

P = the *principal* — a stock of wealth, usually expressed in dollars — equivalent to a sum of money available now

F = the *future value of the principal* — a stock of wealth, usually expressed in dollars

i = the *rate of interest* — percent of the principal, usually on a per annum basis

n = the number of periods funds are borrowed, usually years

R = a periodic equal payment, also called an *annuity* — a flow of wealth, usually expressed in dollars per annum

B = that presently available sum equivalent in value to a series of stated periodic payments, also called the *present value of an annuity* — a stock of wealth, usually expressed in dollars

W = that future sum equivalent in value to a series of stated periodic payments, also called the *future value of an annuity* — a stock of wealth, usually expressed in dollars

The expressions set in italic type help to simplify the terminology. As indicated, equal periodic payments are often referred to as annuities. Assume that such an annuity contract is in effect and that the payments are deposited in a savings account as they are received. Since interest is computed periodically, the account will grow over time to a sum that will be available at the termination date of the annuity contract. The future value of an annuity is that sum. The present value of an annuity is that sum which, if deposited for the length of time that the annuity is in effect and accruing interest at the same rate as the annuity, will equal the future value of the annuity.

Using these simplifications, the essential terms can be defined as follows:

P = the principal, or the present value of a sum

F = the future value of a sum

B = the present value of an annuity

W = the future value of an annuity

R = the annuity

n = the number of periods

i = the rate of interest

The problem of borrowing a sum of $500 at 8% for 2 years may now be formulated algebraically.

The initial step is to compute the value at the end of the first year. This future value can now be derived as follows:

$$F_1 = P + Pi$$

where F_1 stands for the future value at the end of 1 year. Or, simplifying the expression:

$$F_1 = P(1 + i)$$

If this future value is not repaid when due, at the end of 1 year it becomes an amount that is borrowed for the second year. The future value at the end of the second year becomes

$$F_2 = F_1 + F_1 i$$

or, simplifying again:

$$F_2 = F_1(1 + i)$$

But F_1 has already been determined to equal $P(1 + i)$. This expression can be substituted above to obtain

$$F_2 = P(1 + i)(1 + i)$$

This can be expressed as

$$F_2 = P(1 + i)^2$$

Substituting numerical values in the above algebraic expression:

$$F_2 = \$500 (1 + 0.08)^2, \text{ or } F_2 = \$583.20$$

It should be noted that after 1 year the appropriate expression was

$$F_1 = P(1 + i)^1$$

while after 2 years, it was

$$F_2 = P(1 + i)^2$$

The generalized expression for the future value of a sum after compounding for n years at interest rate i can be shown to be

$$F_n = P(1 + i)^n$$

This formula is helpful in organizing the necessary information for rapidly arriving at a solution. Consider, for example, the following problem: What is the future value of an investment of \$1000 at an interest rate of 10% per annum, held for three years? Here $P = \$1000$; $i = 10\%$; and $n = 3$; Hence

$$F_3 = \$1000(1 + 0.10)^3$$

$$F_3 = \$1000 \times 1.1 \times 1.1 \times 1.1$$

$$\underline{F_3 = \$1331}$$

The only cumbersome aspect of this calculation is the computation of the

Table 9 Excerpt from Table A for computing F, the future value of a sum

n\\i	0.07	0.08	0.09	0.10	0.11	0.12
1	1.070	1.080	1.090	1.100	1.110	1.120
2	1.145	1.166	1.188	1.210	1.232	1.254
3	1.225	1.260	1.295	1.331	1.368	1.405
4	1.311	1.360	1.412	1.464	1.518	1.574
5	1.403	1.469	1.539	1.611	1.685	1.762
6	1.501	1.587	1.677	1.772	1.870	1.974
7	1.606	1.714	1.828	1.949	2.076	2.211
8	1.718	1.851	1.993	2.144	2.305	2.476
9	1.838	1.999	2.172	2.358	2.558	2.773
10	1.967	2.159	2.367	2.594	2.839	3.106
11	2.105	2.332	2.580	2.853	3.152	3.479
12	2.252	2.518	2.813	3.138	3.498	3.896
13	2.410	2.720	3.066	3.452	3.883	4.363
14	2.579	2.937	3.342	3.798	4.310	4.887
15	2.759	3.172	3.642	4.177	4.785	5.474
16	2.952	3.426	3.970	4.595	5.311	6.130
17	3.159	3.700	4.328	5.054	5.895	6.866
18	3.380	3.996	4.717	5.560	6.544	7.690
19	3.617	4.316	5.142	6.116	7.263	8.613
20	3.870	4.661	5.604	6.728	8.062	9.646
21	4.141	5.034	6.109	7.400	8.949	10.804
22	4.430	5.437	6.659	8.140	9.934	12.100
23	4.741	5.871	7.258	8.954	11.026	13.552
24	5.072	6.341	7.911	9.850	12.239	15.179
25	5.427	6.848	8.623	10.835	13.586	17.000
26	5.807	7.396	9.399	11.918	15.080	19.040
27	6.214	7.988	10.245	13.110	16.739	21.325
28	6.649	8.627	11.167	14.421	18.580	23.884
29	7.114	9.317	12.172	15.863	20.624	26.750
30	7.612	10.063	13.268	17.449	22.892	29.960

interest factor $(1 + i)^n$. For reasons that will become apparent, designate it as T_A. To simplify even this aspect of the computational process, tables have been prepared that contain the relevant factor. For example, Table A on page 234 contains data for interest rates up to 36% and 30 periods rounded to three decimals. If required even more detailed tables, calculated from 1/64 of a percent in interest per period and extending up to hundreds of periods, are available in libraries and at financial lending institutions. Also, many electronic calculators that have been programed to compute these values are now available.

Table 9 is an excerpt from Table A. To select the proper interest factor, T_A, for the previous example, locate the appropriate interest percentage

(10%) in the top row and the specified number of periods (3) in the left hand column: T_A is the value listed at the point of intersection. The formula $F_n = P(1 + i)^n$ can be restated as $F_n = PT_A$. Substituting $P = \$1000$ and $T_A = 1.331$, we obtain

$$F_3 = \$1000 \times 1.331 = \$1331$$

Consider another example: $3152 is deposited in a savings account promising 6% per annum. What is the value of this deposit after 9 years? In this problem, $P = \$3152$; $i = 6\%$; and $n = 9$ years. From the table $T_A = 1.689$, therefore

$$F_9 = \$3152 \times 1.689$$

$$F_9 = \$5323.73$$

Readers who have a particular affinity for multiplication problems may wish to verify the result by multiplying

$$F_9 = \$3,152 \times 1.06 \times 1.06 \times 1.06 \times 1.06 \times 1.06 \times 1.06$$
$$\times 1.06 \times 1.06 \times 1.06$$

A more complicated type of problem may now be approached. This involves the equivalent sum that one is willing to accept at the present time in lieu of a promise to receive another, usually larger sum in the future. Or, to use the terminology previously introduced, the determination of the present value of a sum. In developing the answer to this problem, the power of algebraic formulation will become particularly evident.

Recall that $F = P(1 + i)^n$. In the problem just stated it is assumed that F, i, and n are all known. The issue is the determination of P. Solving the given equation for P, we obtain

$$P = \frac{F}{(1 + i)^n}$$

or

$$P = F\left[\frac{1}{(1 + i)^n}\right]$$

This becomes the second fundamental equation for compound interest calculations. As for the previous equation, tables have been developed for $1/(1 + i)^n$. These values are designated as T_B. The equation may thus be written $P = FT_B$. An excerpt from Table B on page 237 is presented in Table 10.

A common class of problems can now be handled efficiently. For example: What sum is an individual willing to accept today in lieu of a guaranteed inheritance of $10,000 due him 8 years from now if he believes that he can earn 9% on his investment?

The algebraic formulation results in

Table 10   Excerpt from Table B for computing *P*, the present value of a sum.

$n \backslash i$	0.07	0.08	0.09	0.10	0.11	0.12
1	0.935	0.926	0.917	0.909	0.901	0.893
2	0.873	0.857	0.842	0.826	0.812	0.797
3	0.816	0.794	0.772	0.751	0.731	0.712
4	0.763	0.735	0.708	0.683	0.659	0.636
5	0.713	0.681	0.650	0.621	0.593	0.567
6	0.666	0.630	0.596	0.564	0.535	0.507
7	0.623	0.583	0.547	0.513	0.482	0.452
8	0.582	0.540	0.502	0.467	0.434	0.404
9	0.544	0.500	0.460	0.424	0.391	0.361
10	0.508	0.463	0.422	0.386	0.352	0.322
11	0.475	0.429	0.388	0.350	0.317	0.287
12	0.444	0.397	0.356	0.319	0.286	0.257
13	0.415	0.368	0.326	0.290	0.258	0.229
14	0.388	0.340	0.299	0.263	0.232	0.205
15	0.362	0.315	0.275	0.239	0.209	0.183
16	0.339	0.292	0.252	0.218	0.188	0.163
17	0.317	0.270	0.231	0.198	0.170	0.146
18	0.296	0.250	0.212	0.180	0.153	0.130
19	0.277	0.232	0.194	0.164	0.138	0.116
20	0.258	0.215	0.178	0.149	0.124	0.104
21	0.242	0.199	0.164	0.135	0.112	0.093
22	0.226	0.184	0.150	0.123	0.101	0.083
23	0.211	0.170	0.138	0.112	0.091	0.074
24	0.197	0.158	0.126	0.102	0.082	0.066
25	0.184	0.146	0.116	0.092	0.074	0.059
26	0.172	0.135	0.106	0.084	0.066	0.053
27	0.161	0.125	0.098	0.076	0.060	0.047
28	0.150	0.116	0.090	0.069	0.054	0.042
29	0.141	0.107	0.082	0.063	0.048	0.037
30	0.131	0.099	0.075	0.057	0.044	0.033

$$P = \$10,000 \left[\frac{1}{(1 + 0.09)^8} \right]$$

which is a rather complex expression. Substituting from the table 0.502 for $1/(1.09)^8$ we obtain

$$P = \$10,000 \times 0.502 = \$5020$$

Assume now that a second individual is expecting an inheritance of $10,000 in 8 years, however, she believes that she can earn only 6% on her investment. How much would this second individual require to be willing to settle for today? From Table B, $T_B = 0.627$. Therefore

$$P = \$10,000 \times 0.627 = \$6270$$

The result is interesting and important, and may be generalized as follows:

The lower the interest — sometimes called the discount — rate, the higher the present value of a future payment.

Similarly:

The higher the discount rate, the lower the present value of a future payment.

Finally, only at zero interest is a future payment equal to its present value. An important corollary to this statement is that only at zero interest is it meaningful to add sums due to be received or payed in different time periods. As soon as the interest rate has a finite value, future sums must be appropriately discounted to permit meaningful addition.

An example will clarify this point. How much should an investor be willing to pay for an investment promising $5000 in 5 years, and $2000 in 7 years if, based on his assessment of the risk of the venture, he expects to earn 16% on his investment?

In Table B, at 16% interest, the interest factor for 5 years is 0.476 and for 7 years it is 0.354. Therefore

$$P = \$5000 \times 0.476 + \$2000 \times 0.354$$

or

$$P = \$2380 + \$708 = \$3088$$

Clearly, adding $5000 and $2000 without the appropriate discounting factor would have been an incorrect answer. Remember the following admonition:

Never add monetary units from different time periods without first discounting them appropriately.

Ignoring this caveat will result in computing a number that is not meaningful in an economic sense. Recall the discussion in Chapter 4 regarding assets enumerated on the Balance Sheet!

ANNUITIES

The stage has now been set to develop the concept of an annuity. Recall that an annuity is an equal periodic payment. Examples of annuities are mortgages, level whole-life insurance premiums, social security receipts, and even salaries and wages. To simplify the discussion, suppose that all the annuities specified in the examples are in the nature of contracts that can be bought and sold. This is not a necessary condition, but it helps explain the concepts that have been introduced in this chapter.

The algebraic development of the formula for the present and future values of annuities are concerned with the conversion of a flow of wealth — the annuity in dollars per period — into a stock of wealth. This stock of wealth can be expressed in dollars as a future value or as a present value. The timing of the periodic annuity payment, whether it is made at the beginning or the end of each period, is relevant. To assure consistency of treatment it is generally accepted that most payments are made at the end of a period. Examples of payments at the end of a period are salaries, mortgage payments, and social security receipts. In contrast an example of payments made at the beginning of the period, before services are rendered, are payments on an insurance policy.

Based on the convention that payments are made at the end of the period, the general expression for the future value of an annuity, W, can be developed. Again, view annuity payments as deposits to a savings account. The deposits are made at the end of each year and added to the deposits plus the interest already in the account. The annuity contract is for n years.

The first deposit made is R. Since it is deposited at the end of the first period it will remain in the savings account and draw interest for $n-1$ periods. Assume the annuity contract is for 5 years. The first payment is made at the end of the first year, earning interest for the remaining 4 years. The second deposit will be made at the end of the second year, earning interest for the remaining 3 years. The third deposit earns interest for 2 years, the fourth for 1 year, and the fifth does not earn any interest.

Table 11 on page 78, is an excerpt from a hypothetical savings account earning 6% and meeting the contractual arrangement specified before. The reader may find the stipulation that deposits are made at the end of the period somewhat unrealistic for this particular example. Yet, in a managerial framework, payments on funds borrowed are made after some time has elapsed and not immediately upon the borrowing of funds. Similarly, returns are earned on capital investments considerably after the investment decision is made. This point is discussed further in Chapter 7.

The example presented above may be generalized and can serve as the basis for deriving the algebraic expression for the future value of an annuity. In this example

$$W = \$1000(1 + 0.06)^4 + \$1000(1.06)^3 + \$1000(1.06)^2 + \\ \$1000(1.06) + \$1000 = \$5637.10$$

A generalized expression is:

$$W = R(1 + i)^{n-1} + R(1 + i)^{n-2} + \ldots + R(1 + i) + R$$

The Greek letter Σ customarily denotes the summation of a series. With

Table 11   Scrooge Savings Association

Our motto: A thousand dollars saved is $1500 earned before taxes!

Forced Savings Account # 1

Date opened: January 2, 1980

Terms of savings contract:

$1000 to be deposited at the end of each calendar year for the next 5 years

Interest computed annually at 6%

Date	Deposits	Withdrawals	Interest	Balance
January 2, 1981	$1000.00			$1000.00
December 31, 1981			$60.00	$1060.00
January 2, 1982	$1000.00			$2060.00
December 31, 1982			$123.60	$2183.60
January 2, 1983	$1000.00			$3183.60
December 31, 1983			$191.02	$3374.62
January 2, 1984	$1000.00			$4374.62
December 31, 1984			$262.48	$4637.10
January 2, 1985	$1000.00			$5637.10
January 3, 1985		$5637.10		-0-

this convention, the expression listed above may be presented in shorthand form:

$$W = \sum_{t=0}^{n-1} R(1 + i)^t$$

Using standard algebraic techniques, the formula for the future value of an annuity reduces to:

$$W = R\left[\frac{(1 + i)^n - 1}{i}\right]$$

The expression in the square bracket is interest factor T_C from Table C, page 240. Thus

$$W = RT_C$$

The Scrooge Savings Association example can now be handled more efficiently. From Table C, $T_C = 5.637$. Therefore

$$W = \$1000 \times 5.637 = \$5637$$

Similarly, assume that you have the strength of character to deposit $2500 each year into a savings account paying 7% per annum. What is the account worth after the fifteenth deposit, at the end of 15 years?

$$W = \$2,500 \times 25.129 = \$62,822.5$$

Here is another, more complex, example. An endowment life insurance policy requires 20 equal payments of \$282.30 per annum, with the first payment due upon signing the application for the policy. Suppose that the insurance company earns 6% on its investments. What should the policy be worth at the end of 20 years?

This problem introduces an additional complication. The first payment is made at the beginning of the period, remaining with the insurance company for 20 years and not 19 ($20 - 1$) years. Using the formula $F = P(1 + i)^n$, the future value of this payment may be computed separately. From Table A, T_A for 6% and 20 years equals 3.207. Therefore

$$F_{20} = \$282.30 \times 3.207 = \$905.34$$

The second step is to compute the future value of an annuity for 20 years:

$$T_C = 36.786.$$

Thus

$$W = \$282.30 \times 36.786 = \$10,384.69$$

One additional adjustment must now be made. No payment is due by the policyholder at the end of the twentieth year. Recall that the twentieth payment was made at the beginning of that year. Therefore \$282.30 must be subtracted from the total amount, and the value of policy at the end of the twentieth year is

$$\$905.34 + \$10,384.69 - \$282.30 = \$11,007.73$$

The reader who has followed and mastered this example is in full command of the concepts developed so far in this chapter.

A favorite sales argument offered by whole life insurance salesmen to prospective customers is, "after so many years you can cancel your policy and receive all your payments back," in addition to the fact that you were insured during the entire period. This argument ignores the time value of money, of which insurance companies are most conscious. Thus, if a policyholder in the example presented actually receives \$5646 at the end of 20 years, the insurance company will show a gross profit of

$$\$11,007.73 - \$5646 = \$5363.73$$

Granted that salesmen's commissions, company overhead, and actual risk must be met from this profit, the argument is still spurious. This digression should not be viewed as negating the merits of life insurance; rather it should alert the reader that the tools of financial analysis are as appropriate here as they are in other business applications.

The remaining mathematical problem is the determination of the present value of an annuity. Recall that the future value of an annuity is given by

$$W = R \left[\frac{(1 + i)^n - 1}{i} \right]$$

Also that the future value of a sum is given by

$$F = P(1 + i)^n$$

Equating these two expressions will define P as that sum which, if received today, is equivalent in value to an annuity R, received for n years if the interest rate is i percent per annum. Call that sum the present value of an annuity, denoted by B. Therefore

$$B(1 + i)^n = R \left[\frac{(1 + i)^n - 1}{i} \right]$$

Or

$$B = R \left[\frac{1 - (1 + i)^{-n}}{i} \right]$$

Or

$$B = RT_D$$

where T_D is the computed value of the expression in square brackets, found in Table D.

As an example, compute the annual equal payment due on a $50,000, 30 year mortgage if lender and borrower agree on a 9% interest rate per annum.

From Table D, page 244, T_D = 10.274

$$\$50,000 = R \times 10.274$$

$$R = \$4866.65 \text{ per annum}$$

The reason that this formulation, the present value of an annuity, is appropriate in this example is that $50,000 are advanced to the borrower *today* in exchange for a promise to make a series of payments (annuities) to the lender in the *future*, so that their *present value* equals the value of the loan.

FREQUENT COMPOUNDING

One refinement of these formulas is useful. Often the period of compounding is less than 1 year. For example, savings and loan associations advertise quarterly compounding. The interest rate is usually stated on a per annum basis. A simple adjustment permits the utilization of the previously developed formulas and tables.

Assume for example, that a savings institution advertises 8% per annum interest, compounded quarterly. What will be the value of a $1000 deposit in 5 years? The compounding takes place every quarter, after which 8%/4 = 2% actual interest has been earned on the previous investment. Thus 2% is the relevant interest rate. At the same time the number of periods increased from 5 to the new total number of compounding periods, or 5 × 4 = 20. To solve this problem, T_A is found for 2% and 20 periods, T_A = 1.486, and

$$F = \$1000 \times 1.486 = \$1486$$

Had the savings only been compounded annually, the deposit would have been

$$F = \$1000 \times 1.469 = \$1469$$

The difference is due to the increased frequency of compounding.

A general formulation of this procedure is helpful. Let m be the number of times that the interest stated on a per annum basis is compounded. Then

$$F = P(1 + i/m)^{mn}$$

$$P = F\left[\frac{1}{(1 + i/m)^{mn}}\right]$$

$$W = R\left[\frac{(1 + i/m)^{mn} - 1}{i/m}\right]$$

$$B = R\left[\frac{1 - (1 + i/m)^{-mn}}{i/m}\right]$$

Using the tables, the adjustment required for the determination of the relevant interest rate in the table is a division of the annual interest rate by the number of times interest is compounded per annum. Similarly, the relevant number of periods is the number of years stated multiplied by the number of times interest is compounded per year.

DECISION RULES

Many financial analyses entail the search of an answer to the following question: "Is it worthwhile to invest funds today (in building, equipment, research, etc.), considering the returns that can be expected to be realized in the future from this investment?" The application of the present value framework to this class of decisions is apparent. In essence it involves a comparison of the present value of future receipts to the present outlay of cash, the investment. Let C represent this investment. Thus

C = the investment

B = the present value of expected returns

or

$$B = RT_D$$

where R = annual returns and T_D = the relevant interest factor. Now as long as B is greater than C, the investment is desirable. When C is larger than B, future returns are not sufficient to justify present outlays.

The difference between the present value of expected returns and the initial investment required to generate these returns is termed the net present value (NPV). The decision rule specified above may be stated as follows:

If the NPV is positive, accept the investment proposal.
If the NPV is negative, reject the investment proposal.

An example illustrates this process. Assume that an investment of $15,000 is contemplated. If made, it will generate annual returns of $6000 for 4 years. To justify the risk that this investment entails, a minimum return of 18% is required. Should the investment be made? Here

C = $15,000

R = $6000

T_D = 2.69 (18% for 4 years)

NPV = $6000 × 2.69 − $15,000

NPV = $1140

Since NPV is positive, the investment should be made.

Assume now that another investment requiring $15,000 and returning $6000 per year for 4 years is judged more risky and therefore requires a return of 24%. Should this investment be made? Here

C = $15,000

R = $6000

T_D = 2.404 (24% for 4 years)

NPV = $6000 × 2.404 − $15,000

NPV = −$576

Since NPV is negative, the investment should not be undertaken.

Another decision rule associated with the annual percentage returns expected to be realized on the investment is frequently specified. It is commonly referred to as the internal rate of return (IRR) method. Rather than stipulate a rate of return that must be realized, this approach solves for the interest rate and then compares it to some predetermined rate which takes the risk of the venture into account. If the return computed exceeds the risk adjusted return specified, the decision is to accept the investment. If the expected return is less than the required risk adjusted return, the decision is to reject the investment. A numerical example will clarify this point. Assume:

$$C = \$32,500$$

$$R = \quad \$7000$$

$$n = 8 \text{ years}$$

The investment is judged to be quite safe, as for example, the replacement of an existing machine with a more efficient model so that an IRR of 12% is acceptable. Denote this risk adjusted return as r. Thus $r = 12\%$. Then, solving the equation for T_D:

$$\$32,500 = \$7000 \times T_D$$

$$T_D = 4.643$$

Going across the 8 period row in Table D until $T_D = 4.643$, the actual rate of return realized is found to be almost 14%. Since 14% is greater than the 12% specified, the investment is accepted.

Assume now that new estimate points to expected annual returns of only $6000 instead of the $7000 specified above. Should the investment be made?

$$\$32,500 = \$6000 \times T_D$$

$$T_D = 5.417$$

Going across the 8 period row in Table D until $T_D = 5.417$, the actual rate of return realized is found to be below 10%. Since 10% is less than the 12% specified the investment is rejected.

Although the concept of the IRR is appealing, it is not as widely used as the NPV method. A prime reason for this are the computational difficulties that arise when the annual returns from the project are uneven. While the NPV approach can easily handle this problem (finding the present value of each return separately rather than using the present value of an annuity), the IRR approach requires complex, iterative computational procedures. Therefore most practitioners prefer to deal with the NPV formulation.

A third method for deciding among investment proposals has achieved wide acceptance. It is called the payback method. As the name implies, it identifies the number of periods required to pay back the initial investment. Based on the number of periods thus estimated a decision is made to accept the investment or reject it.

Algebraically, the decision rule is formulated as follows:

Number of payback periods = C/R

Using the example presented initially,

C = \$32,500

R =   \$7000

the number of periods is 4.6, or under 5 years. If the predetermined decision rule calls for a 5-year payback, the investment will be accepted. The second example,

C = \$32,500

R =   \$6000

yields a payback period of 5.4 years, in excess of 5 years. Again, if the predetermined number of periods is 5, this proposal will be rejected.

Payback is appealing in its simplicity, but therein lies its weakness. It ignores the time value of money by allocating equal weight to near term returns and those due later on. It is inconsistent with the time preference concepts developed in this section and may give misleading signals, particularly in instances where returns are uneven over time. Thus the prevailing wide acceptance of the payback method should be discouraged as is stressed in this discussion.

The recommended method for most investment decisions is NPV. It is manageable in its complexity and is readily understood by practitioners, management, and investors. Capital budgeting, discussed in Chapter 8, utilizes the NPV approach for capital investment decisions.

SUMMARY

Interest is the time value of money and must be taken into account in all investment decisions, those requiring outside funds as well as those that are financed internally. The four basic mathematical formulations are the future value of a sum, the present value of a sum, the future value of an annuity, and the present value of an annuity. Tables and calculators that simplify required computations are readily available.

Several decision rules for the analysis of investment decisions have been developed. Although payback is the most widely used criterion it is theoretically deficient. The internal rate of return rule is acceptable in theory but may pose computational problems. The net present value method is theoretically sound, is readily understood, and can be applied to most financial problems. Capital budgeting decisions are usually made within the NPV framework.

7 Financial Planning

A prime function of financial management is to provide general management with the resources required for the attainment of corporate objectives. The financial plan is therefore a key ingredient in any organizational plan. The two purposes of the financial plan are to specify time-phased fund requirements and to identify the likely source of the funds needed.

Any plan requires a view of the future prior to its formulation. This view of the future (commonly termed a forecast) explicitly and implicitly lays out the political and economic conditions that are likely to prevail and are expected to affect business conditions and activity. Since the future is uncertain, judgment is an essential ingredient in the development of forecasts. Chapter 3 outlined some of these considerations.

FINANCIAL FORECASTS

With the development of mathematical programming techniques and the ready availability of computing capacity, econometric forecasting techniques have gained considerable acceptance. These forecasts are predicated on the stability of certain economic relationships and on the ability to capture these relationships in mathematical terms. Even if input data for these formulations are available, certain assumptions regarding political events, tax legislation, demographic factors, technological developments, and consumer preferences must be incorporated into the forecast, either explicitly or implicitly.

Considerable research and computing effort are required to develop econometric forecasts and their cost is therefore relatively high, precluding most small establishments from developing their own capability in this area. The alternative, that of adopting a forecast developed by an outside organization, poses two sets of problems. First, it may not address itself specifically to the business conditions most likely to affect the using organization. Second, as the external environment changes, some of the assumptions implicitly incorporated into the econometric forecast may no longer be proper. Lacking detailed knowledge of all the stipulated relationships, the organization may find it impossible to effect all the alterations required because of changing circumstances. Under these conditions, a sophisticated econometric forecast might be less appropriate than a judgmental forecast, displaying in quantitative terms (such as GNP, employment, interest rates and sales) the expectations of the management team.

Once a sales forecast is presented, company support plans can be developed. The personnel plan, for example, identifies manpower by skill level required to support the sales forecast; the facilities plan time-phases the equipment and building programs required to attain the expected level of output. The financial plan translates all of these support plans into monetary terms, identifies the internal sources of funds, and presents an approach for the raising of capital from external sources, if such is required.

Table 12 displays a typical 6-month sales forecast; Figure 15 is a graphic presentation of this forecast. To facilitate the development of subsidiary plans, sales are grouped by product line. This permits detailed planning to be based on the unique requirements of each product rather than on aggregrate planning factors. For example, assume product A is mobile homes and it requires substantial numbers of semiskilled employees. Also assume that product line D is design services, requiring trained engineering personnel. Thus, although product line A is expected to phase down during the planning period, and product line D is on the ascendancy, the personnel department cannot be expected to shift employees during this period. Rather, both dismissals and hirings can be expected to take place concurrently. Similar conditions apply to facilities and marketing planning.

Since the established product lines of Giant Pigmy Industries in the aggregrate did not appear to promise sufficient growth, management apparently decided to seek the development of new business. This can be accomplished either through the introduction of new products currently in the developmental stage or the acquisition of established product lines from other organizations. The financial plan encompasses these details as well as the cash flow associated with each of the product lines, based on the terms of payment extended by suppliers and those extended in turn to customers. Furthermore, the facility and manpower plans developed separately are time-phased, converted into monetary terms, and added to the fund requirement forecast.

An important part of any planning discipline is the sensitivity testing of the results. This is particularly relevant for financial planning, as deviations in sales expectations are likely to have far reaching influence on

Table 12   Giant Pigmy Industries—sales forecast
January—June 1980 (in thousands of dollars)

Established products	January	February	March	April	May	June	Total
Product line A	500	600	700	600	400	300	3100
Product line B	100	100	150	200	200	350	1150
Product line C	350	250	200	200	150	100	1250
Product line D	50	60	80	100	150	250	690
Total	1000	1010	1130	1100	950	1000	6190
New business	—	50	80	150	350	400	1030
Total sales	1000	1060	1210	1250	1300	1400	7220

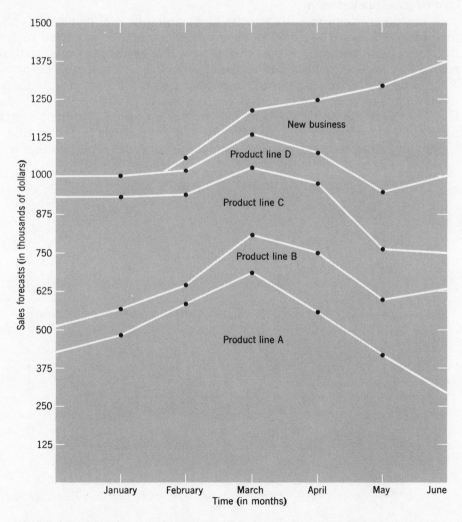

Figure 15. Sales forecast for entire company and four product lines over time.

funds generated internally and on funds required from external sources. Frequently the direction of the change cannot be forecast intuitively. For example, a drop in sales volume may often obviate the need for additional external financing. Financial managers should therefore test the sensitivity of their basic plans to changes in sales volume, product prices, inflation, and so on, to assure themselves that they possess the necessary flexibility to cope with changing financial needs.

While it may not always be feasible to develop support plans for contingency plans as detailed as those developed for the basic forecast, the discipline imposed by approximating the probable impact of changing circumstances is important. Similarly, the early identification of problems that could emerge if sales differ from initial expectations is a practice conducive to good management.

A customary approach to sensitivity planning is to stipulate high and low sales forecasts. These additional forecasts, presented in Figure 16, are developed with the expectation that they will span those events that are most likely to occur. They cannot be expected to cover all contingencies. A hospital, for example, can experience a disastrous fire, or a dramatic sudden increase in demand due to a local epidemic. While operational contingency plans should be available to assure needed service to the community under these extreme circumstances, it is not realistic to expect financial management to concern itself with those financial problems that will

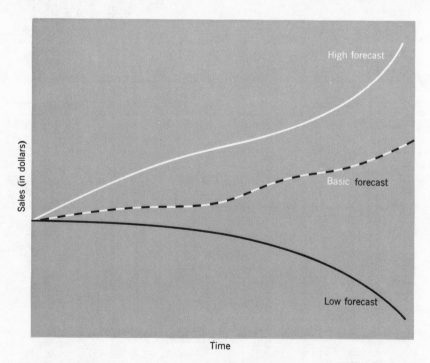

Figure 16. Deviation from basic forecast by high and low estimations.

surface in case disaster strikes. Separate plans should be developed for these unlikely circumstances.

For each of the conditions specified, the basic, high and low sales forecast, financial management must develop corresponding profit forecasts. This requires the development of pro forma accounting statements reflecting the conditions on which the sales forecasts are based. For example, the high sales forecast may require considerable expansion in facilities and manpower. If the required labor tasks are complex, high training expenses may be incurred as sales expand. Profit may therefore equal, or even be less than, that anticipated for the basic sales forecast. Similar special considerations may apply to the lower sales forecast. It is imprudent to predict the impact of changed sales volume on profitability in the abstract; specific situations must be examined prior to the development of profit forecasts.

A useful display of the impact of changing sales revenue is presented in Figure 17. Here the anticipated profit is presented as a deviation from that expected under the basic forecast assumptions. Financial management can thus readily assess the implication of external events on earnings per share and internal cash flow. While managers in not-for-profit organizations are not concerned with earnings per share, internal cash flow considerations

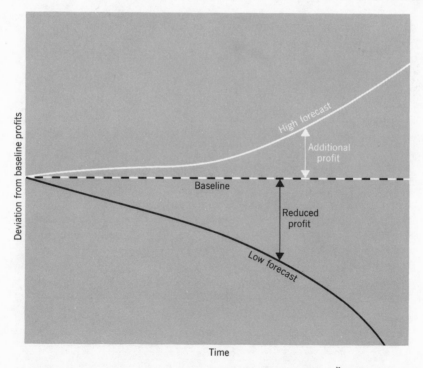

Figure 17. Deviation from profits estimated for baseline forecast.

are at least as relevant to them as to managers in profit oriented organizations. The significance of cash flow is discussed in detail in Chapter 10.

Of key concern to financial management is the early identification of excess and shortages of funds that are likely to occur if business conditions change. Excess funds provide profit potential through timely investments. The nature of the preferred investment instrument is predicated however on the length of time that funds are available for investment purposes. The cash forecast helps to shed some light on this problem.

Even more important is the early identification of fund shortages. As long as the organization is in a healthy financial condition and these shortages are anticipated in a timely fashion, they are not necessarily cause for alarm. Existing relationships with bankers or underwriters can be called upon to meet these deficiencies. Furthermore, excess costs in the raising of outside capital can be avoided if the magnitude and length of time that funds are required can be specified within reasonable limits of accuracy.

Thus the estimation of cash flow for the identification of investment opportunities and potential outside sources becomes a major planning issue for financial management. In addition to the numerical assessment of cash flow outlined in Chapter 10, financial managers find it useful once again to compare the needs emanating from high or low sales revenue against those expected to be encountered in the basic sales forecast. Figure 18 presents the graphics of this approach.

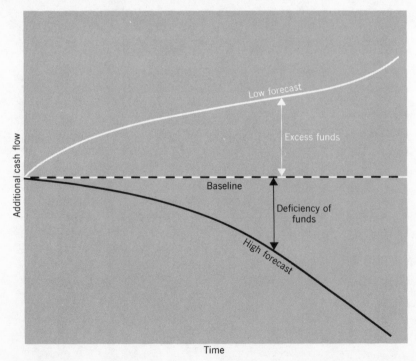

Figure 18. Deviation from cash flow estimation for baseline forecast.

BUSINESS RISK

The uncertainties that make forecasting such a hazardous endeavor are viewed by management as business risk. They are the very essence of being in business. Firms are rewarded by society in accordance with the risk they assume in the pursuit of profits. For example, in the pre-energy-shortage days, electric public utilities assumed very little risk. Their markets were assured by virtue of their monopoly position; their operating cost structure was predictable, and long term interest rates in the economy were stable. Consequently, the return to investors in this industry during that period was limited. By contrast, the high technology industries such as those producing copying machines, cameras, computers, assumed great investors' risk since the technology had not been fully developed, consumer demand had to be created, and the production and distribution cost structure was unknown. In view of this risk exposure, the return to investors (in those companies which prevailed) was usually considerably higher than what they could expect by investing in public utilities.

The assumption and management of risk is one of the key tools of profit oriented business. In a competitive environment riskless investments cannot be expected to earn more than the riskless rate, the return obtained on government bonds. Corporations would be hard pressed for capital if the only promise they could hold out for potential investors were the same return obtainable from investments in government securities. Risk provides opportunities for realizing returns in excess of the minimum level readily attainable. This is the orientation that corporate management must bring to investments in its chosen area of endeavor. It is the role of the financial plan to define more precisely the levels of risk that will be assumed, to assess the expected returns in light of this risk, and to provide a plan of action for managing the risk and realizing the expected returns and thereby justify the exposure of corporate funds to this risk.

Return is easily quantified; it can be viewed either in absolute terms (dollars) or in relative terms (percent return on investment). Risk too may be quantified, although its dimensions require some elaboration. Since the quantification of risk is not as widespread as that of return, its dimensions are not as intuitively obvious to management.

Risk is defined as the deviation likely to be experienced from the expected returns. This is in accordance with the discussion presented in Chapter 3. Consider, for example, two separate projects, A and B, each expected to return $100 to corporate management. Project A, shown in Figure 19 has the following characteristics:

> 25% probability that return will be $80
> 50% probability that return will be $100
> 25% probability that return will be $120

The characteristics of projects B, in Figure 20, are as follows:

    25% probability that return will be $30
    50% probability that return will be $100
    25% probability that return will be $170

Although at first glance it appears that management will be indifferent to the two projects, this is not the case. The reason becomes apparent if the basic high and low sales forecasts are associated with the expected returns. The low forecast is anticipated with a probability of 25%, the basic forecast with a 50% probability, and the high forecast with a 25% probability. If the basic forecast materializes, management will indeed be indifferent. The expected returns are $100 in either case. If, however, events develop so that the low forecast materializes, then project B can be expected to return only $30 while project A promises $80 under those adverse circumstances.

Readers may notice that the dispersion from expected returns cuts both ways. If the high sales forecast materializes, project B will reap higher returns than project A. Financial management cannot, however, attach equal weight to high and low outcomes. Returns that are considerably less than expected may cause the organization acute financial distress, with the possibility of bankruptcy looming in the background. An equal probability of higher than expected return does not adequately compensate management for the risk of financial ruin. Financial management measures risk as the deviation from expected return. Since the deviation from expected return is greater for project B than for project A, the risk of project B is greater.

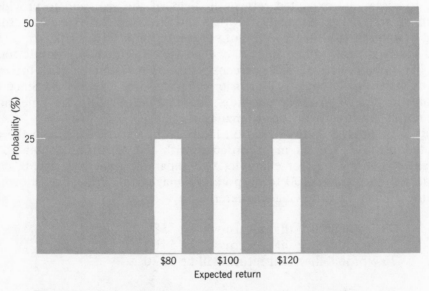

Figure 19. Probability distribution of expected returns: Project A.

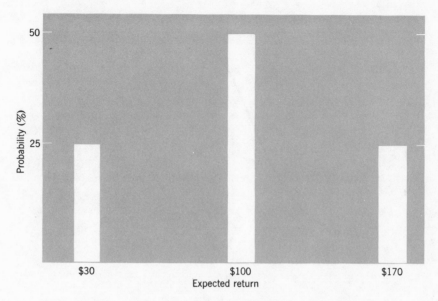

Figure 20. Probability distribution of expected returns: Project B.

Figures 19 and 20 are referred to by statisticians as frequency distributions. They are often developed from observations of actual events. Most events in nature occur with a range of possible outcomes. For example, the average height of a certain group of 35 individuals might be 5 feet 10 inches, yet within that group individuals might range in height from 5 feet 7 inches to 6 feet 1 inch. The tabulation presented in Table 13 groups measurements in increments of 1 inch and lists the number and percentage of individuals in each group.

The graph in Figure 21 plots this data as a frequency distribution. Note, however, that most characteristics in nature are continuous. Thus, for example, individuals are not either precisely 5 feet 8 inches or 5 feet 9

Table 13 Heights of individuals in the group

Height	Number of individuals	Percentage of individuals
5'7''	2	6%
5'8''	3	9%
5'9''	7	20%
5'10''	11	30%
5'11''	7	20%
6'0''	3	9%
6'1''	2	6%
Average 5'10''	35	100%

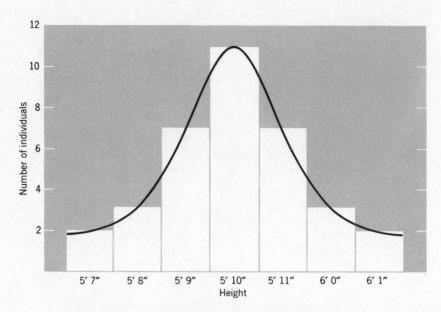

Figure 21.   Height distribution of individuals in group.

inches; some are 5 feet 8 and 1/8 inches, others are 5 feet 8 and 3/16 inches, and so on. Thus it is usually appropriate to connect the midpoints of the bar chart by a continuous curve.

It is often more meaningful to express the number of individuals within a given height class as percentage of total individuals in the group who belong to that height class. Figure 22 illustrates this information. The percentage distribution also becomes the probability that one individual drawn at random from this group will be a stated height. For example, the probability is 20% that an individual picked at random will be 5 feet 11 inches.

The statistical measurement of the dispersion around the mean of a distribution is called the standard deviation and is denoted by the Greek letter sigma (σ). The larger the deviation from the expected return, the larger the risk and the greater is σ. This statistical measure of deviation around the mean has been adopted as the financial measurement of risk. Thus a risk-free investment will have a σ of zero. Similarly a very risky investment will have a relatively large σ.

With available information on expected return denoted by $E(R)$, and risk denoted by σ, financial management may now assess whether the expected return is commensurate with the risk exposure. Conversely, management may assess whether the level of risk required to attain the desired returns is in accordance with management's general mode of operation.

Sufficient empirical evidence has been gathered in recent years to support the contention that the relationship between risk and return is linear,

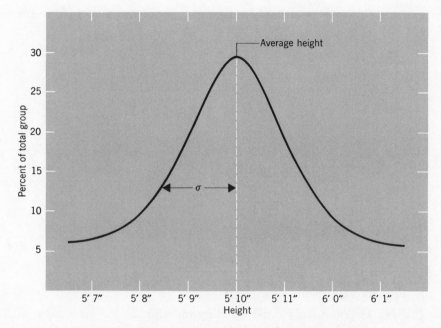

Figure 22. Percentage distribution of heights in group.

as shown in Figure 23. In this figure $E(R)$ on the horizontal scale denotes the expected return. Risk is listed on the vertical scale, increasing from zero upwards. Certain investments can be made without incurring risk; the standard example is federal bonds. The rate realized on a risk-free investment is termed the risk-free rate and is denoted by R_F in the graph. Beyond this, if higher returns are sought, additional risk must be assumed.

Thus, for example, a manager who wishes to achieve a return of R_k, must be willing to accept a risk of σ_k. If he or she accepts that level of risk, the expected return premium is $R_k - R_F$. The risk the manager assumed to generate each unit of return premium is

$$\frac{R_k - R_F}{\sigma_k}$$

the reciprocal of the slope of the straight line.

This line is referred to as the capital market line (CML). Efficient investments can be expected to lie on this line. Efficiency in this usage means that on average the return realized from an investment is commensurate with the risk that has been assumed. Not all investments are efficient. It is the responsibility of financial management to render a judgment regarding the efficiency of proposed investments.

Two special cases merit attention. Project m only realizes a return of R_m, while its risk is σ_m. Since it is to the left of the CML, it is an ineffici-

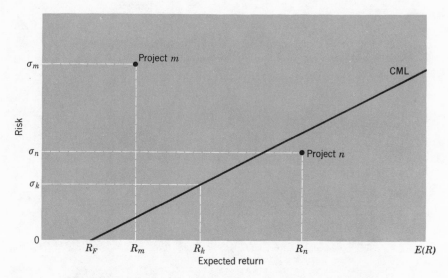

Figure 23. Risk-return relationships for various projects.

ent project. It commands a risk far beyond that which its return justifies and should therefore be rejected. Conversely, project n is to the right of the CML. Its return R_n, is far in excess of what one would expect from its risk σ_n. Being on the right of the CML, it is by definition a most attractive project well worth adopting.

The risk return framework presented above is not only appropriate for financial planning of corporations but also for investors. Actually many of the planning concepts presented are equally applicable to individuals, households, and not-for-profit organizations. The fact that financial return may not be the prime objective of not-for-profit management does not preclude other objectives from being assessed in this framework. For example, an art gallery may risk displaying avantgarde sculpture in the hope of receiving critical acclaim. Such acclaim may actually be the return that the benefactors of the gallery seek!

One final point requires explicit statement. If a manager is willing to accept a high level of risk it is not assured that he or she will necessarily reap the return commensurate with that level of risk in any one period. Recall from Figures 19 and 20 that the expected return is the mean value of the distribution and that values lower (or higher) may be attained. Thus, in a risky project, a lower return than the average value of the distribution can easily materialize. In fact, the higher the risk, the greater the possibility that this will occur. What managers count on is that over many projects and many periods these relationships will stabilize. In the long run it is highly probable that the appropriate return for the risk assumed will be realized.

SUMMARY

The financial plan strives to specify time-phased fund requirements and to identify the likely sources of these funds. Basic to this plan is an assessment of the future environment and the development of a sales forecast. Support plans detailing items such as manpower and facility expenditures provide the information for computing profit expectations and cash requirements. To minimize surprises, alternate forecasts and contingency plans should be developed.

In planning expenditures, financial management is repeatedly confronted with the need to assess expected returns in accordance with the risk to which funds are exposed. The statistical measure of deviations from average returns has been adopted for this purpose. The capital market line displays the linear relationship observed between risk and return for efficient investments. Managers must recognize that the assumption of high risk does not necessarily assure high return on any one investment.

8 Capital Budgeting

Of repeated concern to top management is the allocation of available financial resources for projects that promise to reap returns in the future. This activity represents the very essence of management planning. The long run survival of any organization demands continuing and conscientious attention to this function. The problem is pervasive, applying equally to the management function of both profit oriented and not-for-profit organizations. While profitability is the concern of the former, not-for-profit organizations must be concerned that current resources are allocated so that maximum service is delivered to clients and constituents in the long run, otherwise resources may be denied to the organization in the future.

The deliberate allocation of present resources with the expectation of future returns is termed capital budgeting. The mathematical foundations applicable to this process were developed in Chapter 6. The terminology adopted and the equations developed are:

P = the principal, or present value of a sum
F = the future value of a sum
B = the present value of an annuity
W = the future value of an annuity
R = the annuity
n = the number of periods
i = the rate of interest

Equations:

$$F = P(1 + i)^n$$

$$P = F\left[\frac{1}{(1 + i)^n}\right]$$

$$W = R\left[\frac{(1 + i)^n - 1}{i}\right]$$

$$B = R\left[\frac{1 - (1 + i)^{-n}}{i}\right]$$

Recall that the appropriate numerical entries for the square brackets from the interest tables were designated T_A, T_B, T_C and T_D respectively. Therefore

$$F = PT_A$$

$$P = FT_B$$

$$W = RT_C$$

$$B = RT_D$$

Two decision rules were identified for capital budgeting decisions: the net present value (NPV) and the internal rate of return (IRR). Unless specified otherwise, this discussion will adopt the NPV approach. The formulation of the NPV approach is as follows:

NPV = present value of returns, less the cost of the project

Or

$$NPV = RT_D - C$$

where C is the investment required to generate returns R. The appropriate decision rule is as follows:

If the NPV is positive accept the project

If the NPV is negative reject the project

The following example reviews the basic approach. Assume that management is considering the purchase of a new x-ray unit for $198,000. Estimates indicate that this unit will probably increase cash flow by about $70,000 in each of the next 4 years. Should the investment be made?

To answer this question an appropriate interest rate must be selected. Numerous factors enter into this determination: the cost of capital to the organization, returns that could be realized on other investments (the opportunity cost!), the criticality of the need, and the basic reasons for contemplating the acquisition. Assume that the judgment of financial management is that 20% is an appropriate interest rate for this project.

Therefore the formulation is

$$NPV = \$70,000 \times T_D - \$198,000$$

T_D for 4 years and 20% is 2.589. Therefore

$$NPV = \$70,000 \times 2.589 - \$198,000$$

$$NPV = -\$16,770$$

The decision should be to reject this project.

Assume further that new estimates indicate that these returns might be realized for 5 years instead of 4. T_D now is equal to 2.991 for 20%. Therefore,

$$NPV = \$70,000 \times 2.991 - \$198,000$$

$$NPV = \$11,370$$

The project now appears desirable.

Note how sensitive the results are to the inputs provided to the decision maker. In the example cited, only the number of years was changed. However, had interest rate, or the estimate of costs, or that of returns been altered appropriate changes would have been noticed. The reader may wish to experiment with different inputs to verify this statement. This observation regarding the sensitivity of inputs carries with it significant implications for the application of capital budgeting procedures.

Foremost among these is the need for an impartial and uninvolved review process of the data provided to top management in support of projects recommended for adoption. These proposals are usually developed, proposed, and presented by enthusiastic supporters. Regardless of intended objectivity, advocates are likely to view estimates in a favorable light. Recall that estimates of future returns are made in the face of uncertainty. Advocates will tend to estimate costs at the low end of the range of outcomes and returns at the high end of the range of likely outcomes. Thus, the task confronting management is to provide an impartial assessment of the estimates submitted to it prior to applying the NPV decision rules.

ESTIMATION REQUIREMENTS

Since the estimates provided to management are of crucial importance, it is desirable to explore the source and the nature of the data. Good documentation of the estimation process greatly enhances the credibility of the data submitted. Reviewers should be accorded the opportunity of identifying all significant assumptions that were made in the preparation of the estimates.

A digression from strictly financial considerations is appropriate at this point. By their very nature projects for investment considerations that are conceived, developed, and presented to top management originate mostly in nonfinancial departments. Production may wish to acquire new machinery; marketing may wish to complement the line by the introduction of additional products; research is optimistic about a product in the early stages of development. To receive management authorization for these products and to secure the required funding, it behooves these departments to present their requests in a format and with the necessary detailed documentation that will facilitate the management review process. The probability of selling the project successfully and receiving the desired approval and funding is enhanced by attention to those details on which top management may be expected to focus in its evaluations.

Let us return to the data requirements for the NPV model. The required inputs are as follows:

1. The expected cost of the investment.
2. The expected annual returns. For the sake of simplicity, assume initially that returns are identical in each year, this condition will be relaxed later on.
3. The number of years the project will generate returns.
4. The appropriate interest rate.

In most instances initial data are developed on the basis of engineering characteristics and marketing assessments.

The initial investment costs can entail a variety of outlays. New facilities involve land acquisition, equipment purchase, and construction costs. Research and development usually entail heavy outlays for wages and test equipment. The degree of confidence one can have in the estimate depends on the complexity of the project. Thus it is usually accepted that the costs of research and development are difficult to predict, which implies that the uncertainty is great and the range of possible outcomes is large. Sufficient evidence has accumulated that the ability to predict the cost of one-of-a-kind projects leaves much to be desired. Not only projects requiring sophisticated technology but standard construction projects clearly within the state-of-the-art repeatedly exhibit considerable overruns. The assumption that all phasing and scheduling problems can be worked out without absorbing more than the minimal amounts of labor and material has repeatedly and dramatically been proved unwarranted on a wide variety of projects. Riskier projects requiring research and development for completion must be approached with even greater caution in the estimation.

Costs to be included as part of the original investment are all the expenditures that must be incurred to bring the planned project to the level of completion required before expected returns can be generated. Note that this does not limit investment to the accepted fixed asset categories displayed on the Balance Sheet. Investment in this case can include expenditures for the manpower, advertising, and testing necessary to ready the project for productive use. All costs that would not be incurred in the absence of the project are considered to be investment costs in this context. One final point must be stressed: costs are recognized for the project regardless of how they are financed. Thus whether a special bond is issued to raise capital for the project or available cash is used for that purpose, the expenditures incurred for the project are identical. Initial costs are cash outflows that are required to enable the project to generate expected returns.

Similar considerations apply to the determination of revenue resulting from the project. As mentioned earlier, the analysis focuses on the cash flow resulting from the project, not the accounting profit associated with it. While in the long run the two coincide, in the short run considerable divergence may exist, as has already been demonstrated. An organization realizes returns on the commitment of cash; the proper measure of the return is the cash recaptured within each of the time frames under consideration.

The most apparent difference between cash flow and accounting profit for projects lasting a number of years is depreciation. Recall that for cash flow computations depreciation is not considered an outflow. Yet frequently, the source of information for likely increases in cash flow resulting from a contemplated project is a projection of historical accounting profit. In this case the cash flow is understated to the extent that depreciation is treated as an expense. To arrive at the cash flow expected from the project, depreciation must be added to the projected accounting profit. Note, however, that this is an adjustment to reflect the different treatment of data. A common misconception resulting from this adjustment is that depreciation generates cash flow. This is not the case. The real issue is that accounting profit does not represent cash flow as is generally assumed. The addition of depreciation to reported income is an attempt to arrive at expected cash flow by compensating for depreciation expense deducted on the Income Statement in order to arrive at accounting profit.

Annual cash flow is determined by subtracting from anticipated cash inflows all cash outflows associated with the project. Among cash outflows are labor, materials, and taxes. The latter includes property taxes levied on the facilities and equipment required for the project, and income taxes on the reported accounting income emanating from the project. As stated, the financial analysis focuses only on revenue and costs directly attributable to the pursuit of the project under consideration. It is concerned with marginal revenue and marginal costs. Thus burdening of the project with overhead expenditures is only appropriate if extra overhead expenditures actually result from the addition of this particular project to other existing activities. Normal cost accounting procedures of spreading overhead expenses over all existing activities regardless of expenditures they actually incur must be avoided since they can distort the true cost of the new project.

The life expectancy of the project is primarily a matter of judgment. If it entails, for example, the introduction of a new product that can readily be imitated by the competition, then sizable profits resulting from a dominant market position cannot be expected to last for many years. If, on the other hand, the project consists of additional facilities to meet expanding service needs of a public utility, it appears proper to expect the project to last until it wears out physically or becomes technologically obsolete. Engineering and marketing judgments will direct the selection of the proper life expectancy.

Finally, the issue of the appropriate interest rate must be considered. Recall that expected return should increase as additional risk is assumed.

An assessment of the project risk should therefore be undertaken. Two approaches are used to aid in this assessment. First, different levels of outcomes are postulated and present values are calculated for each of the assumed returns. The dispersions of the values around the most probable return are then noted. Large dispersions will indicate high risk projects; low risk projects, such as the public utility cited earlier, will possess low dispersions. A second, less rigorous approach, is for a management consensus to judge the risk based on past experience with a similar class of projects.

Independent of this, financial management must determine the cost of capital to the organization. A low risk investment can only be justified if its returns equal at least the cost of acquiring additional capital. Riskier investments must generate returns commensurate with the increased risk exposure. Thus, for example, if the cost of capital to the firm is 10%, a moderately risky investment should be expected to generate from 15 to 25% annual returns to merit serious consideration.

NUMERICAL EXAMPLE

Assume that a new production facility for x-ray equipment is under consideration. The facility requires an investment of $8 million, is expected to last for 20 years, and is scheduled to become operational within the year the investment is made. Output of the facility is expected to be four hundred x-ray units annually; income before taxes is estimated to be $10,000 per unit. The accounting department employs straight line depreciation for the facility based on zero salvage value. Management judges the project to be moderately risky, requiring a return of at least 20%. The corporation is in a 40% tax bracket.

Annual depreciation: $8,000,000/20 = $400,000

Expected annual profit before taxes:
$10,000 × 400 = $4,000,000

Annual tax liability: $4,000,000 × 40% = $1,600,000

Expected annual profit after taxes:
$4,000,000 − $1,600,000 = $2,400,000

Expected annual cash flow (after tax profit + depreciation):
$2,400,000 + $400,000 = $2,800,000

Present value of cash flow of $2,800,000 for 20 years at 20%
(interest factor from Table D, T_D = 4.87):
$2,800,000 × 4.87 = $13,636,000

Net present value: PV of cash flow − cost =
$13,636,000 − $8,000,000 = $5,636,000

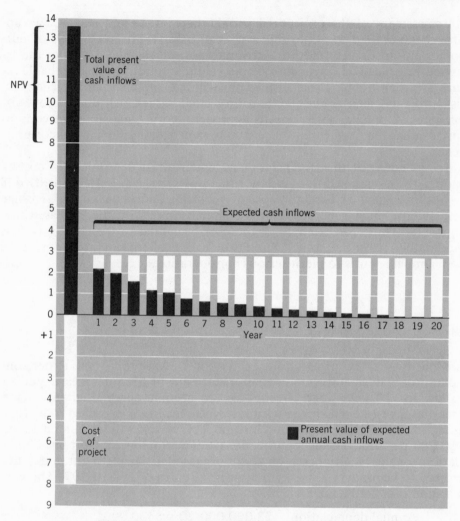

Figure 24. Projected cash flow for an investment.

Since the NPV is positive, the project should be adopted. A graphic representation of expected cash flows and their present values is displayed in Figure 24.

Assume that some of the estimates were to change in an unfavorable direction. Under these conditions the project could rapidly become unattractive. For example, a reduction in the accounting profit to $5000 per unit or a reduction in production volume to two hundred units would result in annual cash flows of $1,600,000 with a present value of $7,792,000; insufficient to justify an investment of $8 million.

INTERNAL RATE OF RETURN

As indicated earlier, the internal rate of return (IRR) is another theoretically acceptable method for determining the desirability of investments.

This method consists of equating the initial investment with the present value of the returns and solving for the interest rate which validates the equation. The resulting interest rate is then viewed in the context of the riskiness of the investment. If the returns are equal to or in excess of those required for the risk class of the investment, the project is accepted. If the expected returns are less than the appropriate risk class, the project is rejected.

From the previous numerical example, we have

Investment required	$8,000,000
Annual cash flow expected	$2,800,000
Number of years	20

Therefore

$$\$8,000,000 = \$2,800,000 \times T_D$$

$$T_D = 2.86$$

Looking across Table D for 20 years, we find that the appropriate interest rate for T_D of 2.86 is around 35%, clearly in excess of the 20% required. The project is therefore accepted.

If, however, expected cash flows are only $1,600,000, the calculations would be:

$$\$8,000,000 = \$1,600,000 \times T_D$$

$$T_D = 5$$

Looking across Table D for 20 years, the relevant interest rate is about 19%, less than the required interest for a project in this risk class.

UNEQUAL RETURNS

So far only projects with equal annual returns were considered. Projects displaying different annual returns are far more representative of actual situations encountered by management. Conceptually, the problem is identical; the difference is only computational. Instead of resorting to the present value of an annuity to ascertain the project benefits, the sum of the present values of each of the project years must be developed.

Consider the x-ray project: investment requirements of $8 million and an annual depreciation of $400,000. Suppose that the expected accounting profits, after taxes, for the first 5 years are as follows:

Year 1 — $400,000
Year 2 — 800,000
Year 3 — 1,200,000
Year 4 — 1,600,000
Year 5 — 2,000,000

While afterward:

Years 6 to 20 — 2,400,000

Based on depreciation charges of $400,000 after tax flow is expected to be:

Year 1   — $800,000
Year 2   — 1,200,000
Year 3   — 1,600,000
Year 4   — 2,000,000
Year 5   — 2,400,000
Years 6 to 20 — 2,800,000

The first task is to find the interest factor for each of the first five cash flows from Table B at 20%.

Year	Interest factor T_B
1	0.833
2	0.694
3	0.579
4	0.482
5	0.402

The second task is to find the present value for each of the 5 years and the sum of these present values.

Year	Cash flow	T_B	Present value
1	$ 800,000	0.833	$666,400
2	1,200,000	0.694	832,800
3	1,600,000	0.579	926,400
4	2,000,000	0.482	964,000
5	2,400,000	0.402	964,800

The sum of these present values is $4,354,400.

The third task is to find the present value of $2,800,000 for 15 years. From Table D, interest factor T_D is 4.675. Therefore

$2,800,000 × 4.675 = $13,090,000

This, however, is the present value of an annuity from year 6 to year 20. Thus $13,090,000 is equivalent to a sum available in year 6. To find the present value of that sum we have to multiply it by the appropriate interest factor from Table B. T_B for year 6 at 20% is 0.335. Therefore the present value of $13,090,000 is

$13,090,000 × 0.335 = $4,385,150.

The total present value is the sum of $4,385,150 and $4,354,400; a total of $8,739,550. Since this is still in excess of the $8 million investment,

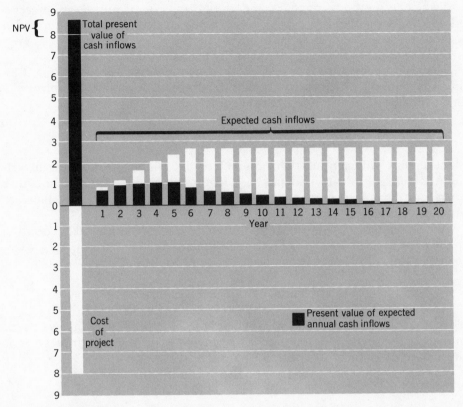

Figure 25.   Projected cash flow for an investment with unequal returns.

the project should be accepted. Figure 25 illustrates this situation graphically.

Note, however, that if returns on the project were expected only after the third year, a situation that is frequently encountered, the project would not have been judged acceptable.

OTHER METHODS IN USE

Although several other decision rules for capital asset investments are utilized, their use, fortunately, appears to be diminishing rapidly. All share two characteristics: attractive simplicity of calculation (and explanation) and faulty theoretical foundation. In general they omit precise calculations of the time value of money; at best they substitute rules of thumb as approximation. The purpose of this discussion is to alert the reader that approaches other than NPV and IRR should not be condoned and that decisions based on such methods can lead to erroneous conclusions regarding the acceptance or rejection of projects.

Two such methods, payback and accounting rate of return, are presented below. Note that *they are to be viewed as strawmen to be avoided* rather than as suitable models for managers to follow. This holds true even if the numerical estimates possess intuitive appeal.

The payback method consists of dividing the cost of the investment by anticipated annual cash flows attributable to the investment. Adopting the the estimates of the first numerical example:

$$\text{payback} = \frac{\$8,000,000}{\$2,800,000} = 2.86 \text{ years}$$

Management judgment is then applied to determine whether the investment is desirable. Note that payback ignores cash flow expected in future years and that it cannot be applied in cases where cash flows increase gradually in the early years.

Accounting rate of return is computed by dividing expected accounting income (not cash flow) from the investment by the cost of the investment. In terms of the same example:

$$\text{accounting rate of return} = \frac{\$2,400,000}{\$8,000,000} = 30\%$$

Note that in this method time itself, and not only the time value of money, is ignored. This method can only provide relevant indicators if the stream of income is expected to perpetuity.

CONCLUDING CONSIDERATIONS

The relevance and importance of capital budgeting techniques to good management cannot be overemphasized. It deals with the very core issue of management: allocation of available resources to secure future returns. This is not only the domain of financial management; every manager is in fact continually faced with capital budgeting decisions.

Although in many instances it may be exceedingly difficult to estimate all necessary inputs to the NPV or IRR models, even in such cases the model can be of great service to the manager. By assuming ranges of likely estimates, judgment as to the apparent reasonability of the project may be formulated. Often, particularly in people oriented programs such as training, recreation, and so on, it may be impossible to arrive at a reasonable estimate of cash flow returns. In these cases the problem may be stated in reverse: What benefits does a certain investment imply?

For example, assume that an employee recreational facility can be leased for 7 years with a one time payment of $500,000; out-of-pocket expenses for upkeep are estimated at $60,000 annually. On average the company earns 16% on its investments.

Assume that the equivalent cash flow to justify the investment is E. Required cash flow is therefore E + \$60,000. Solving for an NPV of zero

$$0 = (E + \$60,000)T_D - \$500,000$$

$$0 = 4.039E - \$257,660$$

$$E = \$63,793$$

The interpretation of this result is that the increased morale and employee good will should increase productivity by \$63,793 annually, otherwise the company's average return on its investments will drop below 16%!

It is recognized that some investments are a "must," not really subject to management discretion. Among them are those required for health and safety, those dictated by competitive practices, and those required by an assortment of government regulations. Yet even in these cases the analysis presented above can be conducted to develop an appreciation for the magnitude of the commitment formulated.

Other projects will vary from those for which the risk is relatively low and estimates can be prepared with great precision, for example, the replacement of existing equipment with newer more efficient models to produce the same products, to high risk ventures into new products or markets. Whatever the situation, all of management is better served by analyses conducted in the capital budgeting framework.

SUMMARY

The allocation of available financial resources to projects that promise to reap benefits in the future is a key concern of management in both profit oriented and not-for-profit organizations. The analysis underlying this task is termed capital budgeting. It employs the mathematics of finance and the decision rules developed in Chapter 6.

Careful attention to correct data estimation is a basic requirement in these analyses. Costs and benefits should be estimated in terms of cash inflows and outflows directly associated with the project under consideration and overhead costs not directly attributable to the project should be excluded from the analysis. The source of financing the project, whether internal or external funds are used, is not relevant to the decision.

Discount rates applied are based on the risk-free rate plus an adjustment for project risk.

9 Performance Budgets

A budget is a quantitative expression of management's plans. Both explicitly and implicitly it presents the intentions and objectives of management to all echelons of the organization and provides a vehicle for monitoring the implementation of plans. In addition, it enables management to assess the adherence of individuals and organizational components to the goals stipulated in the plan and thereby to provide a quantitative basis for measuring and rewarding individual and departmental performance.

At a highly aggregated level the budget provides the financial manager with information regarding organization-wide capital surpluses and shortfalls. This information is essential for the timely recognition of investment opportunities and adequate planning for the acquisition of short and long term capital. A realistic, well managed budgeting process will reduce the errors of omission and commission in the allocation of resources, either one of which can be costly to the organization.

The basic documents in the budgeting process are called the master budget. In essence they represent on a before the fact or, in accounting terminology, on a pro forma basis the results expected to be achieved by the organization and its subcomponents in the ensuing period. The master budget specifies targets for functional activities such as sales and production, translates these activity levels into pro forma Income Statements and, by means of supporting schedules, identifies necessary facility and personnel requirements, and cash excesses and shortages, and traces those expectations to an ending Balance Sheet.

A major drawback of a single master budget is the static nature of the document. Any change in the external environment or in internal efficiencies will cause deviations from expected results in all aspects of the organization's performance. This in turn may result in improper imputations of higher or lower performance than expected to many organizational elements. Thus, for example, a general pay increase granted to employees by corporate management can be expected to result in higher production costs than were initially budgeted. In this case penalizing the production department for the overrun of budgeted labor costs would clearly be inappropriate. To overcome difficulties of this nature flexible budgets are developed.

The tracing of cost behavior during production and distribution is an integral part of the budgeting process. Cost accounting is the activity that strives to relate both direct cost inputs of labor and materials and the requirements for supporting administration and facilities to the cost of the product. These accounting schedules of cost behavior become inputs to the budgeting process and also aid in the development of appropriate pricing strategies for the product or service provided by the organization.

THE MASTER BUDGET

The budgeting process commences with the preparation of a sales forecast. Since supporting forecasts such as production, personnel, and facilities emanate from the sales forecast, its importance can hardly be exaggerated. An excessively optimistic forecast can result in the hiring of superfluous personnel, the acquisition of unneeded facilities, and so on, all incurring increased costs for the organization without being associated with increased revenue and profits. Conversely, an overly pessimistic forecast can also prove costly to the organization. Shortages of personnel and facilities to meet existing customer demand can result in the loss of possible revenue and profits in the short run, and a permanent loss of customers and clients in the long run.

One of the difficulties frequently encountered is that the marketing department, which is best qualified to determine the emerging needs of potential customers, is often viewed as possessing an overly optimistic outlook on market potential. Its forecasts are interpreted as being geared to provide stimulus to the sales organization, without necessarily reflecting a realistic appraisal of customer demand. Thus, these sales forecasts are often "massaged" prior to incorporation into the master budget. This is not a desirable approach since it distorts one of the important benefits of budgeting: common adherence to the stated objectives of management. Budgeting is an interlocking process, closely tied into the long term plans of the organization. One of its considerable side benefits is that it encourages organizational communication on goals, approaches, and resources. The inability to agree on realistic objectives subverts this process.

On the basis of the sales forecast production requirements for the organization are established. These requirements are normally presented in terms of units of product per period of time. Cost accounting methods, described below, are used to translate the unit production requirements into cost of goods sold (COGS). Other costs and expenses are estimated in a similar manner. For example, marketing expenses may be established on the basis of cost per salesman in the field plus administrative expenses. Some costs may be based on contractual agreements such as rents, leases, and executive salaries or on reasonable extrapolation of past experience. Thus next year's electricity bill may be assumed to equal this year's bill plus a percentage growth in consumption plus a percentage adjustment for inflationary cost increases.

These cost estimates are developed with appropriate backup and detail for each activity possessing separate or distinctive characteristics. A metal stamping department in a manufacturing plant, a pharmacy in a hospital or a bookstore in a museum are typical examples of such activities, also called cost centers. In view of the many variables involved it is not particularly meaningful or useful to develop very specific guidelines for the establishment of cost centers. In general terms, to justify the investment of effort, the following conditions should exist before cost centers are established:

1. Management of the cost center should entail some degree of managerial discretion. This can be either in terms of products offered, the labor policies adopted, the ability to change administrative or production processes or in terms of the authority over make or buy decisions that affect the cost center.
2. The total costs involved should be worth the administrative effort required to establish and monitor the cost center.
3. Top management should be prepared to follow through by monitoring, rewarding, and penalizing performance as reported in the cost control system adopted.

Ideally, cost center managers will have full Income Statement responsibilities for their area of activity. If this is accomplished managers will actually be responsible for profit centers and not merely held accountable for cost performance. Although profit centers are discussed in greater detail further on, two problem areas deserve attention here. The first recurring problem with profit centers is the issue of transfer pricing. Many materials and services required by a given profit center in a large organization are supplied by other profit centers within the organization. Examples include x-ray units serving hospital patients, upholstery shops in automobile assembly plants, and data processing services provided within an insurance company. A likely bone of contention is the price that the receiving profit center is charged for the services or products provided by another profit center. The second problem results from the fact that very few profit center managers have full authority over the resources required for their area of responsibility. Thus the acquisition of productive capacity and labor may be beyond their realm of authority although they are responsible for center profitability.

Table 14 X-Ray Unit, Hospital Service Corporation, performance report, March 1980

	Master budget	Actual	Variance
Units	2,000	1,200	800
Sales revenue	$50,000	$30,000	$20,000*
Variable costs:			
Film	16,000	12,000	4,000†
Other material	3,000	2,500	500†
Technician	1,500	1,200	300†
Other labor	500	500	0
Other variable	2,000	1,500	500†
Total variable	23,000	17,700	5,300†
Contribution margin	27,000	12,300	14,700*
Fixed costs:			
Rent	800	800	0
Depreciation	400	400	0
Supervision	2,000	2,000	0
Other fixed	3,500	3,200	300†
Total fixed	6,700	6,400	300†
Operating income	20,300	5,900	14,400*

*Unfavorable.
†Favorable.

Once a pro-forma statement is developed for the entity under consideration, be it a department, a cost center, or a profit center, it becomes the budget for the ensuing period. It can either be presented for the whole period, usually a fiscal year, or for subperiods such as months, weeks, or even days. Performance is then ascertained by measuring the extent to which actual amounts recorded deviated from budgeted amounts. Within the same budget some deviations may be favorable if, for example, actual materials cost less than the budgeted amount. Simultaneously, other deviations may be unfavorable if supervision costs exceed the budgeted amount. Table 14 presents an example of a Master Budget and some of its possible variances.

In presenting the budget it is customary to separate the variable and fixed costs incurred on the Income Statement. This distinction is particularly meaningful for budgetary purposes. Variable costs are directly related to the level of output, while fixed costs can rarely be controlled in the short run. The difference between sales revenue and variable cost is called the contribution margin. It reflects the actual contribution that sales revenue makes towards meeting overhead costs and generating profits. Generally additional sales are desirable as long as the contribution margin is positive. This is the same as stating that additional sales are desirable as long as the price realized per unit is in excess of variable costs per unit.

Analysis of the master budget and performance report in Table 14 can create the impression that although sales revenue and operating income were lower than expected, the performance of the x-ray unit during much of 1980 is commendable since all the other variances are favorable. This impression is misleading. For example x-ray film is budgeted at $8 per plate. The performance report indicates that for the 1200 plates needed $12,000 in costs were incurred. In the absence of other factors (such as inflation in the cost of film) it appears that excessive spoilage occurred. This in turn can demonstrate poor supervision. Note, however, that the performance variance on the master budget is favorable. Unless it is carefully analyzed, this report can give incorrect signals to management. Flexible budgeting is a method that attempts to overcome some of the deficiencies of the Master Budget.

FLEXIBLE BUDGETS

A major shortcoming of the Master Budget is that profit center managers are liable to be rewarded, or penalized, for reasons beyond their control. For example, the x-ray unit may show smaller profits. Yet upon analysis these can be traced to reduced numbers of patients utilizing the facility. Since this unit is only a service function to the hospital it depends on hospital admissions for its patients. It does not engage in independent marketing to assure full utilization of its available capacity. Therefore penalizing the x-ray profit center manager for lower profits resulting from reduced hospital admissions that are clearly beyond his control is not in consonance with good management practice.

The flexible Budget is designed to overcome this deficiency. Table 15 illustrates the underlying concept. The price expected to be attained per unit and the variable cost inputs per unit are identified separately. Different attainable levels of outputs are specified, and revenue and variable costs appropriate for each such level are computed separately. The difference between revenue and variable costs is the contribution margin realizable at each level of output. By subtracting fixed costs from each budgeted contribution margin an operating income budget for each specified level of output is provided.

The unit manager is thus absolved from influences beyond his control, in this instance the number of patients, but he is held accountable for profits that are attainable with the number of patients he was actually called upon to serve. Note that budgeted fixed costs remain constant regardless of the volume of output and consume an ever increasing percentage of the contribution margin as the level of output decreases. Conversely, as output increases, operating income increases more than the percentage increase in volume. The flexible budget strives to judge the unit mana-

Table 15 X-Ray Unit, Hospital Service Corporation, flexible budget, March 1980

Units	Budget amount per unit	Number of x-rays per month						
		2400	2000	1600	1200	800		
Sales revenue	$25.00	$60,000	$50,000	$40,000	$30,000	$20,000		
Variable costs:								
Film	8.00	19,200	16,000	12,800	9,600	6,400		
Other material	1.50	3,600	3,000	2,400	1,800	1,200		
Technician	0.75	1,800	1,500	1,200	900	600		
Other labor	0.25	600	500	400	300	200		
Other variable	1.00	2,400	2,000	1,600	1,200	800		
Total variable costs	11.50	27,600	23,000	18,400	13,800	9,200		
Contribution margin	13.50	32,400	27,000	21,600	16,200	10,800		
Fixed costs:								
Rent		800	800	800	800	800		
Depreciation		400	400	400	400	400		
Supervision		2,000	2,000	2,000	2,000	2,000		
Other fixed		3,500	3,500	3,500	3,500	3,500		
Total fixed costs		6,700	6,700	6,700	6,700	6,700		
Operating income		25,700	20,300	14,900	9,500	4,100		

Table 16   X-Ray Unit, Hospital Service Corporation, performance report, March 1980

	Costs incurred	Budget for volume	Variance explanation
Units	1,200	1,200	0
Sales revenue	$30,000	$30,000	0
Variable costs:			
Film	12,000	9,600	2,400[*]
Other material	2,500	1,800	700[*]
Technician	1,200	900	300[*]
Other labor	500	300	200[*]
Other variable	1,500	1,200	300[*]
Total variable	17,700	16,200	3,900[*]
Contribution margin	12,300	16,200	3,900[*]
Fixed costs:			
Rent	800	800	0
Depreciation	400	400	0
Supervision	2,000	2,000	0
Other fixed	3,200	3,500	300[†]
Total fixed	6,400	6,700	300[†]
Operating income	5,900	9,500	3,600[*]

[*]Unfavorable.
[†]Favorable.

ger solely on his performance and not penalize or reward him for factors beyond his control.

Table 16 presents the performance report under a flexible budgeting system. It provides an opportunity for identifying the cause of the cost variances experienced. Thus it also flags the issue for management's attention and follow-up. In addition it provides information to budget officers regarding justifiable adjustments that should be incorporated into future budgets. Thus the identification of variances triggers appropriate management involvement. This budget, in addition to providing necessary financial information, is a basic tool for management planning and control.

COST ACCOUNTING

The flexible budget demonstrates the importance of asigning proper costs to each stage of the production process. It facilitates management planning and control and permits the development of appropriate reward systems. In addition, of course, proper costing is essential for pricing and the buy-or-make decisions of components required for the product. It is one of the roles of cost accounting to provide appropriate information for these budget systems and thereby for management decisions.

Often costs are directly related to observable and quantifiable physical phenomena: minutes for labor by skill level, pounds of material by type, kilowatt hours of electricity. In these instances standards can readily be developed that will reflect the costs associated with those physical inputs required for the product or the service. Cost standards developed in this fashion are termed engineered standards. Care must be taken with engineered standards to allow for the ordinary slippage in efficiency that occurs in all processes. If this is not done, then the standards specified will be unattainable and could prove harmful to employee morale. Once appropriately engineered standards are developed for each physical input at each step of the production process, an engineered cost per unit of product can readily be developed.

In instances where the inputs are difficult to relate directly to output, strictly engineered standards may not be attainable and observed quantifiable relationships must be modified with judgmental factors. For example, a physician may be expected to see a certain number of patients per hour and a teacher may be expected to be in the classroom for the required instruction. Neither of these standards helps, however, in setting quality objectives in the delivery of service. The establishment of cost standards for this class of activities is therefore substantially different from the establishment of standards for mass production items where quality requirements can be engineered directly into the product and accounted for in terms of cost. Professional discretion is frequently used in setting standards for professional activities; strictly engineered standards might otherwise distort the output objectives to strictly numerical assessment. Judgment is also used in instances where the production runs are limited and the cost of setting engineered standards might be out of proportion with the expected operation income.

Another issue encountered is the allocation of costs incurred by more than one profit center to each of the other profit centers involved. It is customary to identify a measurable unit such as square feet, number of employees, hours of computer time, and so on, which is directly related to the common costs incurred. For example, the relationship between the floor space occupied and the total floor space available to the organization is often an equitable basis for the allocation of total rental costs to each of the individual profit centers.

By documenting variable costs and by providing an equitable basis for the allocation of fixed costs, the dual management objectives of pinpointing accountability and controlling costs can be achieved.

PROFIT CENTERS

The term profit centers has previously been mentioned in passing. It is worth special discussion in the context of budgets since the concept is often abused, causing friction between financial and nonfinancial managers. On the other hand, successful implementation of this concept is one of the major contributions financial management can make to overall management functions of the organization.

The concept originates in the intent of management to provide managers in a large organization with an environment similar to that of independently based managers. The profit center is intended to provide considerable freedom of action to the manager for allocating corporate resources according to his best judgment. It is normally supported by an accounting system that identifies operating income originating in the profit center and assesses the manager for the resources he employs. It is believed that increased competition and cost consciousness on behalf of departmental managers will benefit the parent organization. Conversely, the absence of continued competitive pressures can lead to managerial slackness and may ultimately be detrimental to the organization.

Profit centers are established to foster the spirit of cost consciousness and competitiveness, and also to provide an objective basis for assessing the performance of managers. At the extreme, each profit center manager can be viewed as running his own organization formulating independent product, personnel, and financial decisions. This condition, however, seldom exists. Customarily, the profit center manager operates within a product charter, adhering to personnel policies of the organization and using the facilities, equipment, and financial resources provided him. Actually his freedom of operation is severely circumscribed.

These restrictions are frequently a source of contention between the profit center manager and top management. The manager may argue that the facilities, personnel, and resources assigned to are not suitable for achieving the highest profitability possible in his operations. Top management, on the other hand, is under different pressures, frequently calling for greater uniformity in products, equipment, and policies. These pressures may originate in the demand of investors to demonstrate profits in the short run, they may reflect cash flow deficiencies, or they may merely mirror the political realities within the organization. A reward system that ignores these considerations can result in built-in conflicts and will be ineffective in the long run. Ideally, management will develop budgets for each profit center that reward and penalize the profit center manager only for those variances truly under his or her control.

A related complication arises from the fact that profit centers usually sell their products to other profit centers within the same organization. Since the selling price affects sales revenue of one profit center and the COGS of the second profit center, it influences the realized operating income of both. The determination of an equitable transaction price often becomes a source of contention between the respective profit center managers. A customary resolution of this issue is to solicit independent bids from outside suppliers for the products in dispute and use the prices quoted as the appropriate transfer prices within the organization. Often, however, particularly for intermediate products and special components, market prices do not exist. In these instances transfer prices must be negotiated between departments.

The design of a profit center budgeting system requires careful attention to the impact the system is likely to have on the decision processes of the profit center manager. Attainment of the goals set for the manager must be consonant with the objectives of the parent organization, otherwise profit center budgeting may prove counterproductive. If, however, the budgeting systems are designed with full awareness of the complications discussed above, profit center accounting can provide considerable stimulus to effective management.

The attention devoted to profit center budgeting should not be interpreted as obviating the need for performance budgets in not-for-profit organizations. While fund accounting limitations might make it difficult to establish meaningful profit centers, cost centers can readily be identified and tracked via the budgeting process. The establishment of meaningful relationships between the costs incurred and the service provided has in fact become a cornerstone of the negotiating process between not-for-profit organizations and their funding agencies.

SUMMARY

A budget is a quantitative expression of the plans of management. If properly designed, it facilitates communications and provides an objective basis for exercising control and structuring reward systems. It can improve performance and heighten managerial morale.

The basic document in the budgeting process is the Master Budget. It calls out the expected results for the organization and its components for the period under consideration. Flexible Budgets strive to identify specific causes of performance variance and thereby facilitate remedial actions. Cost accounting provides cost inputs via engineered or judgmental standards to the budgeting system. Profit centers are established to provide managers with discretionary powers. Their implementation requires attention to the complex issues of transfer pricing and operational authority.

10 Cash Flow

Of the many feasible supporting budgeting schedules, none is as important to the financial manager as the cash budget. The reason is simple: regardless of the future potential of the organization, unless cash is available to meet near term obligations such as payroll, power, telephone, notes due, and so forth, the organization is effectively out of business. While in the private sector the organization's long term survival depends on profitability and in the public sector on outside funding, near term survival in either case necessitates the availability of necessary cash to meet immediate requirements.

Budgeting systems for long term planning and control purposes are usually geared to accepted accounting conventions. Thus, for example, sales are recorded at the time the merchandise is shipped, not at the time payment is received. Since most transactions are based on credit, an additional sale will be reflected as increased operating income without necessarily increasing the availability of cash simultaneously. On the contrary, the sale might require short run cash expenditures for labor and material, thus effectively reducing the cash balances available to the organization. At the same time accounting conventions indicate increased profits on the performance reports. The opposite situation may also exist. The performance report of a profit center may indicate a loss based on customary accounting practices of deducting appropriate depreciation expenses. Since, however, depreciation expense is an internal adjustment, and not associated with the disbursement of cash as most other expenses are, the cash position of the entity may actually have improved.

The availability of adequate cash balances to meet the organization's needs is too important an issue to be handled indirectly. Financial management should be guided by a dual criterion: long run profitability subject to the availability of adequate working capital in the short run. The document tracing the flow of cash through the organization is the cash budget. Although of little direct significance to managers of profit centers, it is a key document for financial management.

WORKING CAPITAL

Working capital is a term almost synonymous with current assets and reflects the short term disposition of the organization's capital. In general, as business activities increase, working capital needs of the organization increase. This is caused by increased financing requirements for accounts receivable, increased levels of inventory needed to sustain operations, and higher cash balances required to smooth over the accelerated pace of activity. Some of the increased needs are provided spontaneously by creditors who are likely to permit the organization to increase its levels of Accounts Payable as business activity expands. This, however, is only of limited assistance in the increased demand for funds. The concern of financial management is the rapid increase in the difference between current assets and current liabilities. This difference is referred to as *net working capital.* As the pace of business activity and profitability increases, net working capital needs also increase and sources of funds must be identified in advance to provide the necessary additional capital to meet the needs of the organization. This requirement is of course identical for both profit oriented and not-for-profit organizations.

To permit the early identification of the need for additional funds, financial management requires close monitoring of the organization's cash position at all times. As is the case for most transactions, the acquisition of cash demands a certain amount of lead time. If deficiencies are identified sufficiently early, then as long as the organization is basically in a healthy financial condition the appropriate sources for funds can readily be tapped. The same potential sources of capital are likely, however, to deny those applications for additional funds that are made under conditions of acute fund shortage. Such behavior signals potential lenders and investors that careless planning and poor management practices are in effect, and does not inspire confidence in the organization's capacity to repay the loans at a future date. Lenders and investors are unlikely to respond to such behavior by providing additional funds.

Conversely, good financial management implies that all funds available to the organization are productively deployed. The accumulation of cash balances in excess of those ordinarily required for the short term needs of working capital expansion deprives the organization of income that could otherwise be earned. Financial management must strive to estimate minimum cash requirements and devise plans for borrowing or investing funds so that the cash balances maintained are neither above nor below the needs of the organization at any point in time.

THE CASH BUDGET

The mechanism for gaining the necessary visibility regarding the availability of cash is the cash budget. Although it bears a resemblence to the Master Budget, it is not oriented toward forecasting operating income and profits but is aimed rather at identify the cash balances that will probably exist in future periods. The cash budget traces the flow of funds through the organization, identifying likely sources and expected applications of funds prior to their occurrence. By discerning levels of cash balances ahead of time, financial management is in a position to plan borrowing or investment strategies appropriate for the needs of the organization. The cash budget thus becomes the instrument that permits financial management to plan rather than merely to react to emerging situations, and is therefore a key tool of management.

Table 17 presents such a cash budget. While the format is typical, it should not necessarily be adopted precisely as structured. The layout adopted by financial management should facilitate the identification of likely problems and their possible resolution by highlighting those receipts or disbursements that are particularly important to the organization. Clearly, receipts from patients are not of crucial significance to General Motors!.

In preparing a cash budget only the receipts and disbursements of cash require forecasting. Other entries are either stipulated, reflecting analysis and judgment of financial management, or represent actual account balances. Thus the entry "cash balances desired" is an example of the former, while the "beginning balance" taken from the cash T-account is the entry that would be reported on a Balance Sheet as of December 31, 1979. Other entries in the cash budget are derived via the cash budgeting process described further on.

Lip service is often paid to the need for the continual updating of planning and control documents, yet in actual practice planning documents are usually prepared in a sporadic fashion, often divorced from near term operational developments. If the cash budget is to serve the purposes outlined earlier it cannot be handled in this fashion. It must be updated continually and revised as new information becomes available. At least at the end of each period, in this case a month, a new forecast should be prepared that will extend the full span of cash budget cycle for the budget cycle – in the given example, for 6 months.

These procedures will insure that the cash budget remains an updated, relevant document. Since its implications are very near term, financial management cannot afford to be guided by forecasts and projections that have become outdated by the pace of events. The cash budget may be compared to a flight plan. Even senior airline pilots will reexamine their preferred flight route in line with latest meteorological conditions, fuel levels, and aircraft weight. They will not accept yesterday's flight plan

Table 17 Hospital Service Corporation cash budget January–June 1980 (in thousands of dollars)

	January	February	March	April	May	June
Beginning balances	25	79	26	20	107	207
Cash receipts						
From patients	35	63	70	72	78	82
From insurance carriers	228	248	262	275	285	296
From investments	6	7	7	7	8	9
Other	12	5	–	15	10	–
Total receipts	281	323	339	369	381	387
Total Cash available	306	402	365	389	488	594
Cash disbursements						
Wages	72	75	78	71	85	88
Rent	18	18	18	18	18	18
Interest	–	–	1	–	–	–
Supplies	105	118	175	135	140	162
Capital assets	–	198	–	–	26	–
Taxes	–	25	5	–	–	28
Miscellaneous	32	22	38	8	12	5
Total disbursements	227	456	315	232	281	301
Cash balances desired	20	20	20	20	20	20
Total cash required	247	476	335	252	301	321
Cash excess (deficiency)	59	(74)	30	137	187	273
Borrowing requirement		80	30	50		
Loan repayment						

without updating the information on which it was based and reassessing the contemplated route in the light of recent developments. In general, the higher the stakes and the more crucial the impact of economic events and customer demand conditions on the organization, the more frequently should the cash budget be updated.

Given the opening cash balance of $25,000 in Table 17, the total cash available during January is estimated by adding the expected total receipts of $281,000 to the beginning balance for a total of $306,000. Total disbursements of $227,000 forecast are developed by adding anticipated cash disbursements expected during January 1980. Note that the focus is on the disbursement of cash. A credit purchase of supplies, for example, does not entail the outflow of cash although the accounting system will report it as an expense. The desired cash balance is added to the anticipated disbursement, arriving at a total cash requirement of $247,000. Subtracting this amount from the total cash expected to become available indicates excess cash balances of $59,000 for this period. Based on this analysis, financial management can now invest these in short term financial instruments with maturity dates corresponding to the cash needs identified for future periods. Since these short term investments are usually highly liquid and safe they are treated as cash equivalents and recorded as cash. The beginning balance for February will therefore be the total of $59,000 and $20,000, or $79,000.

Similar considerations apply to the February forecast. Note that among disbursements capital assets of $198,000 are indicated. This is in contrast with an Income Statement that lists depreciation expense but not the expenditures for the acquisition of fixed assets. Since the focus of the cash budget is on the inflows and outflows of cash rather than on the determination of costs, depreciation expense that does not entail an outflow of cash is ignored while the purchase of a fixed asset must be recognized. This outflow contributed to a cash deficiency of $74,000 during the period, which must be obtained from outside sources such as a commercial bank. Assume that the borrowing agreement entered into with the Hospital Service Corporation's bankers calls for the borrowing and repaying in increments of $10,000. In line with this agreement borrowing requirements are forecast at $80,000, since $70,000 would result in a cash balance of $16,000 which is judged by financial management to be inadequate for meeting the organization's needs. Note that through the preparation of the cash budget this need for outside funds is identified considerably in advance of the time they are actually required, enabling financial management to shop and negotiate for favorable borrowing terms.

The borrowing of funds in February will require disbursement for interest in March. Otherwise receipts and disbursements follow the previously established pattern. Note that tax payments are actual disbursements of funds to tax collectors and not the recognition of a liability as they are on the Income Statement. The cash excesses of $30,000 recognized in March are used to partially repay the $80,000 loan. In view of this, the beginning balance in April is precisely the $20,000 balance desired.

SYNCHRONIZATION OF CASH FLOW

As stated above, the cash budget must be continually updated to reflect changing conditions. This will permit early identification of issues of concern to financial management and the development and execution of appropriate plans. Reacting to unanticipated crises situations is costly and should be avoided. The cash budget is a tool geared to the attainment of this objective.

The cash budget presented here presumes that receipts and disbursements are synchronized within each month. This may not be the case. It is conceivable that for some organizations disbursements are required at the beginning of each month, while receipts may only materialize towards the end of the month. This could create severe cash deficiencies during the month even if the budget indicated excess funds.

Three possible approaches can be suggested to resolve this problem. First, and recommended, is to develop a cash budget on a weekly or even daily basis. This will pinpoint the issue for continued management attention. The second possibility is to shift receipts one period out, while leaving disbursements as originally detailed. This will, in essence, present the worst case — all disbursements at the beginning of the period and all receipts towards the end. The third option is to adjust the desired cash balances upwards to provide additional slack for slippage in cash receipts.

SIGNIFICANCE OF CASH FLOW

The cash budget provides much needed information to financial management. While over the long run the flow of cash and of profits can be expected to be synonymous, considerable divergences may occur in the short run. In accordance with GAAP, acountants have considerable latitude in recognizing income and expenses. Therefore the Income Statement is not a suitable indicator per se on the near term financial health of the organization. The cash flow statement too, is not a sufficient measure of financial health per se. Excess cash can readily be attained in the short run by disposing of corporate assets, which does not necessarily signify financial health or improved business conditions! Clearly, a financial manager must chart his course taking into account all pertinent information, rather than focusing exclusively on one indicator. Ignoring cash flow needs in the short run can bankrupt the organization in spite of a highly profitable outlook for the long run!

The significance of cash flow is worth specific mention. Earnings are generated through investments in financial instruments, fixed assets, and motivated personnel. To acquire any of these requires the disbursement of cash. The larger the cash balances, the greater the opportunity to seek out such investments. Conversely, the greater the net cash flow resulting from an investment, the higher the return that has been achieved. Capital budgeting procedures recognize this by focusing on cash flows as the relevant indicator of returns realized in each period. For these reasons astute managers investors and lenders insist on tracing the flow of cash through an organization in addition to examining the performance results achieved consonant with GAAP.

A widely held misconception regarding cash flow was identified earlier. Depreciation charges are often alleged to generate cash flow. That this is not the case can be deduced from the cash budget in Table 17. Depreciation is not a line item in this budget either as a receipt or as a disbursement of cash. The erroneous belief regarding the role of depreciation in cash flow projections emanates from adjustments that are made to the Income Statement. Recall that depreciation expense reduces reported income from what it otherwise would have been without entailing the actual outflow of cash from the organization. Cash flow resulting from operations is therefore greater than accounting income after taxes. The addition of depreciation to accounting income tries to compensate for this discrepancy. In order to use projected profits as a reliable indicator of cash flow many other adjustments will be required. Although many of these adjustments are less significant individually than depreciation their aggregate impact may be sizable, particularly if different reports are prepared for tax and shareholder accounting. Thus, although addition of depreciation to projected profit may provide a quick estimate of cash flow, it is hardly a reliable estimate. This can only be achieved through the preparation of a cash budget.

Cash flow considerations are of equal importance to profit oriented and not-for-profit organizations. The cash budget provides the vehicle for both to focus on expected cash surpluses and deficiencies. The differences are the avenues open to the organization for raising funds if the need arises. Profit oriented organizations cannot hope for emergency appropriations to relieve sudden deficiencies!

SUMMARY

To assure survival of the organization, financial management must have visibility regarding the near term requirements for funds. Working capital needs are particularly prone to increase at a time of expanded business activity and increased profitability. The cash budget is the document that provides the mechanism for the desired visibility. Only expected receipts and disbursement of funds are listed in the budget. These differ from the definition of expenses and receipts customarily adopted for accounting purposes and ordinarily reflected in reported profit.

The cash budget permits deliberate planning for the efficient acquisition of funds and for short term investments. Lenders view careful cash budgeting as an indication of good management practices. Cash budgeting is of equal importance to profit oriented and not-for-profit organizations.

11 Leasing

An increasingly practiced form of long term financing is leasing. The capital budgeting framework developed in Chapter 8 can readily be utilized to resolve a frequently recurring issue confronting financial management: whether to lease or to buy a required fixed asset. Generalized statements of the nature that "leasing is superior to buying" are not particularly helpful. The question cannot be addressed in the abstract but must be asked in the context of specific conditions confronting financial management at the time the issue is raised. In order to analyze an equipment lease properly it is important to understand its nature and function.

Leases can be placed into two categories: those that are purely financial in nature and those that include the provision of selected services as part of the agreement. An example of a purely financial lease is a railroad leasing rolling stock from a bank. Clearly, the bank does not intend to get involved in servicing the equipment. The terms of the lease will probably specify the condition under which the railroad is obligated to maintain the rolling stock; the responsibility for maintenance in this case is shifted totally to the user. An extreme example of a service lease is a telephone. Here the lessor assumes full responsibility for maintaining the instrument in serviceable condition. Actually, in view of its relationship with the Public Utility Commission and the nature of its rate structure, the telephone company has a vested interest in providing good maintenance to each instrument in service.

BALANCE SHEET IMPLICATIONS

To properly understand leasing it must be recognized as a form of long term financing although it does not appear directly on the Balance Sheet. Consider, for example, two airlines in 1970, each with assets worth $500 million exclusive of flight equipment. Assume that half of these assets were financed with debt, the other half with equity. Now assume that each airline considers acquiring 20 wide body aircraft at $25 million each, a total obligation of $500 million. Airline A finances the equipment through the issue of long term bonds. Airline B, however, enters into a leasing agreement for this equipment with a commercial bank. The respective hypothetical Balance Sheets of the two airlines after acquisition of the equipment are shown below.

AIRLINE A
Balance Sheet
December 31, 1970
(millions of dollars)

Current assets	$500	Old debt	$250
		New debt	$500
Fixed assets	$500		
		Equity	$250
Total	$1000	Total	$1000

AIRLINE B
Balance Sheet
December 31, 1970
(millions of dollars)

Current assets	$500	Old debt	$250
Fixed assets	–0–	Equity	$250
Total	$500	Total	$500

An outsider, unfamiliar with the practices of the industry might draw erroneous conclusions from these financial statements. Airline B is not in better financial condition, in spite of its debt to equity ratio of 1 : 1 compared to airline A's ratio of 3 : 1. The leasing obligation is in fact a contingent liability for airline B, the clean Balance Sheet notwithstanding. If airline B defaults on its lease obligation the lessor will most probably withdraw his equipment from the lessee, actually depriving him of his earning assets.

Accountants and financial analysts have recognized the distortion that omission of leases from the Balance Sheet introduces into the analysis. During the mid 1970s the Financial Accounting Standards Board (FASB) circulated a draft proposal for establishing guidelines for capitalizing leases. The intent is to show the lease in effect both as an asset and a liability. Similar treatment will have to be accorded by both lessor and lessee. It is expected that within the decade the conceptual and practical problems associated with the accounting treatment of leases will be resolved and that leases will be uniformly reported on the Balance Sheet, avoiding the confusion which exists at the present time.

FINANCIAL CONSIDERATIONS

The financial issues of a lease versus a purchase involve considerably more than the Balance Sheet considerations. The arguments presented by advocates of leasing can be categorized into three general classes: cash flow, risk, and service. Since all these considerations have financial implications they can be calculated independently. Any evaluation must recognize that regardless of the merits of the leasing arrangement, an additional economic agent who has to be compensated for his services has been introduced into the asset acquisition process.

The cash flow argument is as follows. Rather than make the cash outlay for the acquisition of the asset, thereby encumbering the organization's cash balances, the asset is paid for as it produces revenue, not impacting on available balances and retaining sufficient flexibility for the acquisition of outside capital for other projects. The rebuttal to this argument is the following. Potential lenders are well aware of the contingent liabilities represented by lease agreements and will not ignore leases in effect at the time they contemplate additional lending. The basic argument that operational control over an asset can be acquired without being associated with an outflow of cash cannot be rebutted. It reflects, however, the failure of financial management to plan properly. As stated, with few exceptions, leasing is a more expensive way to go since another party enters the transaction. Proper planning should have identified the need and arranged for long term capital to acquire the fixed asset. Exceptions are at the extreme: an unanticipated, unusual opportunity with insufficient time to raise the required capital, or a desperate move when traditional sources of financing are unavailable and the equipment is essential to the operational survival of the organization.

The second argument, which is frequently advanced in support of lease versus buy decisions, is that leasing reduces the risk of the organization. An example is computer equipment that is rendered technologically and economically obsolete as new generations of computers are introduced. The counter argument is based on the risk return relationships previously observed in many financial decisions. Technological obsolescence is a real possibility and the risk cannot be avoided. The relevant question is, however, who bears the risk. If the lessor bears it, he will expect to be compensated for it and the lease payments will incorporate the risk premium. The lessee's costs will therefore be higher compared to those that would be incurred with outright ownership of the asset. Associated with a reduction in return, however, is a commensurate reduction in the risk of obsolescence.

The third argument in favor of leasing is the service argument. Much of the equipment subject to leasing is specialized in nature (computers and copying machines are good examples) and requires custom tailored maintenance with ready access to spare parts and modification instruction. Thus, manufacturers often insisted on leasing arangements for their equipment, using the argument that improperly operated equipment reflects adversely on their products. Legal action has resulted in requiring manufacturers to offer their equipment for sale as well as for lease and has further discouraged their insistence on requiring a maintenance agreement with them as a condition for supplying the desired equipment. Therefore, the financial manager considering equipment acquisition has the option in most cases of deciding whether or not to enter a service agreement regardless of whether he buys or leases the equipment. The decision may thus be made on its merits: if the proposed service is worth the additional cost it should be purchased; if not, the organization may wish to provide the maintenance itself.

In summary, in a well-run organization leasing should be regarded as one possible way of long term financing and should be evaluated on its merits. If after detailed financial analysis it is demonstrably cheaper or the reduction in risk is worth the extra cost, it should be adopted. If not, it should be rejected in favor of other forms of long term financing. One exception to this rule has been discussed: unexpected opportunities or an unexpected shortage of funds. Some other exceptions emanating from tax regulations and contracting practices also exist and are discussed below.

LEASING ADVANTAGES

A classic example is the distortion introduced into make or buy decisions by the investment tax credit. Recall that 10% of the acquisition cost of most equipment is deductible from the actual tax liability incurred by an organization. Assume that this organization has already incurred a tax liability of $1 million. Thus, for example, if equipment was acquired for $9 million early in the year, then $900,000 (10% of $9 million) is deductible from the tax payments otherwise due, resulting in a required payment of only $100,000 instead of $1 million. Now assume that during the year the equipment was acquired the corporation recorded an operating loss. Recall that the investment tax credit can only be applied against a tax liability in the purchase year and does not yield a tax refund if a tax liability is not incurred. Thus, in the absence of a tax liability, the benefits of the investment tax credit are lost to the corporation that acquires the equipment. Leasing, on the other hand, shifts the advantage of the investment tax credit to the lessor. Based on his costs in acquiring the asset — 90% for him versus 100% for the using corporation — the lessor may be able to offer terms that are more advantageous to the firm than direct acquisition. As a footnote to this point, during the 1970s those airlines that recorded accounting profits frequently purchased new equipment while airlines with accounting losses leased their newly acquired equipment.

Another related exception to the guidelines established earlier is when a contract specifies costs that are reimbursable. Organizations often find it advantageous to lease an item and charge off the total lease cost to the contract rather than purchase it and demand reimbursement for depreciation, maintenance, and other related expenses which might be difficult to identify and document separately.

An additional area exists where the lessor can provide a service which the lessee cannot provide on his own. This occurs with the resale of earlier generations of equipment. Consider the organization wishing to possess the latest generation of computing equipment at all times. If it purchases each new generation of equipment, it will have to expend the required effort to dispose of the newly obsolete previous generation of equipment. The time and effort required to identify potential customers and close the transaction can be substantial and costly. A computing leasing organization, on the other hand, probably has among its customers organizations that are interested in the lower cost of using a previous generation of computing equipment. Over time the lessor can thus establish a "hand-me-down" approach to equipment leasing, reflecting the economies of this approach in cost presentations to prospective lessees.

MATHEMATICS OF LEASING

To facilitate the analysis of lease versus buy decisions an assessment of the value of tie-in maintenance services provided by the lessor in service leases must be made prior to the analysis. Recall that this does not apply in the case of purely financial leases. For the sake of simplicity of treatment the discussion below is restricted to financial leases. If service leases are analyzed, the annual cash benefit of maintenance services must be deducted from the lease payments to arrive at a meaningful basis for comparison.

The capital budgeting framework is appropriate for resolving the lease versus buy issue for financial management. The decision is made on the basis of the present value of the cash flow net of all taxes resulting from either financing approach. In computing the cash flows associated with a purchased asset, depreciation plays an important role: it provides a tax shield as the acquired asset is depreciated without entailing an outflow of cash. This is not true of lease payments. All the recorded payments involve the actual outflow of funds, deductible of course from taxable income.

A numerical example will illustrate this point. Consider the decision facing a financial manager interested in acquiring test equipment costing $100,000 and expected to last 8 years without salvage value. The corporation is in the 40% tax bracket, adopts straight line depreciation methods, and can benefit from the investment tax credit. The corporation can sell an 8 year note at an annual interest rate of 10% to raise the funds required for purchasing the equipment. As an alternative it is considering the option of leasing the equipment for $15,000 annually.

Since the investment credit reduces the initial cash outflow by 10%, the actual borrowing requirement is $90,000. At 10%, annual interest payments on this amount are $9000. This is an expense, deductible from income for income tax purposes. An additional tax deduction is provided by depreciation, which is based on the total listed purchase price of $100,000. Annual depreciation is $100,000/8 = $12,500 annually. Total tax deductible expenses are therefore $9000 + $12,500 = $21,500. At 40%, this reduces corporate taxes otherwise payable by $8600. The net annual outflow from the purchase of the asset is therefore $9000 − $8600 = $400. Finally, in year 8 the note will be due and an additional $90,000 will be paid out. The present value of these outflows are as follows:

present value of an annuity of $400 per year for 8 years

+ present value of $90,000, due 8 years in the future

Or

$$R \times T_D + F \times T_B$$

$$\$400 \times 5.335 + \$90,000 \times 0.467 = \$44,164$$

Figure 26 is a graphic presentation of the cost of ownership. In addition to the annual outflows, a sizable payment is due at the end of 8 years. The present value of that payment is of course substantially less than the cash outflow in year 8.

If financial management leases the equipment, the annual outflow will be $15,000 less a reduction in income tax liability of 40% of these payments, or $6000. Actual cash outflow due to the lease is therefore $15,000 − $6000 = $9000. The present value of these outflows for 8 years is

$$R \times T_D = \$9000 \times 5.335 = \$48,015$$

Figure 27 presents the cost of leasing. While the annual cash outflow is substantially greater in each of the first 7 years, the extra payment due in year 8 is avoided. Since the present value of the outflows for the lease are in excess of the outflows for the purchase, purchase is preferred over leasing in this particular case.

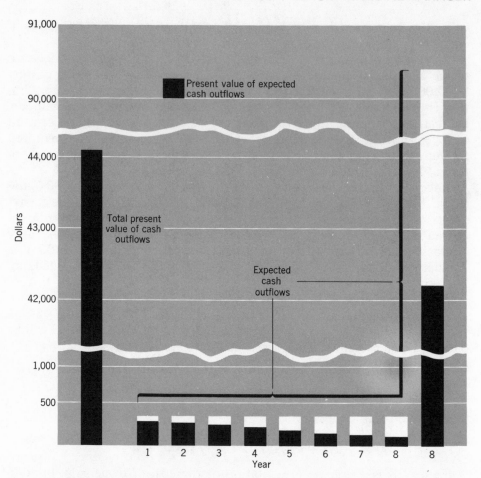

Figure 26. Equipment cost – ownership option with investment tax credit.

Assume now that the investment tax credit cannot be applied. Would purchase still be the preferred solution? Interest payments are now 10% of $100,000, or $10,000 annually. Total tax deductible expenses are $10,000 interest plus $12,500 depreciation, a total of $22,500. The applicable tax savings is 40% of $22,500, or $9000. Therefore the actual annual outflow of cash is $10,000 − $9000 = $1000. The present value of total outflows is the sum of $1000 per year for 8 years and $100,000 in year 8, all discounted at 10% per annum.

$$\$1000 \times 5.335 + \$100,000 \times 0.467 = \$52,035$$

The decision has now changed in favor of the leasing arrangement. Figure 28 represents the ownership situation in the absence of investment tax credit benefits.

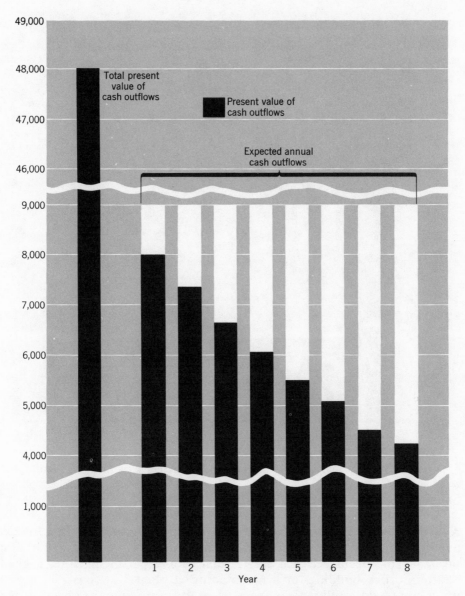

Figure 27. Equipment cost – leasing option.

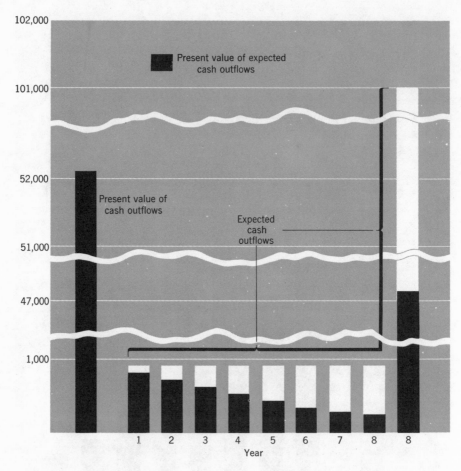

Figure 28. Equipment cost — ownership option less investment tax credit.

SALE AND LEASEBACK

A frequently used form of leasing deserves special comment. It is the sale and leaseback of developed real estate. Under this concept a potential occupant of specialized real estate such as a department store, a headquarters office building, or a manufacturing plant will construct it and, upon completion, sell it to an investor. at the same time the occupant will enter into a long term agreement for the lease of the property. This arrangement presents an additional benefit to the lessee above and beyond those already mentioned. Had the lessee retained title to the property and listed it among other fixed assets on his balance sheet, he would only have been able to depreciate the improvements he made to the property, that is, the cost of construction. Land itself cannot be depreciated. Since the value of land in expensive locations can well amount to 50% of the total value of the asset, the fact that it cannot be depreciated detracts from the desirability of outright ownership. Lease payments, on the other hand, do not differentiate between land and buildings and are fully tax deductible.

Sale and leaseback is thus an instance where leasing can readily be demonstrated to entail the smaller after-tax cash outlays. For this advantage, however, the lessee loses title to the property and the possibility of benefiting from an increase in the market value of the real estate.

Although not-for-profit organizations are not concerned about the tax considerations underlying many of the acquisition versus lease analyses, leasing is also widely practiced in these organizations. The reason lies in fund accounting, which often constrains the ability of organizations to acquire fixed assets on the basis of present worth calculations. Leasing can enable a not-for-profit organization to acquire the services of assets without requiring authorization for capital expenditures.

SUMMARY

Leasing has become an increasingly practiced form of long term financing. Leases may either be purely financial or may include the provision of selected maintenance services. Although the most visible impact of lease financing used to be the absence of the asset acquired and its associated financial claim from the Balance Sheet, this is in process of changing. Three other issues now influence the lease versus buy decision: cash flow, risk, and service.

The capital budgeting framework provides a suitable mechanism for evaluating lease proposals. The present values of the net cash outflows of either proposal are computed and the option with the smaller present value is adopted. Net cash outflows are computed on an after tax basis, taking into account capital service payment and depreciation. Sale and leaseback provides significant leasing advantages in view of the inability to depreciate land.

12   Break-Even Analysis

Break-even analysis is a technique of financial management that has been applied in a wide range of management problems. It is predicated on the observation that some costs vary in direct proportion to output while others remain fixed regardless of the level of output experienced. Examples of variable costs are direct labor and direct material expenses for manufacturing or service organizations and cost of goods sold for retail establishments.

Examples of fixed costs are rent, executive salaries, utilities, and fire insurance.

The concept of variable costs is identical to that of marginal costs in economic theory: they are the costs required to produce one additional unit of output. Break-even analyses assume that these costs remain unchanged over a wide range of outputs. A similar assumption is implied in the definition of fixed costs.

CONTRIBUTION MARGIN

Accountants have recognized the significance of separating variable and fixed costs for management decision purposes. To accomplish this, the contribution Income Statement has been developed. Its acceptance for external reporting has been limited since, for financial reporting purposes, the traditional functional statement has become entrenched. Increasingly, however, the Contribution Income Statement is being used for budgeting and internal control purposes, as discussed in Chapter 9. The illustration presented in Table 18 summarizes the data in Income Statement format.

An important concept directly incorporated in this statement is the contribution margin, which is the difference between the revenue received

Table 18 **International Gadget Corporation,** Contribution Income Statement, January 1, 1980–December 31, 1980

Sales		$8,000,000
Less variable expenses		
Direct material	$3,500,000	
Direct labor	1,500,000	
Total variable expenses		5,000,000
Contribution margin		$3,000,000
Less fixed expenses		
Manufacturing	1,800,000	
Administrative	900,000	
Total fixed expenses		2,700,000
Operating income		$300,000

and the direct cost required to generate this revenue. The presumption is that within a stated range of output additional units can be produced without incurring additional fixed costs. Available facilities, management, distribution channels, and so on, are expected to be able to accommodate the additional production within their available capacity. A purist might argue with this statement: for example, additional production requires additional direct labor and this in turn may increase paper towel consumption, an overhead item treated as a fixed expense. In general, however, this description is a good approximation of cost behavior.

The contribution margin may also be expressed on a per unit basis as the difference between price realized per unit and variable costs incurred per unit. This is a useful formulation for decision purposes. As long as the contribution margin is positive, increasing output contributes to meeting fixed expenses and generating profits. Assume that the International Gadget Corporation sells one million units during the year and that the price realized per unit is $8 and the variable costs per unit are $5. The contribution margin is the difference between the two, $8 - $5 = $3. In order to cover the fixed expenses of $2.7 million, a sufficient number of units must be sold to generate this amount through their contribution margin. This can be determined arithmetically by dividing $3 into $2.7 million, resulting in a unit requirement to cover fixed costs of 900,000 units. If fewer than 900,000 units are sold, the organization operates at an accounting loss. At sales over 900,000 units, the accounting statement shows a profit.

This can readily be displayed graphically. Figure 29 relates fixed costs and variable costs to units sold. Of particular importance to managers is the identification of the point at which the total revenue realized equals the total costs incurred. This is termed the break-even point. Sales above this point generate accounting profits, while sales below this point result

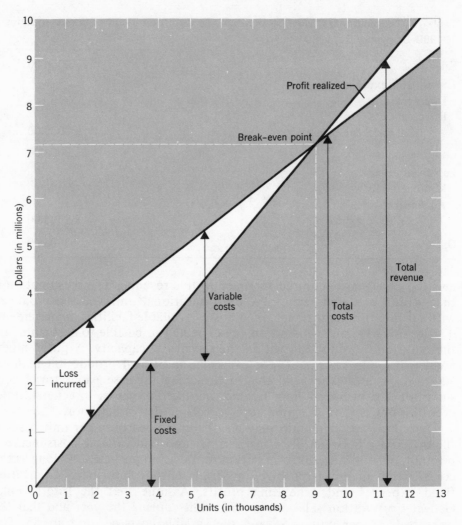

Figure 29. Accounting break-even point.

in accounting losses. The magnitude of profit or loss at any level of output can be determined by the difference between total revenue and total cost at that point.

The graph can also be formulated algebraically. Let

P = price realized per unit

V = variable cost per unit

F = fixed costs

N = quantity sold at break-even

Then by definition, at break even, total revenue = total cost.

But total revenue $= PN$

and total cost $= VN + F$

therefore, at break even: $PN = VN + F$; rearranging terms:

$N(P - V) = F$

Or $\quad N = F/(P - V)$

where $P - V$ is the contribution margin. In terms of the previous example;

$F = \$2,700,000$

$P = \$8$

$V = \$5$

$N = \$2,700,000/(\$8 - \$5) = 900,000$ units as before!

CASH BREAK-EVEN

The break-even model can readily be adapted to the problems of cash management. Certain outflows are invariant with the volume of production, within the relevant range. Rent, light, executive salaries, and insurance are the customary examples. Others, such as direct labor and direct materials, vary directly with the level of output. All of this appears to be identical to the model developed above. There are, however, two major exceptions.

First, in accordance with prevailing trade and accounting practices discussed in Chapter 10, cash receipts and disbursements lag behind accounting revenue and expense portrayed on the Income Statement. If output continues to increase, then actual cash requirements may be considerably larger than those computed on the basis of accounting cost data. Once constant levels of output are achieved, this situation no longer exists and cost data may be used as a reasonable approximation for computing cash requirements.

The second, more significant issue is that of noncash expenses. Preeminent among these, as was mentioned earlier, are depreciation expenses, which although treated as a cost, do not entail an outflow of cash. In effect, therefore, the fixed cash outflows actually incurred are less than fixed costs recorded for profit break-even objectives. The effect of this change is to lower the cash break-even point from the computed profit break-even point.

Consider the previous example. Assume that among the fixed expenses of $2.7 million depreciation expenses total $450,000. Fixed cash disbursements are therefore $2.25 million. Further assume that constant levels of output are planned and will be reached, and thus that $3 adequately represents the cash contribution margin per unit of output.

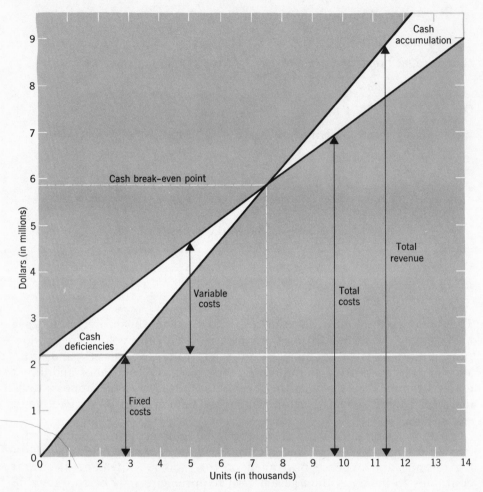

Figure 30.   Cash break-even point.

Figure 30 reflects the cash flow situation as a result of varying levels of output. Note that the cash break-even point is at 750,000 units, 150,000 units below the accounting profit break-even point.

Financial management must be particularly sensitive to output and sales that drop below 750,000 units per year. Should that occur, funds will have to be obtained externally to meet fixed expenses, or ways must be found to reduce the level of disbursements for overhead expenses. Between outputs of 750,000 and 900,000 units per annum a cash surplus is expected to accumulate, although the Income Statement pertaining to this particular product can still be expected to record a loss. Above 900,000 units of output both profit and cash will be positive.

Changing the method of financing fixed assets from ownership to leasing may not have a noticeable effect on the profit break-even point but it can shift the cash break-even point significantly upwards. As discussed earlier, cash flow and profit are not synonymous concepts. Financial management should be guided by considering the implications of its actions on both issues. Break-even analyses provide a suitable mechanism for a preliminary assessment of these implications.

FINANCING BREAK-EVEN

Another useful application of break-even analysis is in determining the relative impact on stockholders of alternate methods of long term financing. The issuance of additional common stock does not entail any new interest expense, consequently total reported income remains identical to that reported before the issuance of additional shares of stock. However, since more shares will be outstanding, the earnings per share (EPS) will be reduced. Conversely, if additional long term financing is obtained through the issuance of bonds the number of shares outstanding will remain unchanged. However, since interest expenses are incurred for the bonds, reported income will be less than in their absence.

An example will illustrate this point. Assume that the International Gadget Corporation has 300,000 shares outstanding. Financial management determines that an additional $2 million of new capital can be employed productively. Underwriters advise that bonds may be sold at an

Table 19 International Gadget Corporation, Pro-forma Income Statement (stock issue)

Sales	$8,000,000	$12,000,000	$16,000,000
Variable expenses	5,000,000	7,500,000	10,000,000
Fixed expenses	2,700,000	2,700,000	2,700,000
Interest expense	—	—	—
Total expenses	7,700,000	10,200,000	12,700,000
Income before taxes	$300,000	$1,800,000	$3,300,000
EPS (346,157 shares)	$0.87	$5.20	$9.53

Table 20 International Gadget Corporation, Pro-forma Income Statement (bond issue)

Sales	$8,000,000	$12,000,000	$16,000,000
Variable expenses	5,000,000	7,500,000	10,000,000
Fixed expenses	2,700,000	2,700,000	2,700,000
Interest expense	240,000	240,000	240,000
Total expenses	7,940,000	10,440,000	12,940,000
Income before taxes	$60,000	$1,560,000	$3,060,000
EPS (300,000 shares)	$0.20	$5.20	$10.20

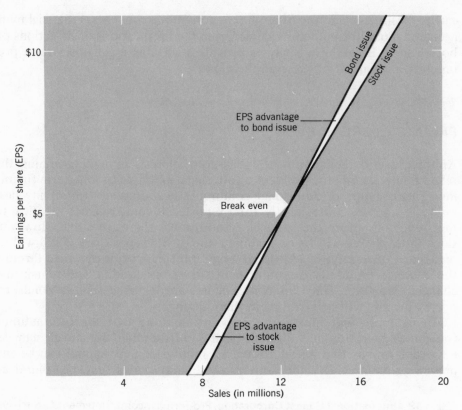

Figure 31.   Financing break-even point.

interest rate of 12%, or common stock may be sold at $43.33 per share. Management expects sales to range between $8 million and $16 million during the next 5 years. Which method is advisable?

Constructing pro-forma Income Statements for the corporation at various levels of sales results in the pro-forma Income Statement presented in Table 19.

EPS in Table 19 is computed on the basis of 300,000 original shares outstanding plus 46,157 new shares ($2,000,000/$43.33 per share) for a total of 346,157 shares. Consider now Table 20, presenting the effect of a bond issue for raising the desired $2 million with annual interest costs of $240,000.

Income before taxes in Table 20 is reduced by the $240,000 in interest expense from that reported in Table 19. However, since no additional stock was issued, only 300,000 shares are outstanding. These results can be presented graphically, as in Figure 31. Analysis reveals that at sales volume below $12 million a stock issue is more desirable insofar as current stockholders are concerned. If sales expectations exceed $12 million, a bond issue appears more desirable from their point of view, while at $12 million old stockholders would be indifferent. Since the role of financial management in a profit oriented orgainzation is to maximize the wealth of stockholders, an assessment regarding the sales outlook for the next few years must be undertaken prior to reaching a decision regarding the nature of future financing.

Most of the examples developed as illustrations of break-even analyses deal with problems of profit oriented organizations. Yet these techniques are equally applicable to problems of not-for-profit organizations. Any financial situation that entails both fixed and variable expenditures and generates revenues can benefit from this approach. It is a widely used tool of analysis for almost all managerial functions.

SUMMARY

Break-even analysis is a technique of financial management that is widely used in many other managerial functions. It is an appropriate tool of analysis whenever differentiations can be made between fixed and variable costs and whenever the contribution margin per unit is positive. The break-even point represents the level of revenue which precisely equals the fixed and variable expenses for the given volume of output.

Other, frequent financial applications include cash break-even analysis and the evaluation of long term financing options. Break-even analyses are equally applicable to managerial problems confronting not-for-profit organizations.

13 Inventory Policy

Ideally, investments in any asset account of the Balance Sheet, be it land, equipment, inventory, or even cash are made solely for the purpose of increasing expected levels of profits in a profit oriented organization or the quality and range of service in a not-for-profit organization. Capital budgeting provides an approach for determining the desirability of acquiring long term assets once the stream of expected returns can be ascertained. The responsibility of financial management in these instances is usually limited to determining the desirability of the proposal. The determination of specific characteristics of the proposed investment, such as size and output, is usually left to operating management.

In current assets financial management frequently doubles as operating management. This is clearly so in the case of cash management, very prevalent for credit management, and frequently includes at least a voice in inventory management. Financial management has a substantial stake in the determination of appropriate levels of inventory. If these exceed levels that may be justified on the basis of financial analysis, funds are in effect tied up in nonproductive activities and the overall profits or levels of service of the organization are less than they could be. The problem facing financial management is to determine the costs associated with alternate inventory policies and to adopt those policies that attain the desired objectives with the least possible expenditures.

The arguments for increasing an organization's level of inventory are readily stated. By holding higher levels the probability of stock-outs is reduced. Customers have a better chance of receiving the precise item they intended to acquire, sales and profit increase, and goodwill is established, enhancing the likelihood that the same customers will engage in additional purchases in the future. With the exception of increased profits, the same argument holds true for the not-for-profit organization, whose ability to serve its clientele is enhanced by higher levels of inventory. Thus it appears that the greater the inventory, the better the service, sales revenue, and profit.

Clearly, there is another side to this issue. The holding of inventory gives rise to a series of costs that would not be experienced without the inventory. Some of these costs are obvious: costs of increased capital requirements to finance the additional inventory; the cost of increased facilities to store the additional inventory; and the cost of increased obsolescence and spoilage resulting from the higher inventory levels. Although other costs may not be as directly apparent, they are nevertheless very real. Among these are increased property taxes for the higher investment in inventory and facilities, increased manpower requirements for paper work, storing, packing, cleaning, and guarding the inventory, and increased insurance costs to reduce the consequences of loss due to theft and fire.

Some of the costs incurred in inventory management decrease on a per unit basis with increased levels of inventory. Predominant among these are ordering costs. As the quantity of each distinct item carried in inventory increases, the number of reorders that must be processed for that particular item decrease per period. Each order has numerous costs associated with it, ranging from the taking of physical inventory to ascertaining shortage to management decision time to request additional units. These are in addition to the costs associated with the typing, processing, and mailing of actual orders, those associated with receiving, sorting, and storing merchandise received, and those of filing accompanying documents and authorizations for payment to suppliers. These types of costs favor the acquisition of sizable levels of inventory at one time over minimal levels, with frequent reordering.

DECISION RULES

The issue confronting the financial manager is where to draw the line, for without any inventory he is clearly not in business. If all inventory that could conceivably add to sales and service is acquired, resources may be so strained that other areas requiring financing, such as the acquisition of fixed assets, expenditures for personnel training, and the recurring costs of advertising, may have to be neglected.

Economic theory provides guidelines for solving this dilemma. In general, output should be increased to the point where marginal revenues equal marginal costs. In this case an additional item should be held in inventory as long as the increase in sales revenue realized by virtue of storing the additional item equals the cost of holding that item. To arrive at a quantitative solution, estimates in terms of costs can be prepared by the controller's staff, while estimates of additional sales realistically attainable with the added inventory can be developed by the marketing organization.

Although it is not anticipated that these analyses will result in a precise number that will be acceptable to all members of management, the joint assessment will lead to the identification of the appropriate range of acceptable inventory levels. This process may also help to highlight costs that are frequently not visible to operating management.

The widespread availability of computing capacity permits management to exercise tight control over inventory levels. A particularly significant utilization of computers for this purpose is the point-of-sale electronic registers in retail operations. These registers have the capability of continually updating inventory information as sales are made and merchandise is received. This information, coupled with the mathematical formulation of cost functions, storage capacity, and sales expectations, permits the rapid calculation of reordering points and quantity per order. As the number of items carried and the magnitude of the investment in inventory have increased, financial managers have relied more heavily on the aid of mathematical decision models for inventory control.

ECONOMIC ORDER QUANTITY

An example of such a mathematical formulation is the economic order quantity (EOQ) model. This model seeks to determine the number of units to be ordered each time an order is placed. Recall that as fewer orders are placed, the costs associated with ordering decreases. On the other hand, by receiving more units with each order that has been placed, the storage and associated costs of holding inventory increase. The EOQ model determines the number of units that should be ordered each time an order is placed, so that the overall costs associated with inventory management are minimized. In the model, let

F = the costs associated with placing one order. These include paper work, merchandise receipt, payment, and so forth, and are judged to be independent of the size of the order

U = sales in units per year of one item being stocked in inventory

C = costs per year associated with carrying one item in inventory. These include, among others, rent of facilities, insurance, and taxes

Then it can be shown that the number of units to be ordered each time so that the overall cost of ordering is at a minimum, that is, the economic order quantity, is

$$EOQ = \sqrt{\frac{2FU}{C}}$$

For example, assume that

F = fixed costs per order   = $5

U = units sold per year   = 5000

C = carrying costs per unit/per year = $0.80

Then

$$EOQ = \sqrt{\frac{2 \times 5 \times 5000}{0.80}} = 250 \text{ units}$$

The interpretation is that good inventory management calls for orders to be placed in lots of 250 units at a time. Precisely when these orders will be placed will depend on the safety levels required and the seasonality of the item. If either smaller or larger orders than the EOQ quantity are placed, unnecessary inventory expenses will be incurred.

Figure 32 displays the behavior of these costs graphically.

While the model specifically addresses a merchandise inventory problem, the concept and approach are applicable to a much wider range of problems. Consider, for example, the problems facing the financial manager in regard to the levels of cash to maintain. In addition to the cash flow considerations discussed in Chapter 10, two other factors should be taken into account. First, excess idle cash has an opportunity cost. It may either be invested in profit generating assets, or some of the outstanding debt-incurring interest charges can be repaid earlier than required. Both these solutions are preferable to letting idle cash earn minimal returns on short term investments. Second, the acquisition of cash often entails sizable legal and administrative costs, some of which are independent of the size of the loan secured. The problem of cash management can thus be viewed as an inventory problem, posing some of the same issues of ordering and holding costs that merchandise and work in process inventories were shown to exhibit. Several mathematical models have been developed to address the particular requirements of cash management.

Another management problem that resembles the issues identified in the EOQ model is created in activities of highly specialized labor services facing fluctuating demand. The prototypes for these are consulting and software firms. During slack times, when employees cannot be billed to client accounts, the dilemma facing management is whether to retain these employees, since their wages become overhead expense without generating sales revenue. The alternative is to dismiss them to reduce the drain on profits and hope that equivalent talent can be acquired when their services are required again. If employees are dismissed and client contracts develop subsequently, considerable hiring costs will probably have to be incurred. Again, the concepts of balancing holding against acquisition costs developed previously can be expected to aid the manager in minimizing total costs within a period. This framework should be applied in addition to the factors that must be considered in personnel decisions.

Inventory policy is another area of financial management that is as applicable to not-for-profit organizations as it is to profit oriented organiza-

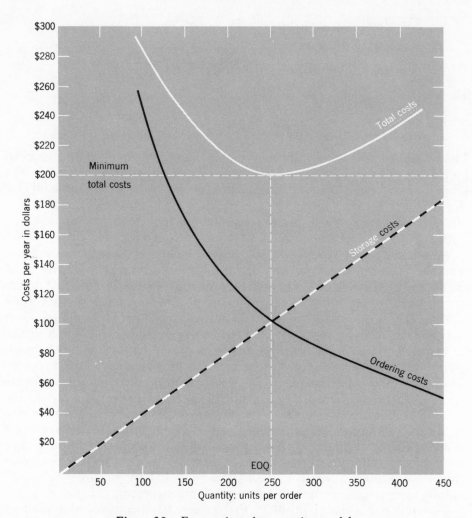

Figure 32. Economic order quantity model.

tions. The approach outlined regarding merchandise decisions, personnel policy, and cash management is equally suitable to the public and private sectors of the economy. The requirement to reduce operating costs without jeopardizing the level of service offered is of continuing concern to all management.

SUMMARY

Inventory policy is an area where financial management often exercises line responsibility. The issue is to minimize the total costs associated with inventory management consistent with the level of service that has been stipulated. The widespread availability of computers and the acceptance of mathematical decision models have assisted in this task. The EOQ model is an example of such a decision rule.

Many activities besides physical inventory can be analyzed in this framework. Cash management and personnel policies are typical applications. Inventory management, with all its ramifications, is equally pertinent to profit oriented and not-for-profit organizations.

14 Cash Management

Cash management is one of the few areas discussed in this book that is exclusively within the domain of financial managers. Although most financial decisions directly influence other managers through budgets, authorized levels of inventory, or approval for the acquisition of capital assets, such is not the case with management. This activity is internal to financial management and does not require negotiations with operating managers under ordinary conditions. If drastic shortages of funds occur, financial management may have to revise budgetary authorizations which were previously approved. Such instances, however, represent crises intervention rather then exemplary management practice. Cash balances and deficiencies are in essence the residual from all the operating decisions that have been taken in prior periods. The difference between good and barely adequate performance is only noticeable in corporate earnings. In not-for-profit organizations the results are even more subtle: good cash management will be reflected in the attainment of higher levels of service for the resources provided to the organization than would be possible with poor or mediocre cash management.

In the previous discussion on inventory the appropriateness of viewing cash as an inventory item was pointed out. Excess cash balances should be invested, to avoid waiving the returns such investment can realize. Economists refer to these foregone returns as the opportunity cost. A proper definition of opportunity cost is the return that may be realized by the next best alternative. Thus, for example, the opportunity cost of investing funds in very low risk internal investments that generate 15% may be viewed as 8%, the return on government bonds. The risk assumed by corporate management is properly viewed in terms of a return of 15% – 8%, or 7%. Another example: the opportunity cost of full time studies incurred by an unemployed worker is the unemployment compensation that he must forego by law!

Idle balances are needed for valid reasons, such as safety levels to protect against deficient planning and as buffer stocks to protect against slower than anticipated receivables. Over time, however, most organizations develop some experience as to the frequency of occurrence of such events and adjust their planning accordingly. Furthermore, capital markets for short term securities have been developed to such an extent that investments will yield a positive return if held for only 1 day. Relinquishing such a return implies an opportunity cost. The true cost of holding cash balances is the return realized on these balances minus the opportunity cost incurred.

NEAR TERM STRATEGY

Several options are open to financial management in reducing the cost of holding cash balances. First, additional long term projects which, on previous investigations, appeared desirable but could not be financed for lack of long term funds might now be considered. Second debt, short term or long term, might be prepaid, enhancing the debt to equity ratio of the Balance Sheet and reducing overall interest costs. Trade credit discounts that could not be accepted before now become feasible. These are the happy dilemma of financial management: how to utilize excess balances. Most of the time, however, certainly in successfully growing organizations, another dilemma prevails: how to manage short term cash deficiencies.

Ignoring for the time being the possibility of issuing additional securities or borrowing short or long term funds, two basic alternatives remain. First, the financial manager may pressure line managers to reduce all asset accounts. This may be reflected in reduction of prevailing inventory levels, curtailment of capital asset expansion and replacement plans, liquidation of securities held for long term investment purposes, tighter credit terms, and pressure on customers to meet their outstanding obligations in order to reduce the balances in accounts receivable.

Each of these solutions raises questions regarding the long term survival of the firm. The issue of reducing inventory levels has already been discussed. Reducing expenditures for fixed assets may have a variety of undesirable effects. First, it may preclude the organization from replacing antiquated equipment with newer, more efficient versions which could increase operating profits. Second, it might restrict the organization from meeting expanding customer demand, thereby placing it at a disadvantage vis-à-vis its competition. Pressuring customers to speed their payments and denying future extensions of credit may improve cash flow initially but can ruin customer relationships in the long run. None of these solutions should ordinarily be pursued beyond the exercise of normal management control over loose practices that are likely to occur periodically in the conduct of any activity.

The second basic alternative open to the financial manager is to delay payments until the last possible due date. This can be costly in two ways: it can impair the credit rating of the organization, raising the cost of future funds, and it can result in the loss of discounts that would otherwise be available. Thus, while a strategy of accelerating receipts and delaying payment should be favored in principle, it should only be pursued to the point where it incurs direct or hidden costs to the organization.

LONG TERM STRATEGY

Beyond the daily problems of cash management, financial management must be concerned with the nature of financing the long term asset requirements of the firm. This discussion is not oriented towards the composition of the capital structure (debt vs. equity) but rather distinguishes between short term and long term funds. By their very nature, however, short term funds are debt, usually commercial bank loans. Equity capital is by definition long term capital, as is long term debt.

To understand the appropriate utilization of short term and long term funds it is useful to view the total capital needs of a representative organization as shown in Figure 33.

Successful organizations require continuing expansion of their assets, particularly during their growth phase. Existing facilities must be enlarged and new equipment must be acquired to facilitate the increased demand for output. In the early years of an organization each of these expenditures probably constitutes a significant addition to the stock of fixed

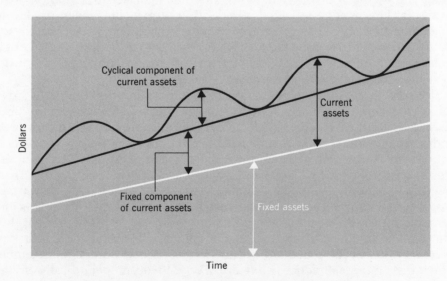

Figure 33. Component view of total capital needs.

assets on hand. Thus the acquisition of a new facility or new computer system may appear as a step increase in the total level of fixed assets. Over time, however, each new fixed asset expenditure is likely to represent a smaller percentage of total fixed assets on hand at the time. Thus, over the long run, the level of fixed assets can be approximated by an upward sloping line.

The same situation does not exist for current assets. Most organizations face cyclical needs for cash, inventory, and accounts receivable. For example, department stores stock their heaviest inventory in the late fall in anticipation of customer demand at Christmas; agriculturally based industries will be in peak inventory position shortly after the harvesting season; accounting firms catering to individuals will have their highest levels of accounts receivable shortly after April 15. This cycle is likely to repeat itself annually. Within each cycle, the difference between peak requirements and off-season needs may be substantial.

The task of financial management is to obtain the necessary funds from internal and external sources to meet these needs. Both short term and long term funds may be utilized for this purpose. As was pointed out in Chapter 2, the cost of short term funds is usually lower than that of long term funds. The temptation to finance all of the organization's needs with short term capital should, however, be resisted. Short term funds are just that; they require the borrower to repay the funds in full or to renew the outstanding loan on its maturity date. Renewal of the loan on the maturity date is, however, not guaranteed to the borrower since one of several adverse situations may arise at that time. Among these are the possibility that the lender may be under pressure from the Federal Reserve to reduce his outstanding loan portfolio. Furthermore, the lender may have become dissatisfied with the financial posture of the borrower and may welcome the opportunity to reduce outstanding commitments. Finally, the lender may have identified more lucrative loan possibilities in the interim and desires to shift his loan portfolio to higher income producing opportunities.

If the borrower has not anticipated this possibility he may find himself in the unpleasant and expensive predicament of having to abandon construction projects prior to completion for lack of sufficient funds. The direct and hidden costs associated with such developments are completely out of line with the slight savings in interest costs that may be associated with the use of short term funds.

As displayed in Figure 33, not all current assets fluctuate cyclically. Usually one finds a permanent component in current assets, composed of minimum required cash balances coupled with the lowest levels of accounts receivable and inventories that must be supported. The discussion regarding the financing of fixed assets also applies here. Since these levels of current assets are always anticipated, the funding required to support them should not be placed in jeopardy, and long term financing is therefore highly recommended for this segment.

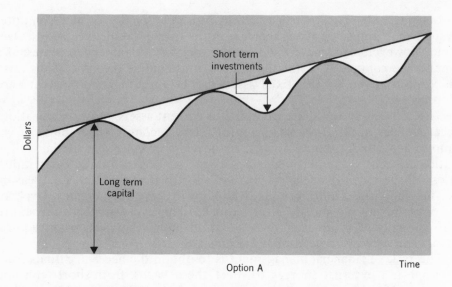

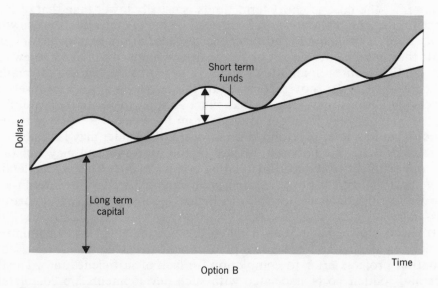

Figure 34. Two options for financing cyclical fluctuation of current assets.

The cyclically fluctuating segment of current assets offers the financial manager far greater discretion. As indicated in Figure 34, two basic options are open. If he or she is extremely averse to risk, all current assets need may be financed with long term capital, as indicated in Option A. During other than peak periods the financial manager will invest excess funds in short term money instruments, redeeming these as capital needs increase and reinvesting proceeds as excess cash accumulated during later phases of the cycle. This is a very conservative strategy, the least risky,

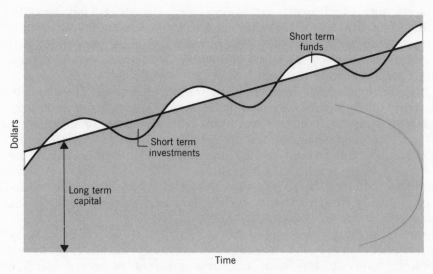

Figure 35. Compromise approach to options for financing cyclical fluctuation of current assets.

and the most expensive, since the cost of long term capital exceeds the periodic returns from short term investments.

Option B, as displayed in Figure 34, is a far riskier strategy. All cyclical needs are financed with short term funds. This saves on interest costs without jeopardizing the completion of long term projects. The main drawback of this strategy is the absence of any slack for financial contingencies. If fund requirements are underestimated, or if lenders renege on their commitments, the financial manager may have to deny funds to previously approved profitable investments. Aside from deliberate high-risk management strategy, organizations often find themselves in Option B due to poor planning. Although this level of risk is tolerable it is not recommended as a deliberate long term approach.

A compromise approach, such as that shown in Figure 35, is frequently practiced and is recommended. It implies the use of long term capital up to about halfway between the peak and the trough of cyclical needs. If cyclical needs are less than the level of financing adopted, the financial manager invests excess funds in short term instruments as indicated in the shaded area. If needs are in excess of the long term financing provided, he or she can supplement long term capital with short term borrowing. Adopting this approach allows sufficient slack for emergencies and for pursuing attractive opportunities that may otherwise have to be ignored. The overall cost of capital is less than with complete long term financing, yet flexibility is almost identical to that of Option A in Figure 34.

Throughout this discussion two points have been stressed repeatedly: short term capital is risky and long term capital is costly. Once again the financial manager is faced with a risk-return tradeoff: If he or she adopts the low risk strategy of financing all fund needs with long term capital, costs are higher and profits are lower. If, on the other hand, he opts for the high risk strategy of financing all current assets with short term capital, costs are lower and resulting profits are higher. As was stated earlier, his risk preference will dictate if and where to compromise and what level of long term financing to adopt.

One additional point merits explicit statement. Excess interest costs for long term funds might be viewed as being similar to the premium paid on a casualty insurance policy. These extra costs assure the financial manager that the necessary financial resources will be available regardless of unfavorable developments in money markets. The role of a casualty insurance policy is to assure that physical assets will be at hand, regardless of calamities that may befall the facilities. The policy premium, while decreasing profits from what they would have been in the absence of such a policy, reduce the business risk to the manager.

Long term capital serves an identical function. It reduces the risk facing the financial manager and frees him to concentrate his effort on the effective long term utilization of resources rather than worry continually whether the resources required for the pursuit of the organization's objectives will be available as needed.

INVESTMENT INSTRUMENTS

If management adopts Figure 35, the compromise approach to cash management in balancing long term and short term funds, periodic needs for the short term investment of excess balances arise. The market for such instruments had become very active in recent years and a variety of public and private organizations offer their debt obligations for investment purposes. In addition to assessing the risk-return relationships of these securities, financial management must consider their marketability, to assure liquidity should sudden needs arise, their maturity dates, and their denominations.

Preeminent among the choices available for these investment purposes are treasury bills and commercial paper. Other issues are available with similar maturity characteristics. Thus for example, various local government and federal agencies other than the U.S. Treasury issue securities with relatively short maturities. Also, as long term debt obligations approach maturity, they act in a manner similar to these instruments and can serve the same purpose.

Treasury bills are issued with maturities ranging from 30 days to 1 year, currently in denominations of up to $1 million. Since there is a very active secondary market for treasury bills, they are highly liquid and are actually viewed as the equivalent for cash. The difference is, of course, that they generate a positive return to the holder that cash in the form of currency or demand deposits does not.

Rather than pay periodic interest as medium term instruments (notes) or long term instruments (bonds) do, treasury bills generate a return to the holder by being offered at a discount and redeemed at face value upon maturity. The discount is established by means of competitive bidding for the bills by dealers and the public.

A simplified example will illustrate this point. Assume that the Treasury is offering $100 million in bills due to mature in 1 year. At a public auction, $94.5 million is offered by dealers and accepted by the Treasury. Investors who paid the indicated amount for the bills or a portion thereof will realize a return of 5.82% on their investment if they hold the bills to maturity, in this case 1 year. In mathematical terms:

$$P = F \times T_B$$

$$\$94,500,000 = \$100,000,000 \, T_B$$

$$T_B = 0.945$$

why no 9.45 howdidyou get 5.82

Interest Tables B are not sufficiently detailed to identify fractional interest rates. To find the appropriate interest rate the reader can interpolate, acquire more detailed tables or, best of all, invest in an electronic financial calculator to verify the answer of 5.82%. Financial managers charged with the continued investment of very large portfolios sharpen their pencils to obtain fractionally higher interest rates. Three-tenths of 1% on a $50 million portfolio is $150,000, almost sufficient to pay the salary of a good financial manager!

Commercial papers are debt obligations similar to treasury bills issued by private sector corporations. In actual practice only the largest and best known corporations, those judged to be in the most solid financial condition, issue commercial paper since others may find the discount requirements too burdensome. Since these issues are not backed by the U.S. government they are more risky than treasury bills. As may be expected from risk-return considerations, the return to investors in commercial paper is higher than that obtainable on treasury bills.

Two types of risk confront the investor. First the basic risk of holding unsecured debt obligations of a going concern. Should the business conditions and the cash flow situation of the issuing corporation deteriorate dramatically, it may not be in a position to redeem the paper at face value. This is not as farfetched as it may appear. The commercial papers of the Penn Central were highly regarded until its bankruptcy in 1970. Upon bankruptcy, these instruments were treated in a manner similar to other corporate payables in bankruptcy proceedings. The second risk of investing in commercial paper is due to the lesser marketability of the instrument if sudden liquidity is required. By their nature commercial paper issues are not traded as actively on the resale markets as are treasury bills. This lessened marketability can result in losses on these investments if they must be liquidated prior to maturity.

Financial managers, particularly those subscribing to Figure 35, are frequently active on both sides of the commercial paper market. They may issue these instruments to investors during their cyclical shortages of cash. During periods of excess cash they invest funds in the commercial paper of other corporations. For maximum effectiveness of this strategy, detailed financial planning with continual updating of these plans based on emerging business and economic conditions is essential. The key document in this effort is the cash budget introduced in Chapter 10. It provides a timely view of expected cash surpluses and shortfalls.

The problems of cash management are equally pertinent for profit and not-for-profit organizations. The largest not-for-profit of all, the U.S. government, is actively concerned with the funding of its cyclical cash needs and is the prime issuer of short term instruments to the rest of the economy. Nonfinancial managers may view the activities of financial management in this area as a effort geared to the management of its prime item of inventory, cash.

SUMMARY

Cash management is an internal operation of financial management that influences operating management only in unusual situations. Good cash management will be reflected indirectly in higher profits and better levels of service than are otherwise attainable. Some idle cash balances are needed as buffers and safety stocks. However, excess balances incur an opportunity cost that should be avoided.

While some flexibility exists in financing current assets, long term assets should only be financed with long term obligations. The extent to which current assets are financed with long term obligations depends on the degree of risk aversion of financial management. Excess short term funds can be invested in treasury bills and commercial paper. Well known and highly regarded corporations can finance short term needs by issuing commercial paper. While specific financial instruments may differ, these concepts apply equally to profit oriented and not-for-profit organizations.

15 Credit Management

The essence of a business relationship is mutual trust with the expectation of gain from exchange. The trust encompasses issues such as delivery dates, quality and other product specifications, and, of course, the extension of credit. Except for a narrow segment of retail sales, primarily supermarkets, almost all business transactions are conducted on a credit basis. Actually it is hard to envision business transactions without the mechanism of credit. It provides the lubricant and the slack necessary for the continuity of transactions regardless of the immediate availability of cash. Without credit, near-term cash flow considerations would override long term needs and the efficiencies accruing from production planning would be lost.

Thus the granting of credit is the rule, not the exception. The problem is not whether to extend it but rather how much to grant, to whom, and under what conditions. As with all business transactions, risk-return relationships must be assessed. The risk in this case is that of extensively delayed receipts, or default at worst. The returns expected are the increased profits anticipated from the additional sales that the ready granting of credit can generate less the costs associated with credit extension. Relevant costs in this case consist of the credit operation itself and include personnel costs, computer services, and the cost of invested capital, plus the cost of goods sold to uncollectible accounts.

If credit is not granted or if the standards applied are extremely tight, thus in effect denying credit to all but a select group, the cost of credit administration may be low and losses will not be experienced. At the same time, however, overall sales may suffer and, as a result, the organization may operate at an inefficient output level. Thus the total profitability of the operation may be far less than otherwise attainable.

At the other extreme, if credit is too loose, the losses resulting from nonpayment by customers may exceed the advantages of increased sales

161

revenue. The role of credit management is to arrive at a policy that will maximize the benefits to the credit granting organization. Recall that according to economic theory output should be expanded to the point where marginal costs equal marginal revenue — a criterion that is also applicable to this case. The problem of credit management then is to determine these marginal costs, view them in the context of the revenue expected to be realized, and develop screening techniques that will maintain the desired balance between marginal costs and marginal revenue.

Unfortunately even in successful organizations, credit management is often regarded as basically a clerical activity. The search for the proper balance between risk and potential return requires an understanding of the structure of costs within the organization, sensitivity to marketing potential, and the ability to interpret the financial posture of customers. Furthermore, statistical techniques are applied increasingly to the development of predictors of customer credit worthiness. These may be based on financial ratios, past repayment record, and general economic conditions. Great progress has been made in this area particularly at the consumer level. Competence in credit management requires knowledge of the economics underlying the granting of credit as well as creativity in the development of screening techniques. Mere clerical competence will certainly not do the job.

The very essence of credit management is the assumption of risk. Management must anticipate that certain losses will be incurred in the extension of credit, and these in effect become part of the cost of extending credit. Total avoidance of all losses can only be achieved if all credit is denied. Thus a credit manager who boasts that under his guidance no defaults occured is obviously not undertaking the trade-off analysis required to arrive at the proper credit policy for the organization.

RELEVANT COSTS

The direct costs of operating the credit function can readily be determined. In addition to personnel and computer costs these include fees for rating services, occasional field investigations, and the cost of the capital required to support accounts receivable. In setting credit policy, it is desirable that the credit manager have an understanding of the cost structure of the product or service for which credit is extended.

The important consideration in this context is that relevant cost of the product is not the price charged to the credit customer but rather the out-of-pocket costs incurred in the production process. Only material and labor costs directly attributable to the product or the service sold on credit are relevant. Thus overhead costs and profit expectations that are built into the pricing structure of any product or service are not relevant costs to the credit-granting decision process.

Recall that the contribution margin is defined as the sales price minus the variable costs of the product. In line with this terminology the credit decision should be based on the variable costs incurred by the item. The contribution margin that is added to the variable cost for pricing purposes should be ignored for this decision. Some reflection at the retail level will readily verify this approach. Generally, in those cases where variable costs constitute a very large percentage of the selling price, the potential cost of credit losses is high and credit screening is relatively severe. Conversely, products and services with high contribution margins are normally associated with less stringent credit controls.

Consider a typical retail merchandising operation such as a supermarket. In this instance the contribution margin realized by the retailer on each sale is relatively low. A retail furniture dealer, on the other hand, is an example of a high contribution margin seller, often exceeding the variable costs of the product sold. Proper economic analysis is reflected in the credit management of these two retail operations. The supermarket does not extend credit since the cost of credit management and possible default cannot be absorbed in the prevailing contribution margin. The furniture dealer, on the other hand, liberally uses credit to attract additional sales. His pricing structure permits him to absorb occasional defaults since the COGS is less than the credit extended.

A related example is the relatively severe screening to which applicants for bank credit cards are subjected. The reason for this procedure is that the gross profit accruing to the issuing bank is a low percentage of the sales price of the merchandise, precluding the banks from absorbing heavy defaults within their pricing structure. In other words, their variable costs are very high. It is far easier to obtain an airline credit card, in spite of the high price of flight tickets. This results from the low variable cost of an occupied seat to the airline: basically, it consists of the cost of the meal served during the flight. Thus most of the ticket price paid accrues to the contribution margin, including airline overhead, aircraft depreciation, flight crew payments and so on, which will be incurred regardless of whether an empty seat is filled or the credit sale is made. This is particularly true at a time when airlines experience low load factors. One would expect that airline credit standards will tighten as load factors on airlines increase, and credit sales can only be realized as a replacement for rather than an addition to cash sales.

CREDIT STANDARDS

Any grantor of credit normally wishes to satisfy himself that three basic conditions pertaining to the borrower are satisfied: capacity, collateral, and character. The risk and return considerations enumerated earlier will dictate the appropriate acceptance thresholds for each of these conditions in screening credit applicants. While some acceptance thresholds can be quantified, others require qualitative assessment. As in all management functions, good judgment is essential.

Capacity is a comprehensive term denoting the ability of the borrower to meet the mutually agreed on repayment obligations. The emphasis is on the expected cash flow of the borrower. While the lender is interested in the profitability of the borrower's operations and may wish to examine past and pro-forma Income Statements, his real concern is whether the cash flow will permit repayment of the debt on schedule. Thus projected cash flow statements of the borrower are often a requirement for securing credit. Lacking these, the lender will find it difficult to determine the borrower's capacity.

In extending credit for merchandise the lender will probe for expected cash receipts to the borrower. Bank loan officers will search for mandated outflows that could take precedence over repayment of the new debt. The payment of taxes, utility bills, and direct labor usually assume paramount importance to a financial manager strained for cash, and repayment of open accounts and notes due are easily ignored under conditions of stress.

The second screening criterion listed above is that of collateral, the possibility of securing a legal claim on a borrower's asset in case he defaults on his obligation. Considerable misunderstanding is associated with the significance and intent of collateral. It is rare that the lender is unaware of the difference between the orderly repayment of the debt and his legal right to repossess the merchandise or seize property or equipment pledged as collateral for a loan. Aside from the many legal and administrative costs associated with repossession and seizure, these actions are often accompanied by considerable aggravation and poor public relations. This, incidentally, is the prime reason why most lenders specializing in general real estate loans are reluctant to accept a mortgage on a church. Repossessing a house of worship is not an action for which lenders wish to be known. Also, the resale market for these properties is not particularly active.

Securing a loan by means of collateral has two prime objectives. First, it forces the borrower to place high priority on meeting his stated obligations. If the borrower defaults on his promises the lender holds the club of depriving him of his earning assets. This raises the priority of loan repayment to the same level as tax and wage payments. The second objective is to provide the lender with some claim in case of a total default. With the exception of real estate loans, lenders stand to lose in most cases of repossession. Even in the case of real estate it is rare that a lender is indifferent between normal continuation of the loan and repossession of the pledged property once he identifies all the direct and hidden costs of repossession. If at all possible he will strive to avoid foreclosure.

The third credit screen is an assessment of the character of the borrower. This is the least quantifiable issue, requiring considerable experience and maturity of judgment by the credit manager. In applying this screening criterion, it is useful to remember that mutually beneficial business relationships are rarely possible if one of the parties is bent on defrauding the other. Regardless of capacity and collateral, if the lender perceives the borrower to be of poor character prudence dictates that a lender/debtor relationship be avoided. No amount of legal protection can safeguard the lender from the aggravation that may be associated with trying to collect previously agreed on amounts.

One of the best ways to judge an individual's character traits towards debt obligations is to examine his track record. This, incidentally, is one of the main functions of the retail credit bureaus and the professional credit reference services. By providing data on past loans and repayment practices, the lender can form a judgment regarding the attitude of the applicant towards honoring outstanding obligations.

CREDIT REFERENCE

An example of a credit reference service furnished by Dun & Bradstreet, Inc. (D & B) is presented in Table 21. It includes much of the information a credit manager requires for decision purposes as well as a suggested composite rating. The rating schedule used by D & B is presented in Table 22.

Entries in the report are categorized by D & B in the following manner:

Summary: A concise analysis, with basic identification of each business's U.S. Standard Industrial Classification code for product line and function, principal executive, line of business, year business started or came under present control, and Dun & Bradstreet Rating. In addition, the "summary" digests important report information.

Report Information: Payments, Sales, Worth, Number of Employees, Record, Condition, Trend. Briefly, the "summary" condenses relevant facts for the credit or sales executive and highlights for review much of the important information detailed in the narrative that follows.

Payments: Shows how the business pays its bills, as reported by suppliers. The section includes approximations of high credit (HC) granted during the past year, amounts owing, amounts past due (if any), terms of sale, manner of payment and supplier comment, such as how long sold.

The Payments section serves several important functions: a supplier intending to open a new account receives a good indication of what to expect when dealing with the prospec-

Table 21 Dun & Bradstreet business information report

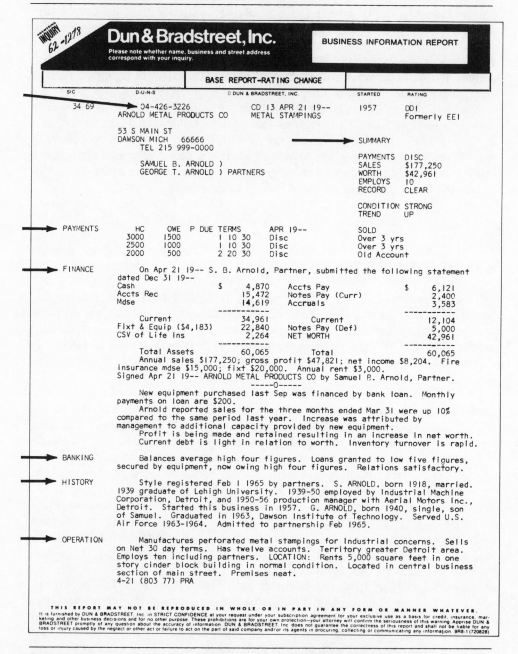

Source. How to Use Your Dun & Bradstreet Service Most Effectively, © 1975 by the Business Economics Division of Dun & Bradstreet, Inc. Used by permission.

166

Table 22 Dun & Bradstreet key business ratings

Key to Ratings

ESTIMATED FINANCIAL STRENGTH			COMPOSITE CREDIT APPRAISAL			
			HIGH	GOOD	FAIR	LIMITED
5A	Over	$50,000,000	1	2	3	4
4A	$10,000,000 to	50,000,000	1	2	3	4
3A	1,000,000 to	10,000,000	1	2	3	4
2A	750,000 to	1,000,000	1	2	3	4
1A	500,000 to	750,000	1	2	3	4
BA	300,000 to	500,000	1	2	3	4
BB	200,000 to	300,000	1	2	3	4
CB	125,000 to	200,000	1	2	3	4
CC	75,000 to	125,000	1	2	3	4
DC	50,000 to	75,000	1	2	3	4
DD	35,000 to	50,000	1	2	3	4
EE	20,000 to	35,000	1	2	3	4
FF	10,000 to	20,000	1	2	3	4
GG	5,000 to	10,000	1	2	3	4
HH	Up to	5,000	1	2	3	4

CLASSIFICATION FOR BOTH ESTIMATED FINANCIAL STRENGTH AND CREDIT APPRAISAL

FINANCIAL STRENGTH BRACKET

1 $125,000 and Over

2 20,000 to 125,000

EXPLANATION

When only the numeral (1 or 2) appears, it is an indication that the estimated financial strength, while not definitely classified, is presumed to be within the range of the ($) figures in the corresponding bracket and that a condition is believed to exist which warrants credit in keeping with that assumption.

ABSENCE OF RATING DESIGNATION FOLLOWING NAMES LISTED IN THE REFERENCE BOOK

The absence of a rating, expressed by two hyphens (--), is not to be construed as unfavorable but signifies circumstances difficult to classify within condensed rating symbols. It suggests the advisability of obtaining a report for additional information.

EMPLOYEE RANGE DESIGNATIONS IN REPORTS OR NAMES NOT LISTED IN THE REFERENCE BOOK

Certain businesses do not lend themselves to a Dun & Bradstreet rating and are not listed in the Reference Book. Information on these names, however, continues to be stored and updated in the D&B Business Information File. Reports are available on these businesses but instead of a rating they carry an Employee Range Designation (ER) which is indicative of size in terms of number of employees. No other significance should be attached.

KEY TO EMPLOYEE RANGE DESIGNATIONS

ER 1	Over 1000 Employees
ER 2	500 - 999 Employees
ER 3	100 - 499 Employees
ER 4	50 - 99 Employees
ER 5	20 - 49 Employees
ER 6	10 - 19 Employees
ER 7	5 - 9 Employees
ER 8	1 - 4 Employees
ER N	Not Available

Source. How to Use Your Dun & Bradstreet Service Most Effectively, © 1975 by the Business Economics Division of Dun & Bradstreet, Inc. Used by permission.

tive customer, based on the previous payment experience of others.

Finance: Includes essential facts for determining the financial condition and trend of a business. Most reports contain financial information which may represent audited figures prepared by a Certified Public Accountant (with or without qualification in the accountant's opinion); unaudited figures from the books of account (not prepared by an outside accountant); or management's own estimate of assets, liabilities, sales, expense and profit. In any event, no audit is conducted by Dun & Bradstreet, Inc. Principals of some concerns decline to furnish detailed figures, and financial figures may therefore be based on bank and supplier comment, investigation of public records or the D & B Business Analyst's estimates of certain Balance Sheet items.

While it is virtually impossible to provide coverage of all public record information, an effort is made to provide information regarding suits, judgments, releases from judgments, Uniform Commercial Code filings and rulings of regulatory agencies. Financial information is also frequently supplemented with information regarding leases, insurance coverage and other pertinent details. Comment in this section is devoted to further necessary explanation of the figures and a description of sales and profit trends. The D & B Rating is based to a large extent upon the degree of financial stability and the trend as reflected in this section.

History: Contains the names, birth dates and past business experience of the principals or owners of a concern. This information is usually obtained from management of the business on which the report is written. Past business experience and outside affiliations of principals are important considerations in evaluating management. In the case of prior business affiliations, D & B files are utilized where feasible to verify and augment the information provided by the management. Other background information is sometimes verified, but that is not usually the case. Criminal proceedings of which D & B learns are reported. Those resulting in convictions are reported indefinitely, but in the other instances, the information is ultimately eliminated from reports.

There are a number of important uses for this history section, including: verifying ownerships, identifying owners, partners or officers and revealing outside interests of the principals.

Banking: Information concerning banking relations may include indication of average balances, previous and current loan experience, whether loans are secured or unsecured, length of time the bank has had the account and whether or not the bank considers the account satisfactory.

Operation: Describes what a concern does and, under the subcaption "location," describes the nature of the premises, the neighborhood and size of floor space. Also described — wherever applicable — are the lines of merchandise sold or kinds of service rendered, price range, classification of customers, selling terms, percentage of cash and crèdit sales, number of accounts, seasonal aspects and number of employees. Usually, the location information is obtained by the reporter's observation while the balance of the information is provided by management.

By describing production and distribution facilities, the operation section gives understanding of the particular business characteristics through which the reader may better judge whether capital is adequate and condition balanced. Also, sales departments find this section valuable for determining whether the subject could be a profitable outlet for their particular lines of merchandise. Purchasing departments find this information useful in determining the capacity of a vender to deliver an order or to support guarantees.*

TRADE CREDIT

To induce customers to expedite their payments, the practice of trade credit has evolved in many lines of business. The intent is to offer the buyer an incentive for early payment of the outstanding balance payable to the supplier. This incentive entitles the buyer to a reduction in the outstanding amount if he makes his payment within a stated time period. An example of trade credit is the designation 2/10 N30. It denotes that the customer can deduct 2% from the face amount of the invoice if he pays within 10 days of the billing date. If he elects instead to postpone payments, he has 30 days from billing date to pay the face amount of the invoice.

The discount rate is often viewed incorrectly as representing a per annum rate. Instead, the 2% is properly viewed as the return earned on 98% of the amount due by accelerating payment from the thirtieth to the tenth day. On an annual basis it may be computed as follows:

*"How to Use Your Dun & Bradstreet Service Most Effectively," © 1975 by the Business Economics Division of Dun & Bradstreet, Inc. Used by permission.

$$\text{annual percent return earned} = \frac{\% \text{ discount}}{100 - \% \text{ discount}}$$

$$\times \frac{360}{\text{last payment date} - \text{discount date}}$$

Thus 2/10 N30 represents an annual return of

$$\frac{2}{100 - 2} \times \frac{360}{30 - 10} = 37\%$$

Similarly, 3/20 N60 should be interpreted as an annual return of

$$\frac{3}{100 - 3} \times \frac{360}{60 - 20} = 28\%$$

These are very substantial returns. Too casual an approach towards utilizing discounts offered by suppliers can deprive the organization of substantial savings. If, after computing the true annual return the financial manager is short of the funds necessary for payment by the early due date, a proper strategy is to borrow the needed funds as long as the annual interest rate on the loan is less than the true annual rate of the discount offered.

Good financial management implies that payments be made only close to either of the two dates. In the first example presented this means either the tenth or the thirtieth day after billing. Payment of the invoice on the twentieth day, for example, does not entitle the organization to take the discount, but does require the outflow of funds that probably could be employed productively internally for another 10 days. The early disbursement implies an opportunity cost without the commensurate reaping of any benefits.

Frequently financial management would like to take advantage of trade credit, but the flow of paper work through the organization may defeat this objective. By the time the merchandise is received, checked, unpacked, quantities verified, and necessary approvals obtained, the time period for taking advantage of the discount may have passed. Often the savings that may be realized by capitalizing on trade credit offered are sufficiently substantial to justify the involvement of financial management in the flow of paper work and revision of existing approval procedures. By updating these procedures financial management can assure itself that all possible returns are realized.

A final word on trade credit. Like many other business practices it is often used for competitive purposes. In periods of recession terms are usually liberalized or their interpretation broadened. For example, customers who deduct the discount even after the indicated day has passed may not be rebilled for that amount in such situations. In times of short supply the same supplier may tighten up on terms and their interpretation, rebilling customers as appropriate. Competitive practices within an industry at the time trade credit is granted will influence the terms and conditions offered to customers.

BOND RATING

A special case of rating debtors' credit worthiness is the rating of bonds offered to the investing public. Recall that a bond is an outstanding obligation that must be serviced by the debtor over time through interest and, perhaps, sinking fund payments. The long term loan is granted to the issuing organization by individuals or institutional investors. It would be highly ineffecient for each investor to analyze the cash flow and profit implications of each bond issue separately in order to formulate an investment decision. The bond rating services perform this function for the investing public. The fee for this service is paid by the issuing organization. This contributes to the marketability of bonds since investors can readily place them in appropriate risk categories.

Two services specialize in rating bond issues: Moody's and Standard & Poor's.While their criteria and designations vary slightly, these services follow basically similar lines of investigation and classification. Their intent is to provide the investor with information regarding the risk class of the bond. Since risk and return go hand in hand, lower ratings imply higher risk classes and will therefore increase the coupon rate that the issuer has to offer the buyer of the bond. Therefore issuing organizations strive to qualify for high ratings and are sensitive to comments pertaining to their financial practices offered by rating organizations.

A word of caution is in order. These ratings, despite heavy reliance on quantitative data, still reflect the judgment of the individuals rating the bond. It is fallible, as all such judgments tend to be. A famous case is the high rating granted a new bond issue of the Penn Central Company about two weeks before it declared bankruptcy. While this case is not necessarily typical, it should be considered by investors. Relying on the judgment of others introduces additional risk. Investors must weigh this risk against the costs associated with duplicating and supplementing the analysis undertaken by the rating agencies.

Finally, financial managers of private as well as public organizations must be in a position to anticipate the observations and comments of the rating agencies since these in turn will influence their cost of capital and cash flow expectations. The well-publicized financial problems of New York City were immediately reflected in lower ratings and higher borrowing costs not only for the city but also for other municipalities and state government agencies that were confronted with similar problems.

SUMMARY

The extension of credit is a widespread tool of sales management. Credit entails a risk and is granted with the expectation that increased sales will increase the organization's profits. The higher the variable costs of the product, the greater the importance of rigorous credit screening. Lenders and suppliers consider the capacity, collateral, and character of the applicant for credit. Credit bureaus and rating agencies supply information pertaining to these three "C's".

Trade credit is the accepted practice of inducing credit customers to accelerate their payments. Since the true annualized return is substantially in excess of the quoted discount, prepayments should be viewed by financial management as investment opportunities. The ratings of corporate and municipal bonds are specialized activities that can have significant impact in the organization's cost of capital in both the private and public sectors.

16 Banking Relationships

Previous discussion stressed the importance of managing the organization's near-term requirements. A banking relationship is a key tool for this activity. Commercial banks provide organizations with the capability of operating with minimal levels of cash and still feel confident to plan financial activities in the face of uncertainty.

Banking services can be viewed as the lubricant of business activity. In the absence of these services organizations are less willing to assume ordinary business risks. This in turn results in lower profits, lower levels of service, and overall lower economic activity. Thus the provision of good banking services has macroeconomic implications.

Banking services in the United States are provided by privately owned commercial banks. While other institutions such as savings and loan associations and credit unions provide some banking services to consumers, most economic activity requires commercial banking services. Commercial banks in turn rely on the Federal Reserve System for liquidity and common services. The functions and trade practices of these organizations are described below.

COMMERCIAL BANKS

Commercial banks are profit oriented organizations in the business of lending funds to individuals, partnerships, corporations, and not-for-profit organizations, including public agencies. They prefer loans with short maturities and would like to see their money paid back in months rather than years, although longer term loans are sometimes extended.

The opening Balance Sheet of a newly organized bank with equity capi-

173

tal of $800 appears as follows, if one ignores requirements for facilities, equipment, and so on:

Cash	$800		
		Equity	$800

Assume now that a customer of the bank opens a checking account with an initial deposit of $1000. The Balance Sheet now appears as

		Deposits	$1000
Cash	$1800	Equity	800
Total	$1800	Total	$1800

Hence deposits are credited to the appropriate account at the bank.
  If the bank extends a loan for $500, its Balance Sheet changes to

Cash	$1300	Deposits	$1000
Loans	500	Equity	800
Total	$1800	Total	$1800

Now assume that a check for $400 is cashed by the depositor, then

Cash	$ 900	Deposits	$ 600
Loans	500	Equity	800
Total	$1400	Total	$1400

Thus a withdrawal is a debit entry to the account.
  Now, if the cash balances of $900 are considered by bank management

to be in excess of immediate needs, some amount, say $600, will probably be invested in short-term, low-risk interest-bearing securities such as treasury bills, as shown below.

Cash	$ 300	Deposits	$ 600
Investments	600		
Loans	500	Equity	800
Total	$1400	Total	$1400

Bank management is deeply concerned with the relationships between investments, loans, and deposits existing at any point in time. Since demand deposits are subject to immediate withdrawal, bank management is hesitant to commit its resources to loans with long maturity dates because it may not be in a position to readjust the relationships between its various assets if large deposit withdrawals occur.

The health of the banking system has implications far beyond the welfare of its stockholders. Failure of a bank jeopardizes depositors and potential borrowers as well. Since most individuals and corporations are both depositors and borrowers the impact of a massive bank failure is far-reaching. As a result of many such debacles during the Great Depression, a substantial body of legislation was passed and is administered by numerous, often overlapping, government agencies. The objective of these regulatory agencies is that banking management use conservative, arm's length business practices. Preeminent among these regulatory agencies are the Comptroller of the Currency in the Department of the Treasury and the Federal Reserve Board, which is independent of the executive branch of the U.S. government.

Good banking relationships are essential to proper financial management. Banks are in business to lend funds to customers they deem credit worthy, and the interest and service charges realized on these loans provides the greatest contribution to their profits. At the same time bank management must safeguard itself against lending to ventures with a high probability of failure. Therefore it applies the tests of credit worthiness discussed in Chapter 15 to its borrowers.

A financial manager applying for a loan can best prepare himself by viewing his company's operations through the eyes of the banker. The lender will clearly be interested in assessing the riskiness of his exposure by means of standard ratios computed on the basis of audited financial statements. He will also want to learn about the competence and tenure of the management team. Most of all, the lender will be concerned with the ability of the borrower to repay the loan as demonstrated in pro-forma cash flow statements. A prudent financial manager will impress the banker by having these documents readily available at the time the loan is discussed and, further, by being able to explain any deviation in his activities from the customary industry ratios the banker uses for his initial assessment.

Bankers are particularly eager to supply funds for self-liquidating, cyclical business needs. If these needs are identified sufficiently in advance, they enable the financial manager to call on banks to meet his peak working capital needs rather than increase his long term capitalization. It is the least costly way for a company to provide adequate working capital during its business cycle. A banker is likely, however, to turn a deaf ear to a loan applicant who has not identified his or her needs ahead of time. Such behavior reveals poor management, increasing the risk associated with the loan.

A long term banking relationship can provide the financial manager with considerably more than periodic funds. Bankers, by virtue of their experience and contacts can suggest improved business practices, identify potential markets, and facilitate international transactions. In recent years bankers have become heavily involved in providing business with long term assets through leasing arrangements. Prior to the 1930s, banks were also active in underwriting long term funds to corporations. Federal legislation has since restricted their activities in this area to municipal issues. It is possible that banks will regain some of their corporate underwriting business in the future.

Every business has its own practices, terminology, and idiosyncrasies; banking is no exception. Financial managers, as a defensive move, must familiarize themselves with these to assure that a true meeting of the minds is reached during negotiations. First among these issues is the term prime rate. This is the rate of interest, quoted on a per annum basis, which the banks charge their best and most credit worthy customers. Very few borrowers can expect to borrow funds at this rate. It is quoted, however, to provide a negotiating framework for funds to borrowers in varying risk categories. Lines of credit are usually arranged long before actual borrowing takes place. In the interim market interest rates fluctuate. Rather than agree on specific interest rates that might prove to be unrealistic at a later date when the actual borrowing takes place, agreements are contracted at the prime rate that prevails at the time the loan is extended plus a premium for risk and service expressed in percentage points above the prime rate prevailing at the time. The prime rate is not specified numerically until actual lending takes place!

An example will illustrate this practice. Assume that a line of credit was arranged at a time when the prime rate was 7¼%. The terms of the agreement call for the loan to carry an interest rate of 1½% above prime rate. Two months later the organization decides to borrow funds. If the prime rate at that point is 8%, then the interest charged by the lender is 8% + 1½%, or 9½%.

Another custom in the trade is the practice of requiring borrowers to maintain compensating balances at the bank extending the loan. Thus, for example, a bank may require a borrower to maintain 20% or $200,000 of the $1 million loan granted to him in his checking account. The net effect of this is twofold. First, if the borrower actually requires $1 million he must in effect borrow $1.25 million in order to have $1 million freely available to him. Second, the effective interest rate paid by the borrower is higher than quoted. In the example cited, suppose that a 10% rate was negotiated on the total loan. Actual interest charges are therefore 10% of $1 million or $100,000. However, the interest rate on the amount under control of the borrower is

$$\frac{\$100,000}{\$1,000,000 - \$200,000} = 12\frac{1}{2}\%$$

This is 25% higher than the nominal amount of 10% negotiated.

If a long-standing banking relationship exists, borrowers can normally expect to qualify for bank loans even in times of general business downturns or during periods of hardship unique to the borrower. However, banks will demand specific actions from management aimed at improving the situation and may also restrict management's freedom to borrow additional funds, invest in capital equipment, or pay dividends to stockholders. These actions have the objective of providing additional security to the lender by enhancing the business posture of the borrower.

THE FEDERAL RESERVE SYSTEM (FRS)

The Federal Reserve System, often referred to as the banker's bank, was established in 1913 to provide central banking facilities for the United States. Over the years interpretation of its original charter has been broadened and additional responsibilities have been assigned to it by congressional legislation or executive fiat.

Among other functions, the FRS has current jurisdiction over the following activities:

- Commercial bank regulatory functions
- Reserve requirements and bank discounts
- Selective credit controls
- Open market operations
- International operations

While the FRS consults and strives to coordinate its activities with other cognizant government agencies, its decisions and actions do not require executive or congressional approval. Appointments to its board of governors are made by the President of the United States with the consent of the Senate. In its operations, however, the Federal Reserve is independent of the executive branch of the government. By law it is required to report on its activities annually to the Congress.

Although the FRS has authority to conduct field examinations of all its member banks, it concerns itself primarily with those that are state chartered since the Comptroller of the Currency has statutory authority over banks with a national charter. The FRS is also responsible for administering the Bank Holding Act of 1956. This act strives to prevent the establishment of monopoly in banking while permitting banks to expand into related, nonbanking endeavors.

Commercial banks are required to keep a fraction of their deposits as cash reserves either in their vaults or with the FRS. The actual percentage varies and is stipulated by the FRS according to its determination of the needs of the economy. By varying this percentage the FRS influences the loan granting capability of its member banks with the level of economic activity. A related instrument for influencing overall economic activity is the FRS discount window. The discount function permits commercial banks to borrow against their loan portfolio to raise funds for extending additional loans. By varying the discount rate, that is the rate of interest it charges member banks for these loans, the FRS can encourage or discourage borrowing according to its determination of the needs of the economy.

The relationship between credit and economic activity serves to explain why the FRS has acquired several related responsibilities in the credit area over the years. Among these are authority to specify which securities may be purchased by investors on credit and the determination of the appropriate percentage of credit or margin that lenders are permitted to extend to investors for the purchase of these securities. In addition the FRS has the responsibility for promulgating regulations to carry out the intent of the congress in the Truth in Lending Act of 1968.

Another important function of the FRS are its transactions in government securities. Among other objectives these are viewed as one of the key mechanisms for pursuing federal government monetary policy. The sale of securities by the FRS to the public draws funds from the banking system, braking economic expansion. The purchase of securities from the public by the FRS provides funds to commercial banks, permitting additional lending and thereby encouraging economic expansion. The responsibility for formulating appropriate policy regarding these transactions lies with the Federal Open Market Committee (FOMC) of the FRS.

The FRS, as fiscal agent of the United States, has numerous responsibilities for international monetary transactions. It handles the mechanics of dealings involving foreign central banks, supervises foreign operation of U.S. banks and U.S. operation of foreign banks and engages, as appropriate, in swap exchanges of foreign currencies. In support of some of these transactions it may simultaneously affect domestic monetary markets through open market operations.

The legal and administrative authority granted by Congress places the responsibility for monetary policy almost totally on the shoulders of the FRS. This is a distinctly different situation from that prevailing in the area of fiscal policy, where the Executive is preeminent in its formulation but actual policy can only be pursued with congressional approval. The results of this asymmetric arrangement are as predictable. When the policy objectives of the administration in power and the FRS differ, considerable tensions develop between them. Conversely, in instances when the FRS and the administration pursue similar objectives in the face of congressional opposition, the threat of new legislation that will restrict the freedom of the FRS is frequently raised.

SUMMARY

Good banking relationships are a key tool in the plan of financial management. By providing liquidity banks foster overall economic activity. Commercial banks are profit oriented organizations, regulated in their activities primarily by the Federal Reserve System (FRS). Bankers are particularly eager to supply funds for self-liquidating, cyclical business needs. As is true of most professions banking has its own terminology and customs of the trade; prime rate and compensating balances are examples of these.

The FRS provides central banking facilities for the United States. It is an independent agency of the government required to report on its activities only to the Congress. Its responsibilities include open market operations, credit controls, and international transactions. Through its open market operations the FRS exercises great influence on monetary policy. This can create occasional friction with the Executive and the Congress.

17 Capital Structure

The acquisition of land, fixtures, inventories, and cash required to sustain the production or services provided by the organization all entail the outlay of funds. These funds are acquired from three basic sources:

1. Equity investors who purchase a share of the corporation with the hope of future returns in the form of dividends and capital gains. Their risk exposure and their expectation of return are the highest.
2. Investors in long-term debt obligations issued by the organization. Their risk is considerably reduced from that to which equity investors are exposed, and so is the return they can anticipate.
3. Suppliers and lenders who provide merchandise on credit or short term loans. Since their exposure is limited and they are in constant close contact with the organization, they can often spot danger signals sufficiently early to avoid substantial loss. Still they too are exposed to risk.

This discussion concentrates on the first two sources of capital: equity and long term debt. The attributes, risk, and rewards of each are identified from the point of view of the investor as well as that of corporate management. Not-for-profit organizations, depending on the nature of their charter, also frequently resort to debt financing. The prime difference between their financing activities and those of profit oriented organizations occurs with respect to equity capital. In not-for-profit organizations the equivalent of equity shares is not acquired for the purpose of financial gain to the supplier of capital but is provided as endowments, charitable contributions, or allocations of tax revenue.

This analysis focuses on the right hand side of the Balance Sheet. The composition of the claims on assets listed on this side is referred to as capital structure. The management of the assets entrusted to the organization, that is the left hand side of the Balance Sheet, have historically been associated with functions of the controller. Activities associated with the right hand side of the Balance Sheet, such as the acquisition of funds and the maintainance of working relationships with suppliers of capital and regulatory agencies, are the responsibility of the organization's treasurer. Financial management encompasses both of these functions.

COMMON STOCK

The most direct form of equity participation by investors in a corporation is through the acquisition of common stock. The accounting entries presented earlier displayed this process well. Recall that the Hospital Service Corporation was organized with the efforts of investors who supplied $5 million in capital to the organization and received 500,000 shares of common stock in return. These stockholders are the sole owners of the corporation. The function of financial management is to maximize the wealth of these investors by its actions. The proper management of assets will contribute to this objective, as will judicious mixing of debt and equity capital to meet the expanding needs for capital.

The board of directors is the legal representative of the corporation's stockholders. An individual stockholder may of course approach an officer of the corporation for information or present his or her recommendations. However, the corporate employee is not bound to cooperate unless the request is channeled via the board of directors. Regardless of these formalities, an investor who possesses a larger percentage ownership of the outstanding stock will have established continuing communication channels with operating management and will exercise considerable influence on the affairs of the corporation if he or she elects to do so. Otherwise, investors do not have a direct say in the affairs of a corporation.

The rights and privileges of common stockholders are summarized and discussed below. The discussion focuses on shareholders of publicly held corporations, each owning a relatively small percentage of the outstanding stock. Large, concentrated holdings of common stock and the ownership of privately held corporations are not discussed since the peculiarities of the particular situation may give rise to many special privileges, which vary according to the specific financial and managerial relationships in force.

Ownership of common stock of publicly traded corporations entitles the investor to the following privileges, listed in increasing order of their importance:

1. Proportionate shares in residual corporate assets in case of corporate failure.
2. Access to the books of the corporation.

3. Attendance and floor privileges at annual meetings.
4. Participation in voting for the board of directors.
5. Proportionate participation in corporate distributions (primarily dividends.)
6. Freedom to sell the securities if desired.

Each of these privileges is explored below. These privileges must be viewed in the context of the underlying legality of common stock ownership. A corporation is an independent entity created by the corporate charter. Thus a stockholder has a proportional claim on the entity but not on any particular asset to which the entity has title.

The privilege of receiving a proportionate share of the residuals in case of corporate failure should not be valued too highly. The probability is considerable that by the time such failure is legally recognized, little equity interest remains to be distributed. Claims of lenders and long term borrowers can be expected to preempt the claims of common stockholders almost totally.

The stockholder's rights to inspect the corporate books fall into a similar category. Actually, an individual stockholder does not have access to more information than the public at large can readily obtain. Although he receives periodically published financial statements, these are also available to nonstockholders. No proprietary or sensitive financial data are likely to be released to anyone solely because he is a stockholder. Competitive pressures justify management's stance in this case. If information such as production costs and customer lists were readily available to all stockholders, it would be impossible to protect the corporation from competitors also availing themselves of this information. If the stockholder presses this issue via legal channels, most corporations tend to respond by engaging in time-consuming legal maneuvers so that the requested information will be obsolete by the time it is released.

Attendance at corporate meetings is seldom restricted to stockholders; all interested parties may usually attend. The associated privileges of questioning management at the meeting, nominating candidates to the board of directors, and voting for the board of directors are restricted to stockholders. Unfortunately, however, the individual stockholder who has not succeeded in forming sufficiently powerful alliances and coalitions with other stockholders prior to the meeting has almost no chance of influencing management decisions or the preordained election of the slate recommended by corporate management. If ego satisfaction is included among the rewards a stockholder seeks, and addressing the annual meeting provides him with such gratification, then it must be considered a privilege. From a strictly financial point of view, however, attendance at meetings is not a tangible benefit.

The election process of the board of directors merits special comment. Large U.S. corporations have historically perpetuated the composition of their board by nominating management personnel, representatives from the financial community, and selected outsiders who are almost professional board members. Representation by the investing public, which in the aggregrate owns the controlling interest in these corporations, has been scant. While there are some indications that this situation may change, the individual who challenges a management slate has little chance of prevailing. A contributing factor is that legal owners of large concentrations of shares such as mutual funds, pension funds, and brokerage accounts have a tendency to vote in favor of nominees of incumbent management if they vote at all. Thus, in the absence of a sizable concentration of singularly motivated private ownership, the possibility of defeating a management nominee is slim. The mechanism for gaining control of the board of directors in the absence of such concentration is a proxy fight. Once again, however, the cards are stacked in favor of incumbent management. The stockholder lists are under the control of corporate officers who can drag their feet via legal maneuvers prior to releasing them. Furthermore, combating insurgent stockholders is a tax deductible expense to the corporation!

The fifth privilege, partaking in corporate distributions when declared by the board of directors, is of significance. Many investors commit their funds with an expectation of participating in dividend distributions, and the fact that no shareholder of the same class of stock may receive preferential treatment is essential to the orderly functioning of security markets and the influx of equity funds into the corporation. Stockholders must recognize, however, that they are only entitled to such distributions if and when they are declared by the board of directors. The fact that operations are profitable does not in itself establish a legal basis for claiming a proportionate distribution.

The final privilege that stockholders in publicly traded shares possess is the ability to dispose of their ownership at their discretion. If their view of the corporation's future is dim, or if their perception of the capabilities of entrenched management is not favorable, stockholders are free to sell their shares and invest the proceeds elsewhere. The liquidity that this provides to investors is also highly important to the corporation since ready marketability eases the corporate problem of raising outside equity capital as the need arises.

These privileges, plus the expectation that the investment will appreciate, constitute the return to the investor. His risk is substantial, since there is no assurance that the corporation will continue to be successful. Thus, the newer and more untried the corporation is, the greater the risk to the investor and the higher his expectation of gain. More mature corporations with proven track records pose a smaller risk; consequently, the expected return to the investor in these corporations is usually less.

The expected return to investors is composed of two portions: the dividend yield, computed as D/P, where D is the expected annual dividend and P is the price of the security, and the growth g, the annual expected increase in the price of security. If we denote the total expected annual return for a share of stock as R_E, then

$$R_E = D/P + g$$

An example will illustrate this point. Assume that a share of common stock is priced at $50, the indicated dividend is $2 annually, and the growth expected in earnings, dividends, and eventually the price of the security is 5%. What is the investor's expected return?

$$R_E = \frac{\$2}{\$50} + 0.05\%; \ R_E = 9\%$$

An investor who seeks this return and is willing to accept the associated risk may for personal reasons prefer to invest in another stock that sells at the same price but pays a higher dividend, say $3.50, despite the fact that the growth expectation at 2% is less than that of the first stock. The return will still be 9%:

$$R_E = \frac{\$3.50}{\$50} + 0.02\% = 9\%$$

A corporation considering the issue of additional common stock will of course look at the other side of the coin. What appears as a return to the investor is a cost to the corporation and has identical components: the dividend cash outflow as a percentage of the price it received for issuing the stock and the percentage growth. The reason that growth is a component of the cost of capital is that by issuing new shares current stockholders are actually relinquishing a portion of their claim on the future growth and profits of the corporation. Therefore the issuance of additional equity capital entails an opportunity cost to their ownership of the corporation. $R_E = D/P + g$ thus not only denotes the return to investors but also the cost to the corporation of issuing equity.

Compared to other long term capital, the issuing of additional common stock appears on the surface to be the expensive way to proceed for a corporation. From a corporate point of view, however, the advantage of financing in this fashion is the absolute commitment that investors have made, since the corporation has no obligation to repurchase the stock in the future. Thus the corporation has truly long term capital at its disposal and can plan accordingly. Furthermore, the issuing of equity capital strengthens the debt to equity ratio on the Balance Sheet. This ratio is closely watched by potential lenders. Their decisions regarding the magnitude of the commitment and the interest rate charged for the loan depends to a certain extent on the relationship that a particular organization's debt to equity ratio bears to others in the same industry. This point is discussed in more detail further on.

LONG TERM DEBT

The promise that an organization makes in exchange for obtaining long term debt capital is twofold: first, to redeem the debt certificate at face value at the indicated date of maturity; second, to pay a fixed periodic, usually semiannual, amount to the holder of the debt certificate. The face value of the certificate is usually but not necessarily $1000; the maturity date of the certificate is usually but not necessarily 10 to 30 years from the date of issue. The periodic payment that the organization makes to the lender is referred to as the coupon. The coupon is usually stated as a percentage of the face value of the certificate, for example, every 6 months the payment on a $1000 face value bond with an 8½% coupon is $42.50.

Bonds are long term debt obligations of the organization. Holders of bonds are creditors, not owners. They may insist that the interest due them is paid on time and that certain other agreements to which the organization committed itself at the time the loan was extended are observed. They cannot, however, vote for the board of directors, nor are they entitled to any dividend distribution made to stockholders. Bondholders, in contrast with stockholders, are outsiders. They are in the same class as suppliers, bankers, and lessors vis-à-vis the organization.

As stated, a bond is a dual promise to pay a periodic payment until maturity and a fixed amount upon maturity. The value of a bond is, therefore, the present value of an annuity, consisting of the periodic coupon payments plus the present value of a sum representing the face value of $1000. In algebraic terms,

$$\text{value of bond} = R\left[\frac{1 - (1 + i)^{-n}}{i}\right] + \frac{1000}{(1 + i)^n}$$

where R = the annuity per period
        n = number of periods to maturity
        i = applicable market interest rate per period

To illustrate, assume that a $1000 face value bond can be purchased. The bond pays $65 annually and matures in 15 years. How much should an investor be willing to pay for the bond if the bond is in a risk class that commands 9% return on invested capital?

$$\text{Value of bond} = RT_D + \$1000T_B$$
$$= \$65 \times 8.06 + \$1000 \times 0.275$$
$$= \$799$$

Note that the face value is not the equivalent of the market value. The face value is the obligation the borrower has to meet upon maturity of the bond. The market value of the bond is determined by the present value of the face value plus the present value of the annuity represented by the coupon. Note also that whenever the market rate of interest (i), is *greater* than the coupon rate ($R/1000$), the bond sells *below* its face value. When the market rate of interest (i) is *smaller* than the coupon rate ($R/1000$) the bond sells above its face value. An example will verify this point.

How much should an investor be willing to pay for a $1000 face value bond maturing in 18 years, with a coupon of $120, if the bond is in a risk class that commands 8% interest per annum?

$$\text{Value of bond} = \$120 \times T_D + \$1000 \times T_B$$
$$= \$120 \times 9.372 + \$1000 \times 0.250$$
$$= \$1375$$

A word on the market rate of interest. This rate is determined by money market conditions at the time the investment is made. It is closely related to the return that other investments in the same risk class yield at that time. Thus, even for the same bond, this rate is liable to change from day to day. It depends on the conditions of the organization issuing the bond as well as on the general economic outlook at the time of issue. For example, if the cash flow position of the organization deteriorates, the risk of lending funds to it increases. If, at the same time, general long-term inflationary expectations for the economy are on the rise, then returns for all risk classes tend to increase. New investors considering the purchase of the existing bonds will therefore apply all of these considerations. Investors holding these bonds will realize a price determined by the present value calculations of new investors, regardless of the price they originally paid or the face value of the bond.

The impact of market interest rates on bond prices can readily be observed by analyzing their effect on perpetuities. Perpetuities are bonds that never mature. Their coupon payment streams stretch to infinity. Since they do not carry a promise of redemption at face value, their market value is determined solely by the present value of an annuity with payments extending to infinity. It can be shown that for such an annuity $B = R/i$. Some U.K. government and several Canadian railroad bonds are perpetuities. Consider the following examples.

What is an appropriate market value for a U.K. perpetual bond, called a Console, issued to pay £50 per annum if the appropriate market interest rate for U.K. government bonds is 12% due to inflation?

$$\text{Market value of Console} = \frac{£50}{0.12} = £417$$

Assume now that inflationary expectations abate and the appropriate interest rate drops to 7%. The new market value is then

$$(£50/0.07) = £714$$

Further assume that massive deflation takes place, and interest rates on government bonds drop to 3%. What is the impact of this on the price of the Console?

$$(£50/0.03) = £1667$$

Bond prices and market interest rates move in opposite directions. As investor risk increases, issuing organizations must compensate investors by paying increasingly higher coupon rates at time of issue. Unless specific provisions are made at that time issuing organizations will have to keep paying the contractually obligated coupon, regardless of changing market conditions.

The special provision that may enable the issuer to reduce high interest payments is the right to *call* the bond for redemption. This right permits the issuer, after the lapse of a specified number of years from the time of issue, to redeem that outstanding bond at face value plus a fixed payment usually equal to 1 year's coupon. Thus, if interest rates drop substantially from the time of issue, the issuer can redeem the old bonds with the proceeds realized from the sale of new bonds. In view of changing market interest rates, these will bear a lower coupon than the old bonds.

The analog to a capital budgeting decision is apparent. The organization will be well advised to call the old bonds and issue new bonds as long as the NPV of this transaction is positive. In calculating the NPV, we must identify the present value of cash outflow and inflow. Consider the following example.

The elders of the First Community Church are concerned about $12,000 in annual interest payments they are required to make on $100,000 face value bonds outstanding and due to mature in 15 years. They are advised that they have the right to call the bonds beginning this year if they pay 2 years' interest in addition to the face value. Legal and administrative costs associated with calling the old bonds and issuing new bonds are estimated at $10,000. In view of the greatly improved financial situation of the church and generally improved market conditions, the new bonds are expected to sell at a 6% coupon rate.

The outlays in this case are as follows:

Excess interest payments:	2 × $12,000	= $24,000
Administrative costs		$10,000
Total costs		$34,000

The present value of the benefits expected to accrue to the church are the difference between the old and the new interest payments, discounted to the present at the *going market rate of interest*. Thus:

Old interest payment	$12,000
New interest payment	6,000
Annual savings	$6,000

Thus the benefits are the present value of an annuity of $6000 for 15 years at 6%, $T_D = 9.712$:

$$NPV = \$6000 \times 9.712 - \$34,000$$

$$= + \underline{\$24,272}$$

Since the NPV is positive, the decision to refinance is beneficial to church finances and should be accepted.

To protect investors and thereby also increase the marketability of newly issued bonds, a legally binding agreement between the organization and its creditors is drawn up at the time a new bond is issued. The document containing this agreement is termed the *indenture*.

The indenture contains all the relevant provisions pertaining to that issue. For example, it will specify payment dates, call provisions (if any), conversion privileges (if any), restrictions on the dividend policy of the corporation (if any), restrictions on future borrowing (if any), and will identify a trustee to act for the bondholders in case the issuing organization defaults on its promises. Recall that individual bondholders are outsiders to the organization and have no legally accountable representative within the organization's formal structure such as stockholders have in the board of directors. The provisions of the indenture assure investors that unilateral and capricious action against an individual or selected group of bondholders cannot readily be undertaken by corporate management since the mechanism for legal redress is fully established should the need arise.

Finally, what are the returns and the costs inherent in a bond issue? Ignoring flotation costs which, are not a substantial percentage for a large bond issue, and assuming that the organization received the full face value of the bond, the cost of a bond to the issuing organization is the annual coupon payment designated as R_I. Since the payment is technically interest on a loan, it is a tax deductible expense for profit oriented organizations. Assuming a marginal tax rate of t, the true cost to an issuing profit oriented organization is

$$R_I(1 - t)/1000$$

The cost to a not-for-profit organization remains

$$R_I/1000$$

Thus, referring to the outstanding church bond with the $120 coupon, the cost of the bond to the church is

$$\$120/\$1000 = 12\%$$

If this bond had been issued by a profit oriented retirement home with a marginal tax rate of 40%, the cost to the issuing corporation would have been

$$\$120(1 - 0.4)/\$1000 = 7.2\%$$

The before tax return that investors expect to realize from purchasing a newly issued bond is essentially

$R_I/1000$

since at the time of issue the coupon rate is almost identical to the market interest rate. Subsequent purchases of previously issued bonds at market prices is determined by the market rate of interest for the risk class appropriate for the bond. This becomes the before-tax return to the investor.

Bonds issued by state and local governmental agencies are referred to as municipals and are exempt from federal income taxes. Since investors are interested in *after* tax return, these issuing agencies are able to issue bonds at a lower rate than organizations and federal agencies not favored by this exemption. Consider an investor subject to a 60% federal income tax rate on additional income. He intends to invest $10,000 and is considering two bonds:

> Bond A: A new corporate issue yielding 8%
>
> Bond B: A new municipal issue yielding 5%

on an after tax basis, the yields are as follows;

> Bond A: 8%(1 − 0.6) = 3.2%
>
> Bond B: 5%   = 5.0%

The municipal is clearly the better investment for him. For an investor in a lower tax bracket, say 20%, bond A would yield the following:

> Bond A: 8%(1 − 0.2) = 6.4%

and would represent the more appropriate investment of the two.

PREFERRED STOCK

Preferred stock has attributes of both bonds and common stock and its impact depends on the point of view of the interested parties. The term preferred stock is an unfortunate one since the preferences to which preferred stock is entitled are few and specific rather than all-encompassing. They are quite limited in scope, and many investors may find that they do not meet their personal preferences and investment objectives.

Since preferred stock appears in the equity section of the Balance Sheet, from the point of view of lenders it is equity capital. The dividend payments of preferred stock take preference (hence the term preferred stock) over the payment of common stock dividends and, if paid, are contractually fixed. Preferred stock dividend payments are not a deductible expense to the corporation as bond payments are. Rather they become deductions from after tax earnings, thereby reducing the earnings available to common stockholders. Ignoring tax implications, preferred stock is quite similar to bonds in this respect. Preferred dividends, like bond interest, are paid out of operating income before earnings to common stockholders are computed. Thus, from the point of view of common stockholders, preferred stock acts in a manner similar to that of a bond.

Preferred stock dividends are declared by the board of directors in a manner identical to that of common dividends. The sole difference is that the amount to be paid is not subject to change. The decision confronting the board is solely whether to pay the stated dividend or to defer payment. If preferred dividends are omitted, however, common dividends may not be declared and paid. In contrast with bond interest, the payment of preferred dividends is not guaranteed. Furthermore, nonpayment of these dividends does not per se provide a basis for preferred stockholder legal action against the issuing corporation.

A slight, very common variation on preferred stock is cumulative preferred. This security is designed to prevent the board of directors from deferring dividends for extended periods of time, then resuming regular preferred dividend payments and subsequently paying a large extra dividend to the common stockholders. Actually such a dividend consists of the cash accumulations due to nonpayment of preferred dividends and therefore constitutes a transfer of wealth from preferred to common stockholders. Cumulative preferred stock provides that common dividend payments can only be resumed after all preferred dividends in arrears have been paid out to the preferred stockholders.

Another modification of straight preferred stock is convertible preferred. At the option of the stockholder this stock can be converted into a predetermined number of shares of common stock. Thus it provides potential participation in corporate growth that straight preferred does not.

Table 23 **National Education Corporation,** Balance Sheet, December 31, 1980

		Current liabilities	$800,000
		Bonds	5,000,000
		Total liabilities	$5,800,000
		Preferred stock $10 PV	1,000,000
		Common stock $1 PV	500,000
		Paid in surplus	6,500,000
		Retained income	600,000
		Total equities	8,600,000
Total assets	$14,400,000	Total liabilities and equities	$14,400,000

Table 24 **National Education Corporation,** Income Statement, January 1 — December 31, 1980

Revenue		
Sales		$38,400,000
Expenses		
Cost of goods sold	$ 5,700,000	
Salaries	23,900,000	
Interest (8% of 5 million)	400,000	
Other	2,300,000	32,300,000
Income before taxes		$ 6,100,000
Taxes (assume 40% liability)		2,440,000
Income after taxes		$ 3,660,000

A numerical example will help illustrate the impact of preferred dividends on common stock earnings per share. Consider the National Education Corporation, whose Balance Sheet and Income Statement are presented in Tables 23 and 24.

Now assume that the preferred stock pays a dividend of $0.90 per share. The Balance Sheet indicates that 100,000 preferred shares and 500,000 common shares are outstanding. Thus total preferred dividend payments due are 100,000 × $0.90 = $90,000. Consequently, income available to common stockholders is $3,660,000 − $90,000 = $3,570,000. Since 500,000 common shares are outstanding, earnings per common share (EPS) are

$$\frac{\$3,570,000}{500,000} = \$7.14 \text{ per share}$$

In the absence of preferred dividends, income per common share would have been

$$\frac{\$3,660,000}{500,000} = \$7.32 \text{ per share}$$

Thus the impact of preferred dividends on the common stockholders is to reduce the EPS which would otherwise be available to them. As stated preferred stock acts vis-à-vis common stockholders in a manner quite similar to that of the bonds outstanding, which require a deduction of $400,000 from operating income to meet interest obligations. However, since bond interest is a deductible expense for tax purposes while preferred dividends are not, the impact of the $400,000 is only

$$\$400,000(1 − 0.4) = \$240,000 \text{ or } \$0.48 \text{ per share}$$

While the impact of the $90,000 preferred dividend is

$$\$90,000/500,000 \text{ shares} = \$0.18 \text{ per share.}$$

Note also that the bonds provided over four times as much capital as the preferred stock in this case while reducing EPS by less than three times the amount they are decreased by preferred dividends.

Why then, would a corporation issue preferred if all these disadvantages exist for common stockholders? In the earlier discussion on common stock it was pointed out that lenders view the debt-to-equity ratio of a prospective borrower as one of the significant indicators of the credit worthiness of the borrower. If the debt-to-equity ratio is below standard, the prospective borrower has the following choices:

1. He can reconsider and forgo the loan.
2. He can probably secure some funds from lenders specializing in high risk loans, with commensurately high interest rates.
3. He can raise the needed capital through the sale of equity.

If he adopts the third choice, he then has two basic options:

1. He can issue additional common stock.
2. He can issue preferred stock.

If he issues additional common stock, the ownership in the corporation is permanently diluted since the new stockholders will share rights and privileges with the original stockholders. Therefore corporate earnings will henceforth and forever be divided among all stockholders, according to their relative percentage ownership.

On the other hand, if a corporation issues preferred stock in order to strengthen the equity section, common stockholders' EPS are reduced by a fixed amount in the future. This amount remains the same, regardless of the actual earnings of the corporation. Thus, if as a result of the infusion of capital resulting from the sale of preferred stock the corporation's after tax earnings rise above the preferred dividend requirements, the increase accrues solely to the original common stockholders, without entailing a perpetual sharing with new stockholders as the acquisition of equity via common stock would require. This is the concept of leverage, which is discussed in greater detail below.

If flotation costs are ignored, then the cost to the corporation of issuing preferred stock is the dividend yield of preferred stock:

$$R_P = D/P$$

Note that this formulation is identical to the cost of common stock;

$$R_E = D/P + g$$

when g, the growth, is zero. Since straight preferred does not share in corporate growth, the formulation

Cost of equity = dividend yield + growth

is therefore a general one, encompassing all equity capital.

The final point requiring assessment is the expectation investors can have with respect to the market price of a preferred stock. Note that once the preferred is issued, it becomes a perpetuity, since its dividend as long as it is paid is invariant of money market conditions. As demonstrated, the market value of a perpetuity is the annual payment divided by the interest rate appropriate for that risk class:

$$\text{market value preferred} = \frac{\text{annual dividend per share}}{\text{market interest rate}}$$

The relevant market interest rate is determined by considering the risk-free rate at the time as reflected in the yield to maturity of government bonds and adding to it a risk premium reflecting the financial soundness of the issuing corporation. For example, if poor business conditions prevail and, consequently, the risk of the deferment of dividends rises, the risk premium will also increase. Similarly, if the risk-free rate decreases the total risk-adjusted market interest rate will reflect this by a commensurate decrease.

Some numerical examples will clarify this issue. Assume a preferred stock paying $2.50 per year is being traded on security markets. On a given day the risk-free rate is 5%, the company appears to be in very good financial position, and the risk premium is determined to be 3%. The appropriate market price is

$2.50/(0.05 + 0.03) = $31.25

Assume further that due to inflationary expectations, the risk-free rate rises to 8% and that the risk premium remains at 3%. The appropriate market price is now

$2.50/(0.08 + 0.03) = $22.73

Now suppose that inflation is affecting the business situation of the issuing corporation adversely and, as a result, rumors abound in the financial community that the preferred dividend may be curtailed. The risk premium consequently jumps to 9%, and appropriate market price now becomes

$2.50/(0.08 + 0.09) = $14.71

Finally, assume that a year later inflationary expectations have abated and business conditions for the issuing corporation improve exceptionally. The risk-free rate is now 4% and the risk premium drops to 2%. The appropriate market price for the preferred stock is now

$2.50/(0.04 + 0.02) = $41.67

The conclusion to be drawn from this exercise is that even a preferred stock paying a fixed dividend may fluctuate substantially in market price.

COST OF CAPITAL

The debt-to-equity ratio of the balance Sheet is of considerable significance to corporate management, investors, and potential lenders. A large amount of debt signals the following: first, in case of default, lenders will be less likely to recover any of the loans extended since there is insufficient equity to absorb the difference between the book value of the assets and their liquidation value. Second, the larger the debt, the larger the cash flow required to service it. Thus, significant operating income may be needed to meet debt service payments without providing an opportunity for new projects or dividend distribution to stockholders. Furthermore, as the business cycle turns down, the impact increases noticeably since operating income may no longer suffice to meet debt service payments. Conversely, however, an economic upswing will be felt positively since once debt service payments are covered excess cash balances are available for internal uses and dividend payments.

Again, numerical examples help to illustrate the point. Consider the dilemma facing the organizers of the National Production Company. Preliminary estimates indicate a requirement for $10 million to finance fixed and current assets with sufficient cash on hand to meet corporate needs until profitable levels of operations are reached. Assume that organizers have the options of

1.   Raising all the required funds through the sale of common stock
2.   Raising 1/3 with debt and 2/3 with common stock

Or

3.   Raising 2/3 with debt and 1/3 with common stock

Possible opening Balance Sheets are presented in Table 25.

Table 25 Opening Balance Sheets under the three alternate capital structures

A

		Equity	$10,000,000
Total	$10,000,000	Total	$10,000,000

B

		Debt	$3,333,333
		Equity	$6,666,667
Total	$10,000,000	Total	$10,000,000

C

		Debt	$6,666,667
		Equity	$3,333,333
Total	$10,000,000	Total	$10,000,000

Assume that the stock has a par value of $10 and is sold at the par value. Further assume that operating income is 5%, 10%, or 15% of total assets depending on whether general business conditions are poor, good, or excellent, respectively. Also, the interest cost of debt is a constant 10%. Taxes are estimated to be 40%. The expected earnings per share (EPS) under each of these financing alternatives are presented in Table 26.

As can be seen, the impact of business conditions on stockholders depends on the capital structure. The greater the debt component, the higher the EPS under excellent business conditions. At the same time, should business conditions turn poor, the high debt approach will result in a loss due to the continuing requirements for interest payments while positive EPS could be generated if the capital structure contained more equity.

Table 26   Relationship between capital structure and EPS

		Business conditions		
		Poor	Good	Excellent
No debt				
	Operating income	$ 500,000	$1,000,000	$1,500,000
	Interest	—	—	—
	Earnings before taxes	500,000	1,000,000	1,500,000
	Taxes	200,000	400,000	600,000
	Earnings after taxes	300,000	600,000	900,000
	Number of shares outstanding	1,000,000	1,000,000	1,000,000
	EPS	$0.30	$0.60	$0.90
1/3 debt				
	Operating income	$ 500,000	$1,000,000	$1,500,000
	Interest	333,333	333,333	333,333
	Earnings before taxes	166,667	666,667	1,166,667
	Taxes	66,667	266,667	466,667
	Earnings after taxes	100,000	400,000	700,000
	Number of shares outstanding	666,667	666,667	666,667
	EPS	$0.15	$0.60	$1.05
2/3 debt				
	Operating income	$ 500,000	$1,000,000	$1,500,000
	Interest	666,667	666,667	666,667
	Earnings before taxes	(166,667)	333,333	833,333
	Taxes	—	—	—
	Earnings after taxes	(166,667)	200,000	500,000
	Number of shares outstqnding	333,333	333,333	333,333
	EPS	($0.50)	$0.60	$1.50

Figure 36 is a graphic illustration of this phenomenon with a wider range of operating income. Note that at $1 million in operating income, stockholders' EPS would be identical under all three financing options.

The phenomenon just described is termed financial leverage. It entails the employment of sources of capital that require fixed payments for their use. Thus the use of preferred stock also entails the utilization of financial leverage. As financial leverage increases, the potential for higher returns to common stockholders increases along with the potential for higher losses. Thus the risk to stockholders and lender increases. This risk is internal to the corporation and is distinct and separate from the ordinary business risk due to changing economic conditions and changing customer demand that face any organization. The risk due to financial leverage is termed financial risk. Recall that higher leverages can hold out the

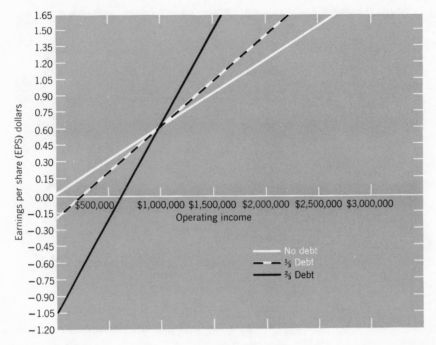

Figure 36. Earnings per share as operating income increases under three different capital structures.

prospect of higher returns to the shareholders; this is in line with earlier statements that for the expectation of higher returns investors must assume higher risk.

The situation is somewhat complicated since investors are not the only group exposed to higher risk when increased leverage is used. Lenders, for the reasons outlined above, are also exposed to increased risk. Recall that the total risk of any organization is composed of business risk plus financial risk. For a given return composed of the interest plus fees charged the borrowing organization lenders are willing to tolerate a stated risk. As the risk appears to increase, either due to increasing business risk or increased leverage, lenders will expect a higher return. One method of portraying this situation is the graph in Figure 37.

In general terms, the business risk faced by firms in the same industry is similar. For example, all oil exploration firms can expect only a limited number of successes in drilling for new wells. All manufacturers in the furniture and appliance industries face the same number of new family formations and new residence constructions. Most fossil fuel electric utilities experience comparable cost functions and demand growth. Thus a lender's approach to a potential borrower is to compare his financial ratios, including the debt-to-equity ratios, to other firms in the same industry. If all

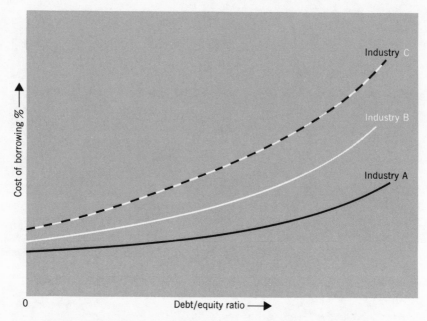

Figure 37.   Different costs for borrowing in different industries.

other comparisons are consonant with the expectations for that industry, the cost to the borrower will vary in accordance with his debt-to-equity ratio as compared to that of the industry. The higher his leverage when compared to the industry, the higher the cost. Note, however, that lenders have different debt-to-equity standards for different industries depending on the business risk to which each industry is exposed. The higher the business risk, the less the financial risk a lender will accept. For example, utilities have a stable, highly predictable demand. This, coupled with regulatory rate setting, assures firms in the industry a reasonably stable return regardless of economic conditions. Lenders to companies in this industry will therefore tolerate considerable financial leverage. The returns of mining companies, on the other hand, are sensitive to world market conditions and commodity prices; experience has shown that these returns can fluctuate rather violently. Hence extractive industries are usually viewed as being exposed to high business risk and lenders are not willing to expose themselves to high financial risk. Consequently, these firms use much less leverage than public utilities and most manufacturing or service industries.

Recall that each component of the capital structure, common stock, preferred stock, and debt, has a distinct cost associated with it. To recap, the cost of common stock is

$$R_E = D/P + g$$

The cost of preferred stock is

$$R_P = D/P$$

The cost of debt is

$$R_I = I(1 - t)$$

As leverage increases, the cost of debt also increases. However, since the interest cost of debt is tax deductible, the substitution of a small amount of debt for equity while the leverage is still low will reduce the *overall* cost of capital to the firm. As leverage increases, debt will require a premium in excess of the cost of equity and the total cost of capital increases. Figure 38 depicts this concept.

As illustrated, with low financial leverage the overall cost of capital to the firm *decreases* as debt is added to the capital structure. After a certain point, however, the premium that must be paid for additional debt more than offsets the savings resulting from the tax deductibility of interest and the overall cost of capital to the firm increases.

Several points are worth mentioning. First, the implications of this evaluation is that some debt in the capital structure is beneficial to the corporation and its stockholders. The puritan ethic that frowns on indebtedness is not consistent with good financial theory or practice. By employing some debt, the overall cost of capital is reduced and, consequently, the returns realized are increased. If, however, leverage is carried too far, the overall cost of capital starts rising.

Second, the optimal region varies from industry to industry and even among firms in a given industry. As was pointed out earlier, it depends on

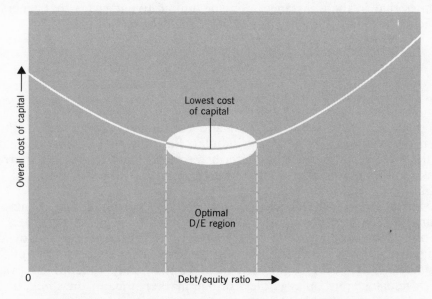

Figure 38. Optimal debt to equity region for an organization.

the business risk to which the firm is exposed. Good financial management implies that the financial manager is able to identify the optimal region for the organization based on knowledge and experience, and via signals received from the financial community.

Third, good financial management entails the adoption of sufficient leverage to reduce the overall cost of capital. Once financial management has identified the optimal region, it should manage corporate expansion by mixing debt and equity issues to continually minimize the overall cost of capital. This implies a flexible attitude towards the raising of capital, rather than an insistence of relying on a single source of outside capital.

Fourth, the professed desire of some financial managers to leverage their organizations to the extreme is not only highly risky but inefficient. The implications of the model presented are that at extreme leverage the cost of capital is higher than necessary. The returns at that point are therefore less than one would expect in view of the risk exposure. This is poor financial management.

A concluding point for managers in not-for-profit organizations. The theory of finance is just beginning to grapple with the cost of capital issues of not-for-profit organizations. At this time it is premature to present definite judgments regarding policy options open to them in this area. In the absence of specific guidelines it appears, however, that limiting extreme leverage must also be considered appropriate guidance for these organizations. This is reinforced by the omission of the primary incentive for debt in profit oriented organizations, tax deductibility. The absence of this advantage should encourage not-for-profit financial managers to adopt very conservative postures, despite the fact that debt may be the only type of capital that management can readily tap. Prudent management dictates that in these instances debt be limited to endeavors that generate sufficient revenue by themselves to meet the debt service costs.

WARRANTS AND CONVERTIBLES

Although in a legal sense warrants and convertibles are securities, their claim on assets and earnings are indirect. Basically they represent claims on the three types of securities described earlier, common stock, preferred stock, and bonds. Warrants and convertibles are useful specialized vehicles for raising corporate funds.

Ownership of a warrant entails the privilege of purchasing corporate securities such as common stock at a predetermined price, regardless of the prevailing market price at the time the warrant is exercised. The owner of a warrant that is itself a marketable security is not a stockholder of the corporation. However, upon paying a contractually determined price, which remains constant regardless of the market price of the stock, he or she can become a stockholder. Most warrants are issued with an expiration date. Prior to that date owners exercise the subscription privilege if the market price of the security in question exceeds the exercise price. If they fail to do so, owners lose all their privileges upon expiration of the warrant and their investment has no further market value.

Warrants are issued by corporate management in situations where it appears advantageous to provide outsiders with a stake in the corporation's welfare, or to provide additional performance incentives to insiders without simultaneously diluting ownership control or earnings per share (EPS). Note that until a warrant is exercised the warrant holder may not vote or receive dividends. Stock options to management constitute a special kind of warrant. Warrants are also used as a method of payment for services rendered, frequently during the organizational phase of a corporation. This method of compensation avoids both cash outflow when it can be ill afforded or dilution of ownership at an early, critical phase in a corporation's life. Finally, warrants are sometimes issued in conjunction with a bond issue. This point will be discussed more fully further on.

Convertibles are securities, primarily bonds and preferred stock, which at the option of the owner may be converted into other securities, usually common stock, at a predetermined exchange rate. For example, a convertible bond might be converted into 20 shares of common stock. While the decision to convert will be influenced by many factors such as risk, dividend payment, interest rates, and so forth, primarily it will hinge on the going market price of the common stock. If the price of the above bond based on the present value of coupon payments and the present value of its face amount is computed to be $900, while the market price of the common stock is $30 per share, bondholders will not find it advisable to convert their bonds. If, however, the stock rises to $55 per share they will consider it far more desirable, particularly if the bonds are about to mature and to be redeemed ar par. If bonds are not near redemption, their market price will reflect the increased value of the stock rather than their value as bonds. Thus if the underlying common stock trades above the conversion value ($50 in this example), the price of the bond will move in gear with the price of the stock. If it is substantially below this value, the market price of the bond will reflect the present value considerations enumerated earlier.

If the issuing corporation desires conversion of the bond, for reasons discussed below, it will call the bond for redemption at a price specified in the indenture. Investors will realize at that point that conversion is a financially more attractive alternative to redemption at face value plus about 1 year interest and therefore convert their holding. Similar considerations apply to the conversion privileges sometimes associated with preferred stock.

Why should a corporation issue convertible bonds at all? A further examination of Figure 38 can provide the answer. Note that as corporations require additional capital for expansion they cannot idenfinitely issue debt instruments since such actions would increase the debt-to-equity ratio beyond the optimal region and raise the cost of capital above its low point. Thus as corporations issue debt, financial management is aware that the next issue of securities to the public will probably have to be equity. By issuing convertible debt, corporations short circuit this process. In effect equity is sold at higher than prevailing prices, since the conversion price is usually about 10 to 25% above the market price, and the groundwork is prepared for future issues of debt.

Consider the following case. Book Learning Institute, Inc. requires $1 million for expansion this year and probably an additional $1 million in 5 years. Its current Balance Sheet is presented in Table 27. Underwriters advise that if the debt-to-equity ratio exceeds 50%, the cost of capital to the corporation is likely to increase. The common stock is currently selling for about $40 per share.

Table 27   **Book Learning Institute, Inc.,** Balance Sheet, April 1, 1980

		Debt	$2,000,000
		Equity	$3,000,000
Total assets	$5,000,000	Total liabilities and equities	$5,000,000

By selling a convertible bond issue the corporation can attain a variety of objectives. First, ownership is not diluted at this point in time. Second, since the conversion features is a special bonus to bond buyers above and beyond the customary privileges of bond ownership, the interest rate the corporation has to pay can be negotiated downward from that paid on a nonconvertible bond in a similar risk class. Third, if the corporation is successful and future expansion is called for it is likely that the price of the stock will rise above its conversion value. In essence, the corporation is selling common stock not at the prevailing market price of $40 but rather at the future conversion price of $50. Finally, by providing for conversion the corporation is keeping its options regarding future financing open. In view of the 50% debt-to-equity ratio, future financing will be limited to equity capital.

The Balance Sheet, after the sale of the convertible bonds in 1980 and after their conversion in 1985, is given in Tables 28A and B respectively.

The debt-to-equity ratio that started out as 2:3 reached the limit of 1:1 with the issue of the convertible bonds. Upon conversion, it actually improved to 1:2. Assuming that all other factors remained unchanged, Book Learning Institute is now able to issue an additional $2 million of debt. Note that if the corporation has issued equity initially to raise the $1 million required in 1980, it would have had to issue $1,000,000/$40

Table 28A **Book Learning Institute, Inc.,** Balance Sheet, December 31, 1980

		Old debt	$2,000,000
		Convertible bonds	1,000,000
		Old equity	$3,000,000
Total assets	$6,000,000	Total liabilities and equities	$6,000,000

Table 28B **Book Learning Institute, Inc.,** Balance Sheet, April 1, 1985

		Old debt	$2,000,000
		Old equity	$3,000,000
		New equity	1,000,000
Total assets	$6,000,000	Total liabilities and equities	$6,000,000

per share = 25,000 shares. In contrast upon conversion it only has to issue $1,000,000/$50 per share = 20,000 shares. Ownership is therefore less diluted than it would have been otherwise. At the same time the needed capital was obtained at a coupon rate less than that required for a straight bond, and upon conversion the Balance Sheet is actually strengthened.

Similar objectives can be accomplished by issuing warrants in conjunction with a straight bond offering if these warrants have an expiration date corresponding to the time an influx of new capital is required. Furthermore, the exercise price of the warrants must be set so the likelihood that the warrant holders will exercise their warrants is high.

Consider the previous opening balance with the following additional information. The stock is currently selling for $40 per share with the expectation that it will rise over $50 within 4 years. Corporate management is not attracted to the suggestion of selling convertible bonds since this will require an additional offering with all the costs and effort that this entails in a few years. Yet since Book Learing Institute cannot productively employ more than $1 million in new capital at this time, it does not wish to raise the $2 million now.

The additional capital can be raised by offering a thousand $1000 face value straight bonds and attaching 20 warrants to each bond. Upon initial sale of the bonds, warrants would be severable from the bonds. The terms

Table 29A   **Book Learning Institute, Inc.,** Balance Sheet, December 31, 1980

		Old debt	$2,000,000
		Bonds	$1,000,000
		Equities	$3,000,000
Total assets	$6,000,000	Total liabilities and equities	$6,000,000

of the warrants specify that, until their expiration date 5 years hence, for each warrant plus $50 the warrant holder may acquire 1 share of common stock.

The December 31, 1980 Balance Sheet, after the issue of bonds with warrants attached, appears in Table 29A. Note that warrants outstanding do not appear on the Balance Sheet since by themselves they do not represent a claim on assets! Also bonds issued in this case are straight bonds without conversion privileges.

Upon exercising the warrants an influx of equity capital will take place, increasing the capitalization above the $6 million achieved without requiring an additional public offering. Thus if the price of the stock improves as forecast, the total capitalization will increase in two stages: first, by the $1 million from the bond offering, and second via a gradual exercise of warrants reaching a total of another $1 million just prior to their expiration.

Another advantage of issuing bonds with warrants attached is that the buyers of these bonds will accept a lower coupon rate than buyers of straight bonds in a similar risk class normally demand. The warrants act as a sweetener to the offering, just as convertible bonds do. Once the warrants are separated from the bonds, the bonds will trade at a market value commensurate with their coupon, face value, maturity date, and risk class.

The Balance Sheet after the exercise of all the warrants issued in 1980 appears in Table 29B. Note also that the exercise of warrants again reduces the debt to equity ratio below 50%, opening the way for corporate management to raise additional capital via short or long term debt if it desires.

Although warrants and convertibles are flexible instruments for meeting specialized financing needs of corporations, they present contingent claims on equity and thereby on the earnings per share of existing stockholders. For this reason, corporate reports to stockholders not only present actual EPS realized but also reflect the possibility of bond conversion or the exercise of warrants by recomputing EPS as if those events had actually taken place. The recomputation requires assumptions regarding the

Table 29B **Book Learning Institute, Inc.**, Balance Sheet, April 1, 1985

		Old debt	$2,000,000
		Bonds	$1,000,000
		Old equity	$3,000,000
		New equity	$1,000,000
		(from exercise of	
		warrants)	
		Total liabilities	
Total assets	$7,000,000	and equities	$7,000,000

date of bond conversion since, after conversion, interest payments to bondholders cease and total corporate earnings fater taxes would therefore increase.

NOT-FOR-PROFIT ORGANIZATIONS

Since the legal status of not-for-profit organizations varies considerably generalized statements pertaining to their capital structure must be formulated with caution. It is appropriate to differentiate between governmental organizations funded out of general revenue and incorporated charitable and educational organizations. Organizational forms combining various characteristics of each also exist. Examples of these are municipal power companies and rapid transit systems.

The common characteristic of these organizations is their inability to issue equity capital readily. This in turn places a limit on the amount of debt they can attract. Lenders recognize that as the debt-to-total asset ratio of these organizations increases their risk exposure in case of default also increases, often beyond a range they are willing to tolerate.

Governmental bodies obtain most funding from general tax revenues and bond issues. Many of these bonds are secured by the general good faith of the governmental unit or by tax receipts that are expected to accrue directly to the body issuing the bonds. Lenders base their coupon rate decisions on the ability of the borrower to meet their debt service payment out of expected tax receipts. When tax receipts are in doubt and other mandated governmental expenditures are substantial, the risk of default increases and lenders may be reluctant to provide funds even at high risk premiums. Thus, in a sense, tax revenues perform some of the function of equity in the case of state and local governmental units. These considerations do not apply to federal government agencies. A U.S. government bond is by definition risk-free regardless of surpluses or deficits incurred. Directly or indirectly the good faith of the federal government is pledged in financing federal agencies. While some federal governmental agencies issue their own bonds they, too, frequently carry an implied moral commitment of federal guarantee. A discussion of the impact and burden of federal debt on prices, employment, interest rates, and output is beyond the scope of this book. It is one of the significant topics of macroeconomics.

Charitable and educational institutions are more similar to profit oriented organizations than to governmental units in their capital structure. Whether they employ standard Balance Sheets or adopt fund accounting, general endowments and continuing contributions provide the function that equity capital provides for corporations. Lenders view their risk in terms of the debt-to-total asset ratio, the legal restrictions of endowment funds, historically experienced contributions, prevailing operating budgets, expected cash flow, computed debt coverage, and collateral provided by the physical plant. Thus, lenders view their risk in a manner similar to their risk perception in lending funds to profit oriented organizations and extend long term debt accordingly.

SUMMARY

The composition of the right hand side of the Balance Sheet is referred to as the capital structure. The long term components of claims on assets are long term debt, common stock, and preferred stock. Common stock ownership is the most direct participation in the fortune of a corporation. The return to common stockholders is the dividend yield plus growth experienced in corporate earnings. Return to preferred stock holders is only the dividend yield, while returns to bondholders are the coupon payments received. With the exception of bonds, which must be computed on an after tax basis, these returns are also the cost of these sources of capital to the corporation. The market value of a bond is the sum of the present values of its coupon payments and its face value, discounted at the appropriate risk-adjusted market rate of interest.

Debt and preferred stock exert financial leverage on the earnings of common stockholders. Generally some financial leverage via debt can lower the overall cost of capital to an organization, while excessive use of such financial leverage can increase the cost of capital above these levels. The characteristics of the industry determine the appropriate degree of financial leverage.

Warrants and convertibles are contingent claims on common stock issued to accomplish specific financial objectives. Since they represent possible claims on equity, EPS are also computed assuming their full exercise and conversion. Not-for-profit organizations cannot raise equity capital directly. To lenders, tax revenues and charitable endowments serve a function equivalent to that of equity in profit oriented organizations.

18 Stockholder Relations

As the discussion of the cost of capital in Chapter 17 pointed out, the price a profit oriented organization receives per share of common stock directly influences its cost of equity and also determines the extent to which ownership in the organization is diluted. Financial management, in accordance with its objective of maximizing the wealth of the shareholders, therefore has a responsibility in undertaking those actions that are likely to impact favorably on the market price of its outstanding securities.

Two interrelated activities are associated with this effort: dividend policy and reporting to shareholders. Both these areas require cooperation between financial management and public relations. Also, in view of reporting requirements imposed by the Securities and Exchange Commission (SEC), the organization's counsel is probably involved in these endeavors.

While the issue of dividend policies is irrelevant to financial managers in not-for-profit organizations, reporting the organization's activities to donors, taxpayers, legislators, and other supporters is at least as important in their case as it is in profit oriented organizations. In either case the providers of capital to the organization wish to be reassured that financial management is exercising proper stewardship over the resources entrusted to it.

DIVIDEND POLICIES

Most financial decisions, particularly those dealing with the management of asset accounts, affect operating management. Not so decisions concerning dividend policy. Their impact will probably be felt by the public relations office of the corporation. Dividends are the one area in which stockholders have seldom hesitated to make their views and preferences readily known to corporate management. Furthermore, dividend decisions influence the market price of common stock and thereby the corporation's long run cost of raising additional capital. For all of these reasons, the dividend decision is based on many considerations in addition to the ready availability of funds for the payment of dividends.

Although dividend payments are customarily presented to stockholders in the context of the Income Statement, the payment of dividends is not directly related to profitability and the generation of income by the corporation. These payments are actually a distribution of a corporate asset, cash, to the stockholders. Ignoring legal constraints that could be imposed by lenders, this distribution may be made at any time upon the action of the board of directors. The pertinent accounting entries are as follows:

        Debit : Retained Income

        Credit : Cash

Note that these are Balance Sheet and not Income Statement accounts.

In declaring and paying dividends, corporations often signal conflicting information to stockholders. On the one hand, the board of directors demonstrates that in addition to the recording of accounting income (of which many stockholders have become quite skeptical in recent years), sufficient cash above and beyond that required for meeting the internal needs of the corporation is available for distribution. This can be interpreted to reflect successful and profitable management stewardship. On the other hand, the very act of distribution may be viewed as an admission by management that it has not been able to identify investment opportunities that can yield to the stockholder substantially higher returns than those the investor may realize by investing the cash distribution himself.

Some of these considerations are reflected in the payment practices of corporations. Mature organizations that expect to continue to be confronted with stable demand and do not seek to increase their share of the market customarily pay sizable dividends. Corporations that are still in a growth phase, and endeavor to increase their product lines and share of the market tend to reinvest their available funds in internal projects and pay only very nominal dividends. Investors thus have the opportunity to accommodate their personal preferences by selecting the type of security that meets their personal investment objectives.

Regardless of the fact that dividends are a Balance Sheet transaction and constitute a distribution of corporate assets, as presented above, the custom of tying dividends to accounting income is deeply entrenched. It is traditional for corporate earnings to be computed on a per share basis. Dividends are customarily reported to stockholders at the time that periodic earnings information is transmitted. A condensed quarterly report usually adheres to the following format:

Income from operations before income taxes
Provision for income taxes
Net income
Earnings per share
Dividends per share

Thus, while to financial management dividends depend on cash flow, to the stockholder they seem to be directly related to earnings per share. Since corporate incomes normally fluctuate in accordance with specific demand and general business conditions, the relationship between dividends and earnings become a policy issue for management consideration.

The solid line in Figure 39 presents a hypothetical corporate earning pattern over time. Some corporations adopt a dividend policy of paying out an approximately fixed percentage of the earnings reported. The stated rationale is that the earnings realized are divided between stockholders for their consumption needs and the corporation for its investment needs. This approach has the drawback that dividends are as cyclical as earnings, moving towards the upside as well as the downside. Stockholders do not cherish unexpected dividend cuts and are likely to make their feelings known to the board of directors. Dividend cuts may also prompt disappointed investors to dispose of their holdings. This in turn may depress the price of the stock and thus have an adverse effect on the corporations image in financial markets.

In lieu of this approach, an increasing number of corporations have opted for a fixed dividend approach. By specifying a fixed annual dividend, cash requirements of dividends can be incorporated into corporate cash budgets and investors do not face undue uncertainties. If conditions warrant it, the stated dividend is increased. As a variation on this theme some corporations such as General Motors, for example, pay a stated fixed dividend plus an extra dividend in those years in which earnings are exceptionally high.

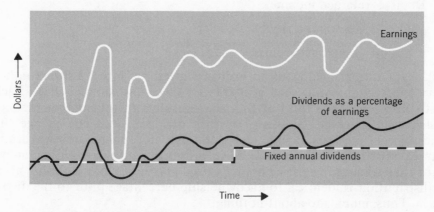

Figure 39. Comparative dividend structures as earnings change over time.

Several dates are associated with the dividend decision. First is the meeting of the board of directors. Recall that dividend payments are not automatically distributed as are interest payments. The duly constituted board must approve the decision to pay, the amount to be paid per share and the eligibility list for the receipt of dividends. This list is determined by selecting a date of record. Any stockholder whose name appears on the books of the corporation as of that stated date is eligible to receive dividends in accordance with the number of shares recorded in his or her name. There remains, however, still another complication. The paper work associated with the purchase and sale of securities does not move evenly or predictably. Thus, unless some convention is adopted, both buyer and seller of the securities would not be certain about their entitlement status vis-à-vis a declared dividend. To overcome this difficulty, the securities industry has adopted the convention that 5 trading days, which usually constitutes one calendar week, before the date of record the security goes ex-dividend. Buyers who purchase the stock subsequent to this date do not receive that particular dividend even if they own the security on the payment date.

STOCK DIVIDENDS

In lieu of, or in addition to, cash dividends some corporations periodically distribute additional shares of stock to shareholders. These distributions are made according to the same rules — declaration date, date of record, ex-dividend date, and payment date — established for cash dividends. Calling the stock distribution a dividend is, however, most misleading. Recall that cash dividends entail a distribution of corporate assets to the stockholders. In the payment of stock dividends no such distribution of assets is made. The accounting entries of a stock dividend demonstrate this. They are internal to the equity section of the Balance Sheet, as follows:

Debit : retained income

Credit : common stock

Credit : paid in surplus

The situation is analogous to slicing a given pie into 12 slivers rather than 6 slices and handing each of 3 guests 4 slivers instead of 2 slices. Each guest still receives one third of the pie, regardless of the number of slices or slivers he is served. Similarly, a stock dividend does not change the ownership claim of any stockholder. Although more shares are owned, the claim exercised per share is reduced in proportion to the additional number of shares issued. The stockholder's total percentage of ownership after the distribution is identical to his ownership percentage prior to the distribution. Thus, much ado about nothing!

Stock splits belong in the same category. While the accounting entries differ slightly, they are still internal to the equity section of the Balance Sheet. In a 2 for 1 stock split, each shareholder receives an additional share of stock for each share that he or she owned prior to the split. This is similar to a 100% stock dividend! The ownership claim per share is cut in half, while total ownership remains the same.

To complete the list of games corporations play in this arena, reverse stock splits are worth mentioning. In cases where the price of the stock dropped below respectable levels, judged to be about $5 per share, corporations try to boost the price by consolidating the outstanding shares, for example 1 new share may be issued for every 10 old shares outstanding. The hope is that henceforth the stock will trade in the more respectable $50 per share region and attract investor interest. The percentage ownership of stockholders remains unchanged by this maneuver. As one might suspect, the record of many such procedures reveals that cosmetic procedures by themselves are insufficient to assure business success. Unless underlying conditions or management practices change, the reverse split securities often sink to their previous, unrespectable levels!

FINANCIAL REPORTING

The second main area outside operating decisions addressed by financial management for the purpose of heightening positive attitudes in the investment community towards the securities issued by the organization is via the reporting of financial and operating data. The most visible example of such reporting is the annual report issued to stockholders. Most organizations also issue quarterly reports to shareholders although these are not as elaborate or detailed as the annual reports.

Annual reports generally have two main parts. The first part contains a summary of financial data and is devoted primarily to the presentation of the organization's accomplishments during the past year and its expectations for the future. It accentuates the positive and rarely dwells on problems or failures. The preparation of this portion of the report is usually coordinated by the public relations department. Long run credibility is the key to sustained success in this effort as in all well-managed public relations endeavors. Overly exuberent expectations that cannot be fulfilled are likely to haunt management in future years and may have an adverse impact on the organization's image and, thereby, on the price of its securities.

The second part of the annual report consists of the financial statements of the organization. This is a joint responsibility of financial management and independent auditors. It is the responsibility of the auditors to verify that the summary schedules presented reflect transactions recorded in accordance with generally accepted accounting principles (GAAP).

Still, even these audited statements contain only scant information for investors who wish to assess the financial posture and performance of the organization. Such investors can avail themselves of the more detailed financial reports filed with the SEC by publicly traded corporations. 10-K, the annually filed report, contains much additional information beyond that customarily released to stockholders. The reason corporations do not release all the data in stockholder reports is not necessarily an attempt to conceal information. Instead, it reflects the limited interest stockholders as a group have exhibited in detailed financial reports. The analysis of these documents is an arduous and time consuming task that few investors are apparently willing to undertake.

INVESTMENT TERMINOLOGY

Rather than plow through detailed financial data, most casual investors base their decision regarding the organization's financial performance and posture on a limited number of statistics that can be computed with ease from the Income Statement and the Balance Sheet. Listed below are some frequently used terms, their method of computation, and their significance.

1. *Price Earnings Ratio (P/E Ratio).* This ratio reflects how many years of currently indicated earnings must be paid for one share of stock. Assume annual earnings per share (EPS) of $2.50. If the stock sells on the market for $50, then the P/E ratio is 20. The more attractive the stock to investors, the higher the P/E ratio is likely to be. Also, the higher the P/E ratio, the less dilution of earnings and ownership of current stockholders in case additional shares of stock are issued.

   High P/E ratios occur if investors expect EPS to increase significantly in the future. In cases where expectations are that EPS will be lower in the future, the P/E ratio will drop below the average observed for that class of security. The P/E ratio is the result of the organization's financial performance and investors expectation of future performance. It does not contain new or different information to management or to investors.

2. *Dividend Yield (D/P).* Dividend yield was introduced in Chapter 17 in conjunction with the cost of capital. It is the percentage annual return of cash that investors in common stock or preferred stock can expect on their investment. Assume that the indicated dividend is $1.20 per share for shares costing $50 each. The dividend yield is

$$\frac{\$1.20}{\$50} \times 100 = 2.4\%$$

3. *Yield to Maturity (YTM).* This concept is applied to bonds. It is significant and contains valuable information for financial management and investors. It represents the internal rate of return of a bond purchased at prevailing market prices and held until its face value is redeemed by the issuing organization. Consider a $1000 face value bond with a $30 annual coupon purchased for $995.75 and maturing in 10 years. Its YTM is given by computing i, the internal rate of return in this formulation:

$$995.75 = \sum_{t=1}^{10} \frac{30}{(1 + i)^t} + \frac{1000}{(1 + i)^{10}}$$

The solution to this equation is YTM = 3.05%. A simplified, less precise computation of the YTM is given by the following:

$$\text{YTM} = \frac{\text{coupon + annual appreciation}}{\text{average investment}}$$

The annual appreciation in this example is

$$\frac{\$1000 - \$995.75}{10} = 0.43$$

The average investment is

$$\frac{\$995.75 + \$1000}{2} = \$997.87$$

Thus $\text{YTM} = \dfrac{30 + 0.43}{\$997.75} = 3.05\%$

The YTM conveys to the investor the true return on his investment in bonds if he purchased the bond at a price differing from face value. To financial management it signifies what the return of bonds in a given risk class is, and thus provides information for establishing the coupon rate for a new issue.

4. *Book Value per Share (BV/Share).* Book value per share represents the sum of the common stock, paid in surplus, and retained income accounts of the Balance Sheet divided by the number of common shares outstanding. Assume that the common stock account is $4 million, paid in surplus is $12 million, retained income is $20 million, and that 2 million common shares are outstanding. Then

$$\text{BV/share} = \frac{\$4{,}000{,}000 + \$12{,}000{,}000 + \$20{,}000{,}000}{2{,}000{,}000}$$

$$= \$18/\text{share}$$

This number may be of historical interest, but does not convey significant information to financial management or to investors about future performance. The fact that the market value per share is below its book value should be a matter of concern to all parties rather than a signal of a buying opportunity as it is frequently represented.

A proper way to view a profit oriented organization is to conceive of it as a black box with a spout and a crank. It is the role of management to turn this crank. If it does so successfully, annuities will spew out of the spout. The value of the organization is not the content of the box (its book value) but rather the present value of the stream of annuities it generates. In most instances book value conveys irrelevant information for investment decisions. This concept can be applied to purchasing decisions of investors as well as to merger and acquisition decisions facing financial management.

SUMMARY

Successful financial management includes the maintenance of appropriate relations with the investment community. Dividend decisions and financial reports are the visible manifestations of this relationship. Not-for-profit organizations also release financial reports to demonstrate that the services they rendered were commensurate with the expenditures incurred.

Dividends are a distribution of corporate assets to stockholders and are independent of earnings realized in any one period. Dividends must be declared by the board of directors. Many corporations adopt regular quarterly payments which are reviewed periodically. Stock splits and stock dividends do not entail a distribution of corporate assets.

Annual reports are geared to the general public and contain only limited financial information. More detailed data is filed with the SEC in the 10-K reports. Investors in general, however, base their decisions on summary financial statistics. The best known of these are price earnings ratio, dividend yield, yield to maturity, and book value per share. The proper way to view an investment is not by computing its book value but rather by computing the present value of the annuities it can be expected to provide to investors.

19 Capital Acquisition

It is useful to compare the stages of organizational growth to biological analogs and then to trace the impact of their respective growth phases on their need for capital, their anticipated financing strategy, and their practices for financial management. To do this, one can differentiate between infancy, adolescence, and maturity. Problems beyond maturity are not discussed since they evolve into issues of political survival for public agencies and bankruptcy courts for private organizations. They are thus beyond the realm of finance and become the concern of politicans and lawyers. It is important to remember that this analog is a pedagogical device and should only be carried as far as useful insights can be gained.

The life cycle of organizations, like that of biological organisms, often follows the S-shaped logistic curve. Figure 40 displays such a typical

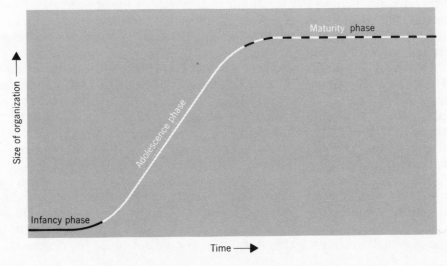

Figure 40. Stages of growth in an organization.

curve, identifying the stages of growth for the organization as infancy, adolescence, and maturity. Size can be stated in any of the commonly measured attributes of an organization: financial statistics, physical assets, or personnel data. Examples of numerical measures of size that are frequently adopted are sales, total assets, profits, square feet of covered space, or number of employees. All of these generally increase simultaneously as an organization moves through its growth stages.

CHANGING NEEDS

The capital needs of organizations are met in different ways during each of the three stages of growth. The customary sources of capital and the usual manner of tapping these sources are discussed below. Distinct differences also arise between methods of financing profit oriented and not-for-profit organizations.

By definition, the financing of not-for-profit organizations excludes the raising of capital by issuing common stock. Their access to outside capital is limited to endowments, donations, tax revenue, and debt. It is unusual for these organizations to tap all of these sources, although each organization is likely to rely on one or two of these methods of financing. However, while their sources of funding may remain the same over their life cycle, their rationale for tapping these sources may vary according to their stage of growth. For example, a new governmental bureau is funded through the appropriation of tax revenues. Although its source of funding will remain the same over its life cycle, the justifications for funding bureau operations will vary between stages. In the early phases of growth, heavy requirements exist for funds to be used for the acquisition of facilities; in the latter phases, heavy demands will accumulate for personnel salaries. The funding of charitable organizations often assumes a similar pattern.

Other not-for-profit organizations may be funded with a large initial endowment at the time of inception, and many foundations follow this pattern. This presents a particularly challenging task to financial management. In essence, the organization's management is provided with the present value of a flow and all future disbursements must come from the corpus of this endowment and its investment income. Further, federal tax legislation specifies that the corpus cannot be carried to perpetuity.

Sometimes there is considerable similarity during the infancy stage between the financing of profit oriented and not-for-profit organizations. A common denominator is strong, emotional sponsorship towards the venture by highly motivated individuals who can attract capital by virtue of the personal confidence they inspire at the inception of the organization.

All available statistics point to the fact that the business risk facing a new organization is extraordinarily high and that conventional sources of capital are not likely to provide the needed financing. If such financing is obtained during the infancy stage, it is usually on the basis of faith in the principals and objectives of the organization.

Usually such faith is only encountered by believers in a cause, who may provide the initial funding of not-for-profit organizations, or by friends and relatives of the principals, who may provide initial capital for profit oriented ventures. On rare occasions specialized sources, such as venture capital firms, may also be available at the initial stages of the venture. Frequently, however, even these firms require some demonstrated initial success of the venture prior to their willingness to partake in it. Debt financing from traditional sources such as banks is not obtainable during the infancy stage since the risk it entails is far in excess of what banks will tolerate.

The challenge of financial management in the infancy stage of a profit oriented organization's life is to tap capital sources outside the established channels of financial markets. No generalized prescription can be presented to solve this dilemma. Financial management must resist the ready issuance of common stock in return for the needed capital for two reasons. First, excess dilution of ownership at that point in an organization's life cycle will remove the financial incentive for success from the founders of the venture. Such incentive is of utmost importance to the success of the venture. Without sufficient motivation of every kind, including financial returns for the principals, it is not likely to succeed. Second, the inclusion of outside investors in the management of the venture might impair the ability and desire of the principals to proceed according to their original intent.

The prescription usually offered is to tap friends and relatives for capital. The financial package offered in exchange for capital may include some common stock, usually less than 50% of the outstanding shares, and a combination of convertible bonds, warrants, and convertible preferred stock. These issues accomplish the objectives of the founders of the venture as well as its investors: they provide capital when needed and attractive returns to investors if the venture succeeds. Yet the danger of outsider involvement in management during the early, critical period is avoided. If the venture is successful, investors will be able to exchange their claims on common stock for direct ownership at a later date.

If the venture survives its infancy, it will exhibit a voracious appetite for capital during its adolescence. Facilities and inventories must be acquired, accounts receivable are building up, cash balances must be maintained at increasingly higher levels, and new products must be financed. It is a common misconception that business success eases the pressures on financial management. The contrary is true: the more successful the venture, the more pressing the need for outside capital. The process of acquiring such capital becomes easier as the venture approaches maturity. Thus, in contrast to the infancy stage, during the adolescence phase the traditional sources of capital become available to corporate management. Underwriters can be approached to facilitate the issuing of securities, be it common stock, preferred stock, or bonds to the public. Normal banking relationships with revolving lines of credit can also be established at this stage. Suppliers are willing to offer customary trade credit and other sources of capital such as mortgage lenders, insurance companies, and lessors can be tapped. A succinct statement would be that from a financial point of view this adolescent phase, as all such phases, is hectic and difficult, yet with proper guidance and good management it too can be overcome!

Although capital needs of corporations continue to grow through the maturity phase, a profound change is taking place. Internal sources of funds, primarily those reflected in retained income and depreciation accounts, are beginning to supply a very substantial portion of the capital needs. As discussed earlier, only a portion of retained income is customarily paid to stockholders in dividends. In the absence of more specific information, half may be accepted as a good planning estimate. In addition, since the corporation now has sizable investments in facilities, depreciation charges are now very substantial. Recall that these charges contribute to the availability of cash. As a first approximation, internal capital accretion between periods can be computed by adding depreciation to retained income. During the maturity phase of an enterprise, the sum of these two can often suffice to meet the capital requirements of the organization. Finally, what is true for all prosperous borrowers is also true for a mature corporation. Its very survival through infancy and adolescence enhances its credibility. By now it has established routine channels with banks, underwriters, insurance companies, and as long as performance continues to be credible it is assured routine and easy access to funds.

To summarize, in profit oriented organizations the tasks facing financial management in the realm of acquiring funds are impossible during infancy, hectic and difficult during adolescence, and become routine management activities during the maturity phase of the organization. They parallel the characteristics of other management activities during these phases by shifting from creative and innovative involvements towards routine and bureaucratic activities.

Similar trends can be observed in not-for-profit organizations. The more mature the organization, the more routine its financial problems. This should not be interpreted as implying that the financial problems of mature organizations are necessarily simple and do not require good financial management. On the contrary, the stakes in large orgainzations are sufficiently high so that even very small improvements in operations and financial management will show measurable and worthwhile results. What has changed, however, is that instead of continual crises management, with emphasis on near term survival and the adoption of solutions that are not necessarily efficient in the long run, long term solutions to financial problems may now be planned and executed.

THE UNDERWRITING PROCESS

To secure long term funds from established financial markets, organizations frequently engage the services of an underwriter. This is particularly important if an organization wishes wide public distribution of the securities it offeres for sale. Banks can act as underwriters but are restricted at this time to municipal issues. Some underwriting firms, particularly investment bankers, specialize in the packaging of the offered securities and the wholesaling aspects of the distribution process. In general the basic economic function of underwriters is to acquire securities from issuing corporations and through their marketing channels to distribute these securities to the investing public. In essence underwriters are wholesalers who, through retail brokerage outlets, retail their merchandise to investors.

The selection of an underwriter is undertaken in the same manner in which any professional service is engaged: word of mouth reputation, experience of associates, interviews and negotiations with interested firms. The underwriting process is regulated by the Securities and Exchange Commission (SEC). In meeting the procedural and legal requirements of underwriting, a first issue can easily take from 6 months to a year. During this period the underwriter will be privy to the inner workings of the organization in financial as well as in related areas. Friction in interpersonal relationships between the underwriter and the organization's management team can handicap the underwriting process and slow down the preparation of the prospectus for SEC approval. Therefore it is important that relationships between corporate management and the underwriters be one of mutual trust and acceptance.

The basic document evolving from the underwriting process is the prospectus. For a new venture it presents the history of the organization, the assessment of the competition, transactions which may have transpired between the principals and the organization, and assorted financial statements. Tentative versions of the prospectus are circulated among prospective buyers to stimulate interest. These documents do not contain the offering price and are issued before SEC approval is obtained for the offering. In the trade they are called "red herrings." When the SEC is satisfied that the prospectus contains all relevant information and that the information presented is accurate, it may grant approval for the proposed offering. Note that SEC approval does not imply that the proposed offering is a financially desirable investment. Approval signifies only that the relevant information has been properly disclosed to the potential buyer. From then on, let the buyer beware!

The price of the securities offered and terms for compensating the underwriter are usually negotiated separately. There is a considerable difference between the first issue of securities of an infant organization and the sale of additional securities of a mature corporation. A mature organization has a track record for the market price of its common stock, and its bonds are rated and fall within well-defined risk classes. The price that can be realized at the offering is reasonably predictable by both the offeror and the underwriter, so that negotiations can take place within bounds of mutual understanding. Not so for a new issue. Its offering price is usually established by comparison with the price of similar securities that are publicly traded. The definition of what constitutes similar securities can lead to considerable misunderstanding and disagreement.

Recall that a basic economic conflict exists between the underwriter and the issuing corporation. The underwriter's objective is to buy the securities at as low a price as possible since this eases his ability to unload his inventory of securities rapidly and avoids the business risk associated with the carrying of any inventory. The issuing corporation desires, of course, to achieve the highest possible price; this increases funds available for corporate purposes, lowers the cost of capital, and minimizes the dilution of current stockholders' ownership. As in all business transactions, the issue will be resolved on the basis of the relative bargaining strength of the parties. The offering price arrived at will constitute an acceptable compromise to all participants in the negotiations.

A second issue for negotiation between the issuer of securities and the underwriter is the compensation of the underwriter, whose expectations are consonant with financial reasoning: the greater the risk, the greater his or her expectation of return to compensate for the risk. Thus mature organizations usually pay a much smaller percentage in underwriting fees than an adolescent organization, and far less than an infant corporation floating its first public issue. The terms of the offer also vary from commitments of the underwriter to purchase all the securities offered by the organization to the public and resell them from his inventory, thereby fully bearing the risk the public may not purchase the issue at the offering price, to a best effort undertaking that totally relieves him of inventory risk. Many underwriting agreements include provisions for supporting the offering price of the securities for a limited period of time through open market purchases by the underwriter, customarily for 30 days.

The nature of compensation for the underwriter is also subject to negotiation. Mature organizations will normally agree to let the underwriter deduct a fixed commission from each security sold as total compensation. For new issues of infant companies such agreements are seldom negotiated. The reason is the risk exposure of the underwriter and the return required to compensate for this risk. If the return were paid to cash, a very high percentage of the capital raised through the public offering would have to be used for payments to the underwriter. This would of course defeat the very purpose the corporation had in mind in deciding on the sale of securities: the raising of capital for corporate purposes. A corporation is chronically short of cash during the early phases of its life cycle and any avoidable cash outflow should indeed be avoided.

Therefore a customary arrangement is to compensate the underwriter in cash for out-of-pocket expenses and also to grant him warrants on newly issued common stock. If the venture is successful the underwriter is well rewarded; if not, his out-of-pocket costs have been met. By owning the warrants, he becomes in essence an interested party in the well-being of the venture. This in turn is advantageous from the issuing corporation's point of view since it provides an incentive for the underwriter to assure the success of the public offering. His final compensation will thus depend directly on the public's acceptance of the securities offered.

PRIVATE OFFERINGS

Not all long term capital is raised through public offerings. Often organizations find it advantageous to raise this type of capital outside such channels. The most common example of this is a mortgage, a secured long term loan that may be granted to the organization by private investors, lending institutions, and frequently life insurance companies. These same individuals and institutions may also invest in other securities such as common stock and general obligation bonds. However, such private investments come under the scrutiny of the SEC, which is concerned that private offerings not be used to circumvent the security laws and that they are actually transactions between knowledgeable equals. Two tests are used for this purpose. The first is a consideration of the sophistication of the potential investor. Each offeree must possess and demonstrate the necessary knowledge for assessing the risks and rewards inherent in the offering. Further, the offeree must demonstrate through examination of corporate books and other investigations that he possesses the necessary degree of sophistication for making an investment without relying on the prospectus. This document, which accompanies a public offering of securities is not required for a private offering. This is the reason for the insistence on sophistication and investigation.

The second requirement is a limitation on the number of offerees. Again the SEC's concern is that a private offering not be used as a conduit to channel securities into public hands without engaging in full disclosure. As a general rule a private sale to more than 35 investors is viewed with suspicion. Furthermore, prospects for these investments cannot be solicited via public advertising but must be approached directly. Each offeree thus approached must possess characteristics that qualify him or her as a sophisticated investor.

The issues involved in all offerings and particularly in private offerings are not limited to the field of finance. They have heavy legal overtones and require expertise in security laws and regulations. This requirement often leads to a preference for individuals with legal backgrounds to be appointed to the treasurer function in an organization. If the required legal expertise is not available within an organization it should be engaged by financial management prior to the formulation of any issue of securities, public or private. This applies equally to profit oriented and not-for-profit organizations.

SUMMARY

The capital needs of an organization change over its life cycle. During infancy, capital needs are best supplied by believers in the competence of the principals in the case of profit oriented organizations or believers in the cause to which not-for-profit organizations subscribe. Capital needs increase during the adolescent phase but can be met via the public offering of securities. Many of the capital needs of mature organizations are funded from internal sources.

A public offering of securities requires the preparation of a prospectus that presents all pertinent information regarding the organization and is subject to approval by the SEC. Underwriters assist in the preparation of the prospectus and purchase securities wholesale from the organization, to be retailed to investors via brokerage offices. Private offerings do not require a prospectus but must meet tests with regard to the sophistication of offerees and the restrictions of publicity concerning the investment. Legal advice is required for a successful offering of securities.

20 Security Markets

For close to 200 years the trading of securities had been conducted in a manner that changed only imperceptibly with time. Although legislation arising out of the depression restricted some brokerage activities, and newly developed communication devices accelerated the operational tempo, the essential characteristics of the auction market — the specialist system and the fixed commission structure — remained unchanged until recently.

The introduction of the computer and its peripheral equipment in the 1960s created capabilities for conveying, storing, manipulating, and displaying information that had not existed earlier. Consequently, institutional arrangements that had prevailed for prolonged periods were suddenly challenged and altered. This state of affairs is expected to continue well into the 1980s. The changes in the making are so profound and rapid in coming that a detailed description of the institutional arrangements existing at any point in time may provide misleading information to the reader. In lieu of this, a generalized view of security trading is presented here.

TRADING PRACTICES

An individual holding securities such as stocks, bonds, and options that have been cleared for public trading according to the security laws is entitled to negotiate with another individual regarding the conditions of sale including sales price, delivery dates, and so forth. In the absence of an organized visible and accessible securities industry, these individuals would have severe difficulty in locating an interested and qualified buyer to consummate a binding transaction within reasonable time limits and without incurring excessive charges. The function of the security markets is to facilitate this process.

223

Until recently trading activities on organized exchanges almost totally eclipsed alternative systems. The advent of new technology has created trading capabilities outside the exchange framework that are increasingly utilized by institutions. Nevertheless, since it is expected that organized security exchanges will retain an important role in securities trading, a brief description of their floor practices is appropriate.

To be accepted for trading on an exchange, securities must meet certain criteria such as capitalization, number of shares outstanding, and volume of trading. The specific requirements for admission to trading vary among exchanges. Only securities that have been admitted to trading on a given exchange can be traded there, and then only by representatives of member firms of the exchange. This limitation arises from the charter provisions of security exchanges. They are owned and operated by their members. If otherwise qualified, individuals and firms acquire membership through the purchase of a seat from a departing member. The price of the seat is negotiated according to prevailing market conditions. Member firms must abide by the rules of their exchange regarding trading practices, capitalization, and so on.

On an exchange, actual personal contact is established between representatives of the buyer and the seller; negotiations take place in accordance with the instructions left by buyers and sellers with their respective brokers. If agreement is reached between the parties, the transaction is displayed in the tape of the exchange and relayed to the buyers and sellers through their brokers.

When the demand and supply of a given security are not in balance the missing side of the transaction is handled by a specialist. An example of this is the high public interest generated in a security by a favorable news release, which may increase demand in the investment community for this security. While the current owners of the security may not be interested in selling their holdings. The specialist is a member of the exchange charged by the governing body with maintaining an orderly market in the securities assigned to him. To accomplish this, the specialist trades in these securities for his own account. This requires the holding of a sizable inventory in the security to meet the demand of prospective buyers and also sufficient cash on hand to absorb the supply offered by sellers. Additional responsibilities of the specialist include the maintenance of records for offers by investors to sell and buy the security at prices other than the prevailing market price.

Publicly traded securities that have not been admitted for trading at organized exchanges are traded in the over-the-counter (OTC) market. In contrast to the organized exchanges, representatives of buyer and seller do not negotiate face to face; a market maker assumes many of the functions of the specialist and any member of the National Association of Security Dealers has access to the communication network for information and trading purposes.

In the OTC market, most transactions are executed between the investor and the market maker. This is a brokerage firm which, in addition to its normal retail and wholesale securities business, trades in selected securities for its own account. The market maker advises other brokerage firms, and through them the investment community at large, of the price he is willing to pay at a given point in time for the security. This is the bid price. The price for which he is willing to sell the same securities is the ask price. Generally the more active the market for any security, the less the spread between bid and ask.

A sizable percentage of trading in securities is between institutions with substantial block holdings. In terms of negotiating strategy as well as total cost, these investors find it efficient to deal directly among themselves. A special communication network serves these traders.

Current technology permits serious consideration of expanded trading options such as direct access to international security markets, individual investors' direct participation in trading, and so on. The problems and issues are legal and administrative rather than technological and economic. Thus, it can be expected that significant changes will continue to evolve in the characteristics and function of security markets.

THE SECURITY AND EXCHANGE COMMISSION

The federal agency that has prime cognizance over the functioning of security markets is the Securities and Exchange Commission (SEC). From its establishment in 1934 until the late 1960s, the emphasis of the SEC's activities was in the area of underwriting and disclosure. By assuring full disclosure in the offering of securities to the investment community and policing against fraudulent activities in this and the subsequent trading process, the SEC expected to assure equal access to relevant information for potential investors.

In recent years the SEC has broadened its involvement to include the operation of organized exchanges and the monitoring of accounting practices of reporting corporations. To facilitate competitive trading, the SEC has been instrumental in reducing the monopolistic trading practices in effect on security exchanges, especially the restriction on minimum commissions charged to the public. To further its objective of assuring full disclosure the SEC has attempted to remedy the lack of consistency in reporting accounting income to stockholders. This required increasing involvement with generally accepted accounting principles (GAAP) and the exercise of professional leadership in areas where a professional consensus was lacking.

Through this involvement the SEC has transformed itself in recent years from an agency pursuing the limited objective of full disclosure to one directly affecting – via regulation, admonishment, and leadership – the economic and professional posture of accounting and security brokerage firms. Issues raised by the SEC have significantly influenced reporting practices of corporations, redefined the responsibility of outside auditors, and contributed to the consolidation of brokerage firms.

The SEC has not shied away from vigorously prosecuting those individuals and firms it considers in violation of the security laws. Section 1b of the Security and Exchange Act of 1934 is of particular relevance to corporate managers. It curtails the trading activities of insiders in corporate securities. The definition of insiders has been consistently broadened over the years and is no longer limited to top corporate officials. All corporate managers should be sensitive to the implications of this act in the trading of securities of corporations with which they have close affiliations.

INVESTMENT ANALYSIS

This book is addressed to nonfinancial managers, outlining the functions and responsibilities of financial management. Yet much of the material presented is fully applicable to the formulation of investment decisions by individuals. This is not a coincidence but reflects the situation as it should be. Financial management and investments are two sides of the same coin.

Recall that the function of financial management is to maximize the wealth of the investor. Through management of working capital investments in long term assets and the adoption of a proper capital structure, financial management should achieve returns for its stockholders commensurate with the risk to which it has exposed stockholder capital. These returns should translate into increased value of the outstanding common stock and a flow of dividends to investors. The present value of that flow plus the appreciation in the price of the common stock constitute the increase in the wealth of stockholders.

To attain this objective, financial management must be sensitive to the interpretation that investors through their decisions on security markets make regarding the actions of management as they pertain to the future of the firm. Thus, to be effective, financial management will attempt to view its own actions through the eyes of the investment community.

Investors who wish to be successful in their pursuit of returns must adopt the opposite stance. Much of the activity of investment analysis consists of identifying the future prospects of the firm under consideration, its expected decisions, its likely sources of capital, its long term investments, its dividend policy, and so forth. Thus, outside investment analysis essentially duplicates and attempts to forecast the management decision process. It must consider accounting policies, depreciation methods, risk and return relationships, discounting factors, market interest rates, and general economic conditions in order to arrive at return expectations for investors. To undertake this task, investment analysts must master the topics identified in this book.

Recall that a profit oriented organization can be viewed as a black box with a spout and a handle. It is the role of management to turn the handle; based on its efforts, returns are expected to gush from the spout. Investment analysis has as its objective the independent estimation of the amount and duration of these returns. Financial management must proceed with full awareness of the interpretation that security markets are likely to apply to its decisions. Through the dividend and disclosure actions discussed in Chapter 18 management can aid in the formulation of appropriate perceptions of financial performance and expectation for the organization by investment analysts. If investors as a group share these expectations, then the market prices that prevail for the securities of the organization are actually in accordance with risks facing the organization. Under these conditions, the ownership and earnings of existing stockholders do not suffer undue dilution as new securities are issued to raise funds for the organization. To successfully discharge these responsibilities financial management must view its actions in accordance with the criteria applied by the investment community in formulating investment decisions.

SUMMARY

The organization and function of the security exchanges is changing rapidly. These changes may be attributed to the increased ability of storing, manipulating, and displaying information by virtue of available computer technology and the growing involvement of the SEC in the operations of the security industry. In organized exchanges the specialist is charged with the maintenance of an orderly market. This and other functions are combined by the market maker in the over-the-counter market.

The SEC discharges its responsibilities under the security laws through the fostering of full disclosure of relevant information by financial management and the vigorous prosecution of fraud. In recent years, the SEC has also become involved in the organization and trading practices of the security industry and has exercised leadership in the accounting practices adopted by financial management. Corporate managers should be particularly sensitive to the SEC's position on the trading of securities by insiders.

Investment analysis is the mirror image of financial management. It consists of identifying the future prospects of the organization and anticipating financial decision processes. To assure that its securities are properly priced in the market, financial management must view its actions in accordance with criteria applied by the investment community. This will prevent undue dilution of the ownership of existing stockholders as new capital is raised in security markets.

21 Financial Management

Finance is the common language of management. The goals, objectives, and plans of the organization, the allocation of the organization's resources, and the accomplishments and failures of organizational components are increasingly presented and assessed in this language. Effective communication between organizational components requires that managers understand this language and use it in the performance of their assigned responsibilities. The absence of sensitivity to this means of communication and to the issues highlighted in this book may handicap managers in presenting their objectives, plans, and requirements for approval to top management in a convincing and salable manner.

It is striking to observe the close correspondence between the activities of financial management in profit oriented and not-for-profit organizations. Contrary to popular impressions the role of financial management is at least as important in the public as it is in the private sector. The lack of the discipline that competitive market prices provide to profit oriented management actually requires a heightened explicit concern by the management of not-for-profit organizations for the practice of good financial management. In the absence of reported profits the results of poor practice are not as readily discernible to the public as they are in the private sector. The application of financial concepts and practices to management transcends the legal form adopted by the organization.

In profit oriented organizations stockholders and their elected representatives as well as lenders and suppliers also have a legitimate need to assess the performance of the enterprise. The language of finance becomes the vehicle for these assessments. Performance assessment in not-for-profit organizations is undertaken by lenders, suppliers, legislative bodies, benefactors, and trustees. Again, most of the information presented for assessment is cast in financial terms. In general, outsiders charged with the responsibility of reviewing organizational performance require familiarity with and mastery of fundamental financial concepts.

The objective of this book is the development of the concepts and procedures that underlie the practice of financial management. By detailing the origin of finance, developing the tools of analysis, and highlighting current areas of investigation, pertinent concepts and procedures are developed and some of their applications are demonstrated. Although the functions of financial management are discussed, this book is intended for nonfinancial managers. Perhaps even practicing financial managers may find explanations and applications that are novel and useful to them.

Rarely can the theory and practice of a field of knowledge be compartmentalized neatly into mutually exclusive packages. Finance is no exception. Thus some issues merit discussion in a variety of theoretical and situational contexts. Rather than impose a burden on the reader, this occasional overlap of explanatory material should actually be helpful to the learning process. An analog to this can be found in the ascending of a spiral staircase. With each turn, a slightly different panorama of the scenery below unfolds and the functions of a variety of elements in the view below become clearer. In this book, for example, interest rates were discussed under the headings of economic concepts, accounting conventions, mathematics, capital budgeting, leasing, banking, and long term securities. Each time a concept was introduced a different aspect of the underlying relationships unfolded in order to contribute to a better understanding of the intricacies of the economic phenomenon of interest. Financial management must concern itself with all the observed nuances in formulating its decisions. The appreciation of existing interrelationships requires exposure to the field of finance as a whole rather than a mere mastery of certain specialized techniques.

Two issues that were handled only by implication should be discussed specifically at this point. First, the role of the financial manager versus the role of financial management and, second, the role of judgment versus analysis in performing the financial management function.

Financial management does not operate as part of the management team in splendid isolation. It concerns itself with macroeconomic problems, volume of output determinations, pricing considerations, implications of government regulation, and assorted related issues. These issues are identical to those that other members of the management team, whose prime interest may lie in marketing, production, law, or personnel are concerned about. Thus the activities a financial manager actually concentrates on may vary from organization to organization depending on the tenure of the incumbents, their capabilities, and the inclinations of the chief executive officer. For the purposes of this discussion, however, what is important is that the function in its totality be properly discharged and that all members of the management team realize that proper financial management is essential to the organization's success and survival.

The financial manager is charged with a dual set of responsibilities.

First, he or she deals with areas for which he alone has line responsibility, such as financial accounting and cash management. Second, he functions as an energizer and motivator, and through persuasion, education, and admonition establishes a climate within the organization that fosters contributions from all members of the management team to financial decision making. Success in exercising the financial management function requires as much devotion to the second set of activities as to the first, and depends, among other factors, on the tone of management cooperation set by the chief executive officer for the organization.

The other issue deserving explicit treatment at this point is the role of judgment versus analysis in financial management. Whenever appropriate and possible, quantitative relationships and models developed by economists and financial theorists were identified in this book. As presented, however, the theory has two defects. First, it is spotty and incomplete. Many aspects of financial management, particularly those dealing with institutional and macroeconomic issues do not have rigorous, empirically testable formulations. Second, it is very difficult to acquire input data for many variables in these models. The use of the standard deviation as a measure of risk is a prime example of this issue. While the standard deviation enhances conceptual exploration of risk as an issue in financial decision making, its computation often requires the stipulation of many, often quite tenuous, assumptions.

However, the fact that specific models or detailed inputs may not readily be available to aid in the solution of a given problem does not diminish the value of quantitative analysis. The role of the financial manager is to exercise his judgment as it pertains to the solution of the problem under consideration. As in any such situation judgment reflects exposure to applicable theory, past experience, and intuition. The greater the exposure of the financial manager to the theory of finance and the broader his experience in financial management, the more appropriate will be the judgment applied to given situations. Financial management does not provide cookbook style approaches with guaranteed results for successful recipes if instructions ar followed! Rather, it should be viewed as a creative approach to the solution of complex problems facing all organizations. Financial management is an organized way of facing financial uncertainties.

This book identified the theory underlying financial management, presented its tools of analysis, discussed applicable concepts, and demonstrated commonly used practices and procedures. For many readers the mastery of this material required considerable expenditure of time and effort, and constituted an investment undertaken with the expectation that the benefits accruing to the reader would exceed the costs! Perhaps the reader concurs at this point that such is the case.

Throughout this book it has been demonstrated that the point of view of financial management can be employed productively by managers in profit and not-for-profit organizations. The application of this approach to problems facing investors has also been identified. Beyond this, readers may find that the concepts developed can readily be adopted to financial planning in small business and even in households. Finally it is another tool in the arsenal of taxpayers who desire the means of checking on the performance of those who allocate an increasing portion of national income. The deliberate allocation of resources, which is the hallmark of good financial management, enhances the level of benefits that can be derived from any organized endeavor. Thus managers, employees, investors, benefactors, and taxpayers all have a stake in the practices adopted by financial management.

Appendix
Interest Tables

Table A   Interest factors $T_A = (1 + i)^n$ for computing F, the future value of a sum

$n\backslash i$	0.01	0.02	0.03	0.04	0.05	0.06
1	1.010	1.020	1.030	1.040	1.050	1.060
2	1.020	1.040	1.061	1.082	1.103	1.124
3	1.030	1.061	1.093	1.125	1.158	1.191
4	1.041	1.082	1.126	1.170	1.216	1.262
5	1.051	1.104	1.159	1.217	1.276	1.338
6	1.062	1.126	1.194	1.265	1.340	1.419
7	1.072	1.149	1.230	1.316	1.407	1.504
8	1.083	1.172	1.267	1.369	1.477	1.594
9	1.094	1.195	1.305	1.423	1.551	1.689
10	1.105	1.219	1.344	1.480	1.629	1.791
11	1.116	1.243	1.384	1.539	1.710	1.898
12	1.127	1.268	1.426	1.601	1.796	2.012
13	1.138	1.294	1.469	1.665	1.886	2.133
14	1.149	1.319	1.513	1.732	1.980	2.261
15	1.161	1.346	1.558	1.801	2.079	2.397
16	1.173	1.373	1.605	1.873	2.183	2.540
17	1.184	1.400	1.653	1.948	2.292	2.693
18	1.196	1.428	1.702	2.026	2.407	2.854
19	1.208	1.457	1.754	2.107	2.527	3.026
20	1.220	1.486	1.806	2.191	2.653	3.207
21	1.232	1.516	1.860	2.279	2.786	3.400
22	1.245	1.546	1.916	2.370	2.925	3.604
23	1.257	1.577	1.974	2.465	3.072	3.820
24	1.270	1.608	2.033	2.563	3.225	4.049
25	1.282	1.641	2.094	2.666	3.386	4.292
26	1.295	1.673	2.157	2.772	3.556	4.549
27	1.308	1.707	2.221	2.883	3.733	4.822
28	1.321	1.741	2.288	2.999	3.920	5.112
29	1.335	1.776	2.357	3.119	4.116	5.418
30	1.348	1.811	2.427	3.243	4.322	5.743

$n\backslash i$	0.07	0.08	0.09	0.10	0.11	0.12
1	1.070	1.080	1.090	1.100	1.110	1.120
2	1.145	1.166	1.188	1.210	1.232	1.254
3	1.225	1.260	1.295	1.331	1.368	1.405
4	1.311	1.360	1.412	1.464	1.518	1.574
5	1.403	1.469	1.539	1.611	1.685	1.762
6	1.501	1.587	1.677	1.772	1.870	1.974
7	1.606	1.714	1.828	1.949	2.076	2.211
8	1.718	1.851	1.993	2.144	2.305	2.476
9	1.838	1.999	2.172	2.358	2.558	2.773
10	1.967	2.159	2.367	2.594	2.839	3.106
11	2.105	2.332	2.580	2.853	3.152	3.479

Table A (Cont'd)

$n\backslash i$	0.07	0.08	0.09	0.10	0.11	0.12
12	2.252	2.518	2.813	3.138	3.498	3.896
13	2.410	2.720	3.066	3.452	3.883	4.363
14	2.579	2.937	3.342	3.798	4.310	4.887
15	2.759	3.172	3.642	4.177	4.785	5.474
16	2.952	3.426	3.970	4.595	5.311	6.130
17	3.159	3.700	4.328	5.054	5.895	6.866
18	3.380	3.996	4.717	5.560	6.544	7.690
19	3.617	4.316	5.142	6.116	7.263	8.613
20	3.870	4.661	5.604	6.728	8.062	9.646
21	4.141	5.034	6.109	7.400	8.949	10.804
22	4.430	5.437	6.659	8.140	9.934	12.100
23	4.741	5.871	7.258	8.954	11.026	13.552
24	5.072	6.341	7.911	9.850	12.239	15.179
25	5.427	6.848	8.623	10.835	13.586	17.000
26	5.807	7.396	9.399	11.918	15.080	19.040
27	6.214	7.988	10.245	13.110	16.739	21.325
28	6.649	8.627	11.167	14.421	18.580	23.884
29	7.114	9.317	12.172	15.863	20.624	26.750
30	7.612	10.063	13.268	17.449	22.892	29.960

$n\backslash i$	0.14	0.16	0.18	0.20	0.22	0.24
1	1.140	1.160	1.180	1.200	1.220	1.240
2	1.300	1.346	1.392	1.440	1.488	1.538
3	1.482	1.561	1.643	1.728	1.816	1.907
4	1.689	1.811	1.939	2.074	2.215	2.364
5	1.925	2.100	2.288	2.488	2.703	2.932
6	2.195	2.436	2.700	2.986	3.297	3.635
7	2.502	2.826	3.185	3.583	4.023	4.508
8	2.853	3.278	3.759	4.300	4.908	5.590
9	3.252	3.803	4.435	5.160	5.987	6.931
10	3.707	4.411	5.234	6.192	7.305	8.594
11	4.226	5.117	6.176	7.430	8.912	10.657
12	4.818	5.936	7.288	8.916	10.872	13.215
13	5.492	6.886	8.599	10.699	13.264	16.386
14	6.261	7.988	10.147	12.839	16.182	20.319
15	7.138	9.266	11.974	15.407	19.742	25.196
16	8.137	10.748	14.129	18.488	24.086	31.243
17	9.276	12.468	16.672	22.186	29.384	38.741
18	10.575	14.463	19.673	26.623	35.849	48.039
19	12.056	16.777	23.214	31.948	43.736	59.568
20	13.744	19.461	27.393	38.338	53.358	73.864
21	15.668	22.575	32.324	46.005	65.096	91.592
22	17.861	26.186	38.142	55.206	79.418	113.574

Table A (Cont'd)

n^i	0.14	9.16	0.18	0.20	0.22	0.24
23	20.362	30.376	45.008	66.247	96.890	140.831
24	23.212	35.236	53.109	79.497	118.205	174.631
25	26.462	40.874	62.669	95.396	144.210	216.542
26	30.167	47.414	73.949	114.475	175.937	268.512
27	34.390	55.000	87.260	137.371	214.643	332.955
28	39.205	63.800	102.966	164.845	261.864	412.864
29	44.693	74.008	121.500	197.814	319.474	511.952
30	50.950	85.850	143.370	237.376	389.758	634.820

n^i	0.26	0.28	0.30	0.32	0.34	0.36
1	1.260	1.280	1.300	1.320	1.340	1.360
2	1.588	1.638	1.690	1.742	1.796	1.850
3	2.000	2.097	2.197	2.300	2.406	2.515
4	2.520	2.684	2.856	3.036	3.036	3.421
5	3.176	3.436	3.713	4.007	4.320	4.653
6	4.002	4.398	4.827	5.290	5.789	6.328
7	5.042	5.630	6.275	6.983	7.758	8.605
8	6.353	7.206	8.157	9.217	10.395	11.703
9	8.005	9.223	10.605	12.167	13.930	15.917
10	10.086	11.806	13.786	16.060	18.666	21.647
11	12.708	15.112	17.922	21.199	25.012	29.439
12	16.012	19.343	23.298	27.983	33.516	40.038
13	20.175	24.759	30.288	36.937	44.912	54.451
14	25.421	31.691	39.374	48.757	60.182	74.053
15	32.030	40.565	51.186	64.359	80.644	100.713
16	40.358	51.923	66.542	84.954	108.063	136.969
17	50.851	66.461	86.504	112.139	144.804	186.278
18	64.072	85.071	112.455	148.024	194.038	253.338
19	80.731	108.890	146.192	195.391	260.011	344.540
20	101.721	139.380	190.049	257.916	348.414	468.574
21	128.169	178.406	247.064	340.450	466.875	637.261
22	161.492	228.360	321.184	449.394	625.613	866.675
23	203.480	292.300	417.539	593.200	838.321	1178.680
24	256.385	374.144	542.800	783.024	1123.350	1603.000
25	323.045	478.905	705.640	1033.590	1505.290	2180.080
26	407.037	612.998	917.332	1364.340	2017.090	2964.910
27	512.867	784.637	1192.530	1800.930	2702.900	4032.280
28	646.212	1004.340	1550.290	2377.230	3621.880	5483.900
29	814.228	1285.550	2015.380	3137.940	4853.320	7458.110
30	1025.930	1645.500	2619.990	4142.080	6503.450	10143.000

Table B   Interest factors $T_B = \dfrac{1}{(1 + i)^n}$ for computing P, the present value of a sum

$n\backslash i$	0.01	0.02	0.03	0.04	0.05	0.06
1	0.990	0.980	0.971	0.962	0.952	0.943
2	0.980	0.961	0.943	0.925	0.907	0.890
3	0.971	0.942	0.915	0.889	0.864	0.840
4	0.961	0.924	0.888	0.855	0.823	0.792
5	0.951	0.906	0.863	0.822	0.784	0.747
6	0.942	0.888	0.837	0.790	0.746	0.705
7	0.933	0.871	0.813	0.760	0.711	0.665
8	0.923	0.853	0.789	0.731	0.677	0.627
9	0.914	0.837	0.766	0.703	0.645	0.592
10	0.905	0.820	0.744	0.676	0.614	0.558
11	0.896	0.804	0.722	0.650	0.585	0.527
12	0.887	0.788	0.701	0.625	0.557	0.497
13	0.879	0.773	0.681	0.601	0.530	0.469
14	0.870	0.758	0.661	0.577	0.505	0.442
15	0.861	0.743	0.642	0.555	0.481	0.417
16	0.853	0.728	0.623	0.534	0.458	0.394
17	0.844	0.714	0.605	0.513	0.436	0.371
18	0.836	0.700	0.587	0.494	0.416	0.350
19	0.828	0.686	0.570	0.475	0.396	0.331
20	0.820	0.673	0.554	0.456	0.377	0.312
21	0.811	0.660	0.538	0.439	0.359	0.294
22	0.803	0.647	0.522	0.422	0.342	0.278
23	0.795	0.634	0.507	0.406	0.326	0.262
24	0.788	0.622	0.492	0.390	0.310	0.247
25	0.780	0.610	0.478	0.375	0.295	0.233
26	0.772	0.598	0.464	0.361	0.281	0.220
27	0.764	0.586	0.450	0.347	0.268	0.207
28	0.757	0.574	0.437	0.333	0.255	0.196
29	0.749	0.563	0.424	0.321	0.243	0.185
30	0.742	0.552	0.412	0.308	0.231	0.174

$n\backslash i$	0.07	0.08	0.09	0.10	0.11	0.12
1	0.935	0.926	0.917	0.909	0.901	0.893
2	0.873	0.857	0.842	0.826	0.812	0.797
3	0.816	0.794	0.772	0.751	0.731	0.712
4	0.763	0.735	0.708	0.683	0.659	0.636
5	0.713	0.681	0.650	0.621	0.593	0.567
6	0.666	0.630	0.596	0.564	0.535	0.507
7	0.623	0.583	0.547	0.513	0.482	0.452
8	0.582	0.540	0.502	0.467	0.434	0.404

Table B (Cont'd)

$n \backslash i$	0.07	0.08	0.09	0.10	0.11	0.12
9	0.544	0.500	0.460	0.424	0.391	0.361
10	0.508	0.463	0.422	0.386	0.352	0.322
11	0.475	0.429	0.388	0.350	0.317	0.287
12	0.444	0.397	0.356	0.319	0.286	0.257
13	0.415	0.368	0.326	0.290	0.258	0.229
14	0.388	0.340	0.299	0.263	0.232	0.205
15	0.362	0.315	0.275	0.239	0.209	0.183
16	0.339	0.292	0.252	0.218	0.188	0.163
17	0.317	0.270	0.231	0.198	0.170	0.146
18	0.296	0.250	0.212	0.180	0.153	0.130
19	0.277	0.232	0.194	0.164	0.138	0.116
20	0.258	0.215	0.178	0.149	0.124	0.104
21	0.242	0.199	0.164	0.135	0.112	0.093
22	0.226	0.184	0.150	0.123	0.101	0.083
23	0.211	0.170	0.138	0.112	0.091	0.074
24	0.197	0.158	0.126	0.102	0.082	0.066
25	0.184	0.146	0.116	0.092	0.074	0.059
26	0.172	0.135	0.106	0.084	0.066	0.053
27	0.161	0.125	0.098	0.076	0.060	0.047
28	0.150	0.116	0.090	0.069	0.054	0.042
29	0.141	0.107	0.082	0.063	0.048	0.037
30	0.131	0.099	0.075	0.057	0.044	0.033

$n \backslash i$	0.14	0.16	0.18	0.20	0.22	0.24
1	0.877	0.862	0.847	0.833	0.820	0.806
2	0.769	0.743	0.718	0.694	0.672	0.650
3	0.675	0.641	0.609	0.579	0.551	0.524
4	0.592	0.552	0.516	0.482	0.451	0.423
5	0.519	0.476	0.437	0.402	0.370	0.341
6	0.456	0.410	0.370	0.335	0.303	0.275
7	0.400	0.354	0.314	0.279	0.249	0.222
8	0.351	0.305	0.266	0.233	0.204	0.179
9	0.308	0.263	0.225	0.194	0.167	0.144
10	0.270	0.227	0.191	0.162	0.137	0.116
11	0.237	0.195	0.162	0.135	0.112	0.094
12	0.208	0.168	0.137	0.112	0.092	0.076
13	0.182	0.145	0.116	0.093	0.075	0.061
14	0.160	0.125	0.099	0.078	0.062	0.049
15	0.140	0.108	0.084	0.065	0.051	0.040
16	0.123	0.093	0.071	0.054	0.042	0.032
17	0.108	0.080	0.060	0.045	0.034	0.026
18	0.095	0.069	0.051	0.038	0.028	0.021
19	0.083	0.060	0.043	0.031	0.023	0.017

Table B (Cont'd)

$n\backslash i$	0.14	0.16	0.18	0.20	0.22	0.24
20	0.073	0.051	0.037	0.026	0.019	0.014
21	0.064	0.044	0.031	0.022	0.015	0.011
22	0.056	0.038	0.026	0.018	0.013	0.009
23	0.049	0.033	0.022	0.015	0.010	0.007
24	0.043	0.028	0.019	0.013	0.008	0.006
25	0.038	0.024	0.016	0.010	0.007	0.005
26	0.033	0.021	0.014	0.009	0.006	0.004
27	0.029	0.018	0.011	0.007	0.005	0.003
28	0.026	0.016	0.010	0.006	0.004	0.002
29	0.022	0.014	0.008	0.005	0.003	0.002
30	0.020	0.012	0.007	0.004	0.003	0.002

$n\backslash i$	0.26	0.28	0.30	0.32	0.34	0.36
1	0.794	0.781	0.769	0.758	0.746	0.735
2	0.630	0.610	0.592	0.574	0.557	0.541
3	0.500	0.477	0.455	0.435	0.416	0.398
4	0.397	0.373	0.350	0.329	0.310	0.292
5	0.315	0.291	0.269	0.250	0.231	0.215
6	0.250	0.227	0.207	0.189	0.173	0.158
7	0.198	0.178	0.159	0.143	0.129	0.116
8	0.157	0.139	0.123	0.108	0.096	0.085
9	0.125	0.108	0.094	0.082	0.072	0.063
10	0.099	0.085	0.073	0.062	0.054	0.046
11	0.079	0.066	0.056	0.047	0.040	0.034
12	0.062	0.052	0.043	0.036	0.030	0.025
13	0.050	0.040	0.033	0.027	0.022	0.018
14	0.039	0.032	0.025	0.021	0.017	0.014
15	0.031	0.025	0.020	0.016	0.012	0.010
16	0.025	0.019	0.015	0.012	0.009	0.007
17	0.020	0.015	0.012	0.009	0.007	0.005
18	0.016	0.012	0.009	0.007	0.005	0.004
19	0.012	0.009	0.007	0.005	0.004	0.003
20	0.010	0.007	0.005	0.004	0.003	0.002
21	0.008	0.006	0.004	0.003	0.002	0.002
22	0.006	0.004	0.003	0.002	0.002	0.001
23	0.005	0.003	0.002	0.002	0.001	0.001
24	0.004	0.003	0.002	0.001	0.001	0.001
25	0.003	0.002	0.001	0.001	0.001	0.000
26	0.002	0.002	0.001	0.001	0.000	0.000
27	0.002	0.001	0.001	0.001	0.000	0.000
28	0.002	0.001	0.001	0.000	0.000	0.000
29	0.001	0.001	0.000	0.000	0.000	0.000
30	0.001	0.001	0.000	0.000	0.000	0.000

Table C   Interest factors $T_C = \dfrac{(1 + i)^n - 1}{i}$ for computing W, the future value of an annuity

$n\backslash i$	0.01	0.02	0.03	0.04	0.05	0.06
1	1.000	1.000	1.000	1.000	1.000	1.000
2	2.010	2.020	2.030	2.040	2.050	2.060
3	3.030	3.060	3.091	3.122	3.153	3.184
4	4.060	4.122	4.184	4.246	4.310	4.375
5	5.101	5.204	5.309	5.416	5.526	5.637
6	6.152	6.308	6.468	6.633	6.802	6.975
7	7.214	7.434	7.662	7.898	8.142	8.394
8	8.286	8.583	8.892	9.214	9.549	9.897
9	9.369	9.755	10.159	10.583	11.027	11.491
10	10.462	10.950	11.464	12.006	12.578	13.181
11	11.567	12.169	12.808	13.486	14.207	14.972
12	12.683	13.412	14.192	15.026	15.917	16.870
13	13.809	14.680	15.618	16.627	17.713	18.882
14	14.947	15.974	17.086	18.292	19.599	21.015
15	16.097	17.293	18.599	20.024	21.579	23.276
16	17.258	18.639	20.157	21.825	23.658	25.673
17	18.430	20.012	21.762	23.698	25.840	28.213
18	19.615	21.412	23.414	25.645	28.132	30.906
19	20.811	22.841	25.117	27.671	30.539	33.760
20	22.019	24.297	26.870	29.778	33.066	36.786
21	23.239	25.783	28.677	31.969	35.719	39.993
22	24.472	27.299	30.537	34.248	38.505	43.392
23	25.716	28.845	32.453	36.618	41.430	46.996
24	26.974	30.422	34.427	39.083	44.502	50.816
25	28.243	32.030	36.459	41.646	47.727	54.864
26	29.526	33.671	38.553	44.312	51.113	59.156
27	30.821	35.344	40.710	47.084	54.669	63.706
28	32.129	37.051	42.931	49.968	58.403	68.528
29	33.450	38.792	45.219	52.966	62.323	73.640
30	34.785	40.568	47.575	56.085	66.439	79.058

$n\backslash i$	0.07	0.08	0.09	0.10	0.11	0.12
1	1.000	1.000	1.000	1.000	1.000	1.000
2	2.070	2.080	2.090	2.100	2.110	2.120
3	3.215	3.246	3.278	3.310	3.342	3.374
4	4.440	4.506	4.573	4.641	4.710	4.779
5	5.751	5.867	5.985	6.105	6.228	6.353
6	7.153	7.336	7.523	7.716	7.913	8.115
7	8.654	8.923	9.200	9.487	9.783	10.089
8	10.260	10.637	11.029	11.436	11.859	12.300
9	11.978	12.488	13.021	13.580	14.164	14.776

Table C (Cont'd)

n^i	0.07	0.08	0.09	0.10	0.11	0.12
10	13.817	14.487	15.193	15.937	16.722	17.549
11	15.784	16.646	17.560	18.531	19.561	20.655
12	17.889	18.977	20.141	21.384	22.713	24.133
13	20.141	21.495	22.953	24.523	26.212	28.029
14	22.551	24.215	26.019	27.975	30.095	32.393
15	25.129	27.152	29.361	31.773	34.405	37.280
16	27.888	30.324	33.003	35.950	39.190	42.753
17	30.840	33.750	36.974	40.545	44.501	48.884
18	33.999	37.450	41.301	45.599	50.396	55.750
19	37.379	41.446	46.019	51.159	56.940	63.440
20	40.996	45.762	51.160	57.275	64.203	72.052
21	44.865	50.423	56.765	64.003	72.265	81.699
22	49.006	55.457	62.873	71.403	81.214	92.503
23	53.436	60.893	69.532	79.543	91.148	104.603
24	58.177	66.765	76.790	88.497	102.174	118.155
25	63.249	73.106	84.701	98.347	114.413	133.334
26	68.677	79.955	93.324	109.182	127.999	150.334
27	74.484	87.351	102.723	121.100	143.079	169.374
28	80.698	95.339	112.968	134.210	159.817	190.699
29	87.347	103.966	124.136	148.631	178.397	214.583
30	94.461	113.283	136.308	164.494	199.021	241.333

n^i	0.14	0.16	0.18	0.20	0.22	0.24
1	1.000	1.000	1.000	1.000	1.000	1.000
2	2.140	2.160	2.180	2.200	2.220	2.240
3	3.440	3.506	3.572	3.640	3.708	3.778
4	4.921	5.066	5.215	5.368	5.524	5.684
5	6.610	6.877	7.154	7.442	7.740	8.048
6	8.536	8.977	9.442	9.930	10.442	10.980
7	10.731	11.414	12.142	12.916	13.740	14.615
8	13.233	14.240	15.327	16.499	17.762	19.123
9	16.085	17.519	19.086	20.799	22.670	24.713
10	19.337	21.322	23.521	25.959	28.657	31.643
11	23.045	25.733	28.755	32.150	35.962	40.238
12	27.271	30.850	34.931	39.581	44.874	50.895
13	32.089	36.786	42.219	48.497	55.746	64.110
14	37.581	43.672	50.818	59.196	69.010	80.496
15	43.842	51.660	60.965	72.035	85.192	100.815
16	50.980	60.925	72.939	87.442	104.935	126.011
17	59.118	71.673	87.068	105.931	129.020	157.253
18	68.394	84.141	103.740	128.117	158.405	195.994
19	78.969	98.603	123.413	154.740	194.254	244.033
20	91.025	115.380	146.628	186.688	237.989	303.601

Table C (Cont'd)

n^i	0.14	0.16	0.18	0.20	0.22	0.24
21	104.768	134.840	174.021	225.026	291.347	377.465
22	120.436	157.415	206.345	271.031	356.444	469.057
23	138.297	183.601	244.487	326.237	435.861	582.630
24	158.659	213.977	289.494	392.404	532.751	723.461
25	181.871	249.214	342.603	471.981	650.956	898.092
26	208.333	290.088	405.272	567.377	795.166	1114.630
27	238.499	337.502	479.221	681.853	971.102	1383.150
28	272.889	392.502	566.480	819.223	1185.750	1716.100
29	312.094	456.303	669.447	984.068	1447.610	2128.970
30	356.787	530.311	790.947	1181.880	1767.080	2640.920

n^i	0.26	0.28	0.30	0.32	0.34	0.36
1	1.000	1.000	1.000	1.000	1.000	1.000
2	2.260	2.280	2.300	2.320	2.340	2.360
3	3.848	3.918	3.990	4.062	4.136	4.210
4	5.848	6.016	6.187	6.362	6.542	6.725
5	8.368	8.700	9.043	9.398	9.766	10.146
6	11.544	12.136	12.756	13.406	14.086	14.799
7	15.546	16.534	17.583	18.696	19.876	21.126
8	20.588	22.163	23.858	25.678	27.633	29.732
9	26.940	29.369	32.015	34.895	38.029	41.435
10	34.945	38.593	42.620	47.062	51.958	57.352
11	45.031	50.399	56.405	63.122	70.624	78.998
12	57.739	65.510	74.327	84.321	95.637	108.438
13	73.751	84.853	97.625	112.303	129.153	148.475
14	93.926	109.612	127.912	149.240	174.065	202.926
15	119.347	141.303	167.286	197.997	234.247	276.979
16	151.377	181.868	218.472	262.356	314.891	377.692
17	191.735	233.791	285.014	347.310	422.954	514.661
18	242.586	300.252	371.518	459.449	567.758	700.939
19	306.658	385.323	483.973	607.473	761.796	954.278
20	387.389	494.213	630.165	802.864	1021.810	1298.820
21	489.110	633.592	820.214	1060.780	1370.220	1767.390
22	617.278	811.998	1067.280	1401.230	1837.100	2404.650
23	778.771	1040.360	1388.460	1850.620	2462.710	3271.330
24	982.251	1332.660	1806.000	2443.820	3301.030	4450.010
25	1238.640	1706.800	2348.800	3226.850	4424.380	6053.010
26	1561.680	2185.710	3054.440	4260.440	5929.670	8233.090
27	1968.720	2798.700	3971.770	5624.780	7946.760	11198.000
28	2481.590	3583.340	5164.300	7425.710	10649.700	15230.300
29	3127.800	4587.680	6714.590	9802.940	14271.500	20714.200
30	3942.030	5873.230	8729.970	12940.900	19124.900	28172.300

Table D   Interest factors $T_D = \dfrac{1 - (1 + i)^{-n}}{i}$ for computing B, the present value of

an annuity

$n\backslash i$	0.01	0.02	0.03	0.04	0.05	0.06
1	0.990	0.980	0.971	0.962	0.952	0.943
2	1.970	1.942	1.913	1.886	1.859	1.833
3	2.941	2.884	2.829	2.775	2.723	2.673
4	3.902	3.808	3.717	3.630	3.546	3.465
5	4.853	4.713	4.580	4.452	4.329	4.212
6	5.795	5.601	5.417	5.242	5.076	4.917
7	6.728	6.472	6.230	6.002	5.786	5.582
8	7.652	7.325	7.020	6.733	6.463	6.210
9	8.566	8.162	7.786	7.435	7.108	6.802
10	9.471	8.983	8.530	8.111	7.722	7.360
11	10.368	9.787	9.253	8.760	8.306	7.887
12	11.255	10.575	9.954	9.385	8.863	8.384
13	12.134	11.348	10.635	9.986	9.394	8.853
14	13.004	12.106	11.296	10.563	9.899	9.295
15	13.865	12.849	11.938	11.118	10.380	9.712
16	14.718	13.578	12.561	11.652	10.838	10.106
17	15.562	14.292	13.166	12.166	11.274	10.477
18	16.398	14.992	13.754	12.659	11.690	10.828
19	17.226	15.679	14.324	13.134	12.085	11.158
20	18.046	16.351	14.878	13.590	12.462	11.470
21	18.857	17.011	15.415	14.029	12.821	11.764
22	19.660	17.658	15.937	14.451	13.163	12.042
23	20.456	18.292	16.444	14.857	13.489	12.303
24	21.243	18.914	16.936	15.247	13.799	12.550
25	22.023	19.524	17.413	15.622	14.094	12.783
26	22.795	20.121	17.877	15.983	14.375	13.003
27	23.560	20.707	18.327	16.330	14.643	13.211
28	24.316	21.281	18.764	16.663	14.898	13.406
29	25.066	21.844	19.188	16.984	15.141	13.591
30	25.808	22.397	19.600	17.292	15.372	13.765

$n\backslash i$	0.07	0.08	0.09	0.10	0.11	0.12
1	0.935	0.926	0.917	0.909	0.901	0.893
2	1.808	1.783	1.759	1.736	1.713	1.690
3	2.624	2.577	2.531	2.487	2.444	2.402
4	3.387	3.312	3.240	3.170	3.102	3.037
5	4.100	3.993	3.890	3.791	3.696	3.605
6	4.767	4.623	4.486	4.355	4.231	4.111
7	6.389	5.206	5.033	4.868	4.712	4.564
8	5.971	5.747	5.535	5.335	5.146	4.968
9	6.515	6.247	5.995	5.759	5.537	5.328

Table D (Cont'd)

$n \backslash i$	0.07	0.08	0.09	0.10	0.11	0.12
10	7.024	6.710	6.418	6.145	5.889	5.650
11	7.499	7.139	6.805	6.495	6.207	5.938
12	7.943	7.536	7.161	6.814	6.492	6.194
13	8.358	7.904	7.487	7.103	6.750	6.424
14	8.745	8.244	7.786	7.367	6.982	6.628
15	9.108	8.559	8.061	7.606	7.191	6.811
16	9.447	8.851	8.313	7.824	7.379	6.974
17	9.763	9.122	8.544	8.022	7.549	7.120
18	10.059	9.372	8.756	8.201	7.702	7.250
19	10.336	9.604	8.950	8.365	7.839	7.366
20	10.594	9.818	9.129	8.514	7.963	7.469
21	10.836	10.017	9.292	8.649	8.075	7.562
22	11.061	10.201	9.442	8.772	8.176	7.645
23	11.272	10.371	9.580	8.883	8.266	7.718
24	11.469	10.529	9.707	8.985	8.348	7.784
25	11.654	10.675	9.823	9.077	8.422	7.843
26	11.826	10.810	9.929	9.161	8.488	7.896
27	11.987	10.935	10.027	9.237	8.548	7.943
28	12.137	11.051	10.116	9.307	8.602	7.984
29	12.278	11.158	10.198	9.370	8.650	8.022
30	12.409	11.258	10.274	9.427	8.694	8.055

$n \backslash i$	0.14	0.16	0.18	0.20	0.22	0.24
1	0.877	0.862	0.847	0.833	0.820	0.806
2	1.647	1.605	1.566	1.528	1.492	1.457
3	2.322	2.246	2.174	2.106	2.042	1.981
4	2.914	2.798	2.690	2.589	2.494	2.404
5	3.433	3.274	3.127	2.991	2.864	2.745
6	3.889	3.685	3.498	3.326	3.167	3.020
7	4.289	4.039	3.812	3.605	3.416	3.242
8	4.639	4.344	4.078	3.837	3.619	3.421
9	4.946	4.607	4.303	4.031	3.786	3.566
10	5.216	4.833	4.494	4.192	3.923	3.682
11	5.453	5.029	4.656	4.327	4.035	3.776
12	5.660	5.197	4.793	4.439	4.127	3.851
13	5.842	5.342	4.910	4.533	4.203	3.912
14	6.002	5.468	5.008	4.611	4.265	3.962
15	6.142	5.575	5.092	4.675	4.315	4.001
16	6.265	5.669	5.162	4.730	4.357	4.033
17	6.373	5.749	5.222	4.775	4.391	4.059
18	6.467	5.818	5.273	4.812	4.419	4.080
19	6.550	5.877	5.316	4.844	4.442	4.097
20	6.623	5.929	5.353	4.870	4.460	4.110

Table D (Cont'd)

n^i	0.14	0.16	0.18	0.20	0.22	0.24
21	6.687	5.973	5.384	4.891	4.476	4.121
22	6.743	6.011	5.410	4.909	4.488	4.130
23	6.792	6.044	5.432	4.925	4.499	4.137
24	6.835	6.073	5.451	4.937	4.507	4.143
25	6.873	6.097	5.467	4.948	4.514	4.147
26	6.906	6.118	5.480	4.956	4.520	4.151
27	6.935	6.136	5.492	4.964	4.524	4.154
28	6.961	6.152	5.502	4.970	4.528	4.157
29	6.983	6.166	5.510	4.975	4.531	4.159
30	7.003	6.177	5.517	4.979	4.534	4.160

n^i	0.26	0.28	0.30	0.32	0.34	0.36
1	0.794	0.781	0.769	0.758	0.746	0.735
2	1.424	1.392	1.361	1.332	1.303	1.276
3	1.923	1.868	1.816	1.766	1.719	1.673
4	2.320	2.241	2.166	2.096	2.029	1.966
5	2.635	2.532	2.436	2.345	2.260	2.181
6	2.885	2.759	2.643	2.534	2.433	2.339
7	3.083	2.937	2.802	2.677	2.562	2.455
8	3.241	3.076	2.925	2.786	2.658	2.540
9	3.366	3.184	3.019	2.868	2.730	2.603
10	3.465	3.269	3.092	2.930	2.784	2.649
11	3.544	3.335	3.147	2.978	2.824	2.683
12	3.606	3.387	3.190	3.013	2.853	2.708
13	3.656	3.427	3.223	3.040	2.876	2.727
14	3.695	3.459	3.249	3.061	2.892	2.740
15	3.726	3.483	3.268	3.076	2.905	2.750
16	3.751	3.503	3.283	3.088	2.914	2.758
17	3.771	3.518	3.295	3.097	2.921	2.763
18	3.786	3.529	3.304	3.104	2.926	2.767
19	3.799	3.539	3.311	3.109	2.930	2.770
20	3.808	3.546	3.316	3.113	2.933	2.772
21	3.816	3.551	3.320	3.116	2.935	2.773
22	3.822	3.556	3.323	3.118	2.936	2.775
23	3.827	3.559	3.325	3.120	2.938	2.775
24	3.831	3.562	3.327	3.121	2.939	2.776
25	3.834	3.564	3.329	3.122	2.939	2.777
26	3.837	3.566	3.330	3.123	2.940	2.777
27	3.839	3.567	3.331	3.123	2.940	2.777
28	3.840	3.568	3.331	3.124	2.940	2.777
20	3.841	3.569	3.332	3.124	2.941	2.777
30	3.842	3.569	3.332	3.124	2.941	2.778

Glossary

Annuity A series of periodic payments, not necessarily annual. Usually they are of equal magnitude and paid at identically spaced time intervals.

Assets Economic resources controlled by an entity to meet its objectives in future periods. While most assets are tangible, such as equipment, facilities, and claims on cash, some intangible legal and accounting entitlements such as patents and goodwill are also regarded as assets.

Assets, current Cash and other assets readily converted into cash or consumed in the normal course of business activity. These assets include accounts receivable, inventories, and short term investments. Also referred to as working capital.

Assets, fixed Economic resources with a life expectancy of over 1 year, utilized in meeting the objectives of the entity. Among these are land, building, and equipment.

Average cost The total costs incurred in the production or distribution of an item divided by the number of units produced or distributed. Average costs usually decline with larger volumes of output, reach a minimum level and increase beyond that volume.

Balance sheet An accounting statement reflecting the financial status and stock of wealth of an entity at a given point in time.

Book value See **Equity**

Book value per share The total equity of the corporation, exclusive of preferred stock, divided by the total number of common shares in the hands of the public. Not an indicator of the market value of common stock.

Bond A long term debt instrument, usually promising to pay its face value on a specified date and a periodic fixed amount in the interim.

Break-even analysis A mathematical and graphic technique that aids in the determination of desired levels of output and appropriate methods of financing. Suitable whenever differentiation between fixed and variable costs are appropriate.

247

Budget   A quantitative expression of a contemplated plan of action. Useful in the formulation of plans, the allocation of resources, and the evaluation of organizational and managerial performance.

Budget, cash   The accounting document delineating expected cash flows. Essential for the determination of cash deficiencies or excess cash balances.

Budget, flexible   The budget that identifies required resources as a function of the level of activity actually experienced.

Budget, master   The document that integrates subsidary budgets of an organization.

Capital budgeting   The process of assessing the desirability of proposed investments.

Capital market line (CML)   A line depicting the relationship between risk and return for efficient investments.

Capital structure   The composition of the right hand side of a corporate Balance Sheet.

Cash budget   See **Budget, cash**

Cash flow   The tracing of cash balances as a result of historical or expected organizational activity.

Commercial paper   Short term, negotiable financial instruments issued by the most prominent corporations to meet cyclical capital needs. Generally regarded as low in risk although clearly riskier than treasury bills.

Compensating balances   Deposits that a borrower leaves with the lending bank throughout the contract period. The borrower pays interest on these balances, thus raising the effective cost of the funds which he actually uses.

Contribution margin   The difference between prices realized in the market and the variable costs of production such as direct labor and direct materials.

Convertible bonds   A bond convertible at the option of its holder into a predetermined number of other securities, usually common stock.

Cost accounting   The procedure concerned with attributing appropriate cost elements to an activity or a product.

Cost benefit analysis   The assessment of the costs incurred and the benefits realized from the adoption of a course of action. It is the essence of the managerial decision making process and has received renewed publicity as a tool for governmental decision making. In organizations that are not profit oriented, benefits are often very difficult to quantify.

Cost center   An organizational unit responsible for the control of costs but not the generation of revenues.

Credit entry   Transaction recorded on the right hand side of an account.

Current assets   See **Assets, current**

Current liabilities See **Liabilities, current**

Debit entry Transaction recorded on the left hand side of an account.

Demand curve The relationship between the price at which a commodity is offered and the quantity demanded at that price. Usually shown as a downward sloping line.

Depreciation The procedure of allocating a portion of the acquisition cost of fixed assets to each of the time periods in which they are utilized.

Dividend A distribution of corporate wealth to shareholders. Stock dividends are a misnomer, since no wealth is distributed.

Divident yield The annual cash return that investors in common or preferred stock can expect on their investment. Computed by dividing expected annual dividend by prevailing market prices.

Economic agent A decision-making organizational unit that arrives at allocative decisions in accordance with its perceived needs. Among others, it may consist of an individual, a household, a corporation, or a not-for-profit insitiution.

Economic order quantity (EOQ) The number of units ordered at one time to minimize the overall cost of inventory management.

Economics The discipline concerned with the allocation of resources — one of the social sciences.

Economics, macro The study of interaction of economic agents in society and the role of government in affecting their decision making process.

Economics, micro The study of the decision processes of individual economic agents in producing, distributing, and consuming goods.

Economies of scale The economic phenomenon observed when average costs per unit decrease as a result of increasing the level of output.

Entity An organizational unit whose financial status or performance is being assessed. The unit may consist of a household, a department a corporation or a governmental subdivision.

Equity The difference between the assets of an entity and its liabilities. Also termed net worth or book value. Typical accounts comprising this difference are common stock, retained income, paid in surplus, and preferred stock.

Equilibrium price The price at which the quantity of commodity offered for sale equals the quantity demanded for purchase. Transactions are consummated at this price.

Federal reserve system (FRS) The central banking institution of the United States. It is administratively independent of the executive branch of the federal government.

First in first out (FIFO) An accounting procedure by which the cost of goods sold are valued at their earliest incurred prices on record. In inflationary times this procedure tends to overstate operating income.

Fiscal policy Measures under the control of central government policy-makers that impact on economic activity. Among these are tax policy, the magnitude of the central government budget and its associated surpluses and deficits, and direct stimulus of economic activity through governmental expenditures in target areas.

Fixed assets See **Assets, fixed**

Flexible budget See **Budget, flexible**

Forecast A view of the future.

Fund accounting Accounting procedures adopted by many governmental and charitable organizations. They are characterized by the absence of a Balance Sheet and depreciation accounts.

Future value The stock of wealth an investor is willing to accept at a stated future time in lieu of promised payments prior to that date.

Generally accepted accounting principles (GAAP) The professional judgment of accountants prevailing at the time financial statements are audited. These principles are not verifiable experimentally, nor are they theoretically unambiguous or embedded in law.

Gross national product (GNP) A measure of the total spending of all economic units on final products during a stated period, customarily a year. It excludes products passing through intermediary production phases and also services such as housewifely chores, which are not sold on the market. It is frequently used as the prime indicator of the overall health of the economy.

Income statement An accounting statement reflecting the financial performance of an entity between two periods in time. A delineation of the flow of wealth from operating receipts and disbursements.

Indenture A legal agreement between the issuers of bonds and the bondholders.

Internal rate of return (IRR) The interest rate that equates the cost of an investment to the present value of the expected returns from the investment.

Investment tax credit A direct reduction in federal income tax liabilities resulting from the acquisition of fixed assets.

Last in first out (LIFO) An accounting procedure by which the cost of goods sold are valued at their latest recorded prices. In inflationary periods this procedure tends to reduce operating income and tax liability.

Leasing The practice of contracting for the services of an asset instead of acquiring its ownership. Minimizes the initial cash outflow to the using organization.

Liabilities Claims for specific amounts, secured or unsecured, held by outsiders against the entity. Examples of these claims are accounts payable, bank loans, mortgages, and bonds outstanding.

Liabilities, current Claims held by outsiders against an entity that are expected to be discharged in less than a year. Accounts payable and bank loans are prominent examples.

Liabilities, long term   Claims held by outsiders against an entity for specific amounts due beyond 1 year. Typical examples of such claims are bonds and mortgages.

Macroeconomics   See **Economics, macro**

Marginal costs   The additions to total costs necessary to produce one additional item above the prevailing level of output. Marginal costs equal average costs when average costs are at their minimum level and increase above average costs at higher levels of output.

Marginal tax rate   The tax rate applicable to the next dollar of income. This is the relevant rate for managerial decision purposes.

Master budget   See **Budget, master**

Microeconomics   See **Economics, micro**

Monetary policy   Measures oriented toward influencing the supply and cost of money in the economy. Adovcates of extensive use of these measures belong to the school of economic thought that believes the supply of money determines overall economic activity and price levels. They often recommend limiting the discretionary authority of the Federal Reserve System in expanding the money supply to increases in the output of the economy.

Net present value   The difference between the present value of an expected annuity and the present value of the investment required to acquire the annuity.

Net worth   See **Equity**

Opportunity cost   The profits sacrificed by not pursuing the next best alternative available.

Over-the-counter market (OTC)   A network of brokers and dealers dealing in securities without the face-to-face encounter of the auction market on an organized exchange.

Paid in surplus   The amount realized by the issuing corporation for its common stock in excess of the total par value of the shares issued.

Par value   The value assigned to authorized common stock for legal reasons. It bears no relationship to a share's market value.

Preferred stock   An equity instrument that promises to pay its holders a fixed dividend if declared by the board of directors. This dividend is not guaranteed.

Present value   The stock of wealth an investor is willing to accept today in lieu of promises to receive returns at future dates.

Price earnings (P/E) ratio   The market price of a security divided by its expected annual earnings.

Prime rate   The rate of interest charged by banks to their best and most credit worthy customers.

Private offering   Security offerings to a limited number of investors that do not require the preparation and dissemination of a prospectus. Offerees must be judged to be sufficiently sophisticated to determine the merits of the proposed investment.

Profit centers An organizational unit responsible for the generation of revenue and the control of costs for which financial statements can be prepared.

Pro-forma statement Financial statements prepared on the basis of stated assumptions rather than strictly on historical events. While most pro-forma statements are prepared for future periods and are predicated on forecasts, some are retroactive determinations. An example is the development of financial statements as if a merger had taken place prior to the date of its actual consummation.

Prospectus A document issued in conjunction with the security registration process that details all pertinent information regarding the proposed issue.

Relevant costs Those costs that are affected by proposed actions and should be considered in the decision process.

Retained income The sum total of accounting profits realized from the inception of the entity less dividends paid to shareholders. (No funds are available in this account for investment purposes!)

Risk Deviation from expected results. As risk increases, investors demand higher returns.

Sales and leaseback The practice of constructing a facility to particular specifications, selling it, and entering a long term lease contract with the buyer. Advantages arise from the nondepreciability of land.

Specialist A member of an organized security exchange charged with the maintenance of an orderly market in the securities assigned to him. To accomplish this he trades for his own account.

Supply curve The relationship between the price offered for a commodity and the quantity supplied at that price. Usually shown as an upward sloping line.

Trade credit The practice of granting discounts to clients to encourage the early settlement of accounts.

Transfer prices Imputed prices of intermediate products for recording transactions between departments in an organization. In the absence of equivalent market transactions, these prices are internally negotiated.

Treasury bills Short-term negotiable financial instruments periodically auctioned off by the U.S. Treasury. The return to investors is the difference between the purchase price of these bills and their face value realized upon redemption. Regarded as the safest short-term investment vehicle.

Underwriter A financial intermediary specializing in aiding organizations in issuing and distributing securities.

Warrant A security that promises its holder the acquisition of another security, usually common stock, at a predetermined price. Equivalent in many attributes to a long term option.

Index